T0330449

Environmental Regulation in a Federal System

NEW HORIZONS IN ENVIRONMENTAL ECONOMICS

Series Editors: Wallace E. Oates, *Professor of Economics, University of Maryland, USA* and Henk Folmer, *Professor of General Economics, Wageningen University and Professor of Environmental Economics, Tilburg University, The Netherlands*

This important series is designed to make a significant contribution to the development of the principles and practices of environmental economics. It includes both theoretical and empirical work. International in scope, it addresses issues of current and future concern in both East and West and in developed and developing countries.

The main purpose of the series is to create a forum for the publication of high-quality work and to show how economic analysis can make a contribution to understanding and resolving the environmental problems confronting the world in the twenty-first century.

Recent titles in the series inlude:

Environmental Regulation in a Federal System

Framing Environmental Policy in the European Union

Tim Jeppesen

Project Manager, Kommunernes Revision, Denmark

NEW HORIZONS IN ENVIRONMENTAL ECONOMICS

Edward Elgar

Cheltenham, UK • Northampton, MA, USA

Published by
Edward Elgar Publishing Limited
Glensanda House
Montpellier Parade
Cheltenham
Glos GL50 1UA
UK

Edward Elgar Publishing, Inc.
136 West Street
Suite 202
Northampton
Massachusetts 01060
USA

A catalogue record for this book
is available from the British Library

ISBN 1 84064 944 5

Printed and bound in Great Britain by Biddles Ltd, *www.biddles.co.uk*

Contents

List of figures

List of tables

Preface

This book originates from my PhD dissertation completed at Odense University in 1998. It was hard work to finish the thesis and it has been hard work to rewrite it in a more readable form. Both of these processes involved several people to whom I would like to say how much I have appreciated their input, their support and their help.

First of all there are a number of co-authors with whom I wrote parts of the dissertation and thus, also, parts of this book. Without the work of Henk Folmer (Universities of Tilburg and Wageningen), Rien Komen (Wageningen University) and Per Andersen (University of Southern Denmark) there would have been no dissertation and, hence, no book.

In the autumn of 1995 I had the great opportunity to stay at The Beijer International Institute of Ecological Economics, The Royal Academy of Sciences, Stockholm. Beijer is a centre of environmental economics, and if you cannot find the information you want, you will always be guided to the relevant people. Karl-Göran Mäler is a great resource, and his numerous comments and questions, which I could not always answer, have improved part of this book considerably. Ing-Marie Gren, Christina Leijonhufvud, Astrid Auralsson, Carl Folke and Tore Söderqvist were most obliging and helped me to feel at home immediately.

Sweden has been good to me. It was at the sixth EAERE conference in Umeå, 1995, that I met Henk Folmer. Over a couple of beers one night, we found out that we were working on similar subjects, and Henk immediately invited me to Wageningen. Since then I have discussed my work with him many, many times (Henk would probably say daily). He has shown me what it takes to write a good paper: never be satisfied before every ambiguity has been removed. 'Tim, it must be CRYSTAL clear.' However, just a superficial reading of this book will show that Henk was on a 'Mission Impossible'. Needless to say, the remaining ambiguities are my sole responsibility.

My supervisor on the dissertation, Per Andersen, has been my mentor in many respects since 1988, when I started to study economics. He has had a hard time, having to live with my numerous questions, some of which were more relevant than others. His faith in the project has in difficult times been stronger than my own, and his persistent encouragements have prevented me from dropping the reins.

In August 1995 I participated in a course on 'Environmental Problems and Ecological Consciousness: Historical and Social Perspectives', arranged by Professor Sverker Sörlin, Department of the History of Science and Ideas, Umeå University. The methodological point of departure was history, and since I was the only economist, the topics that came under lively debate had little in common with my work. However (or more likely: therefore), the course was extremely inspiring and helped me to see both the limits and the potentials of environmental economics. Today, I still reflect on the discussions we had on the course, and I would particularly like to thank Sverker Sörlin, Richard B. Norgaard, Kristin Asdal and Anders Öckerman.

My colleagues in the Economics Department at the University of Southern Denmark, Anna Jarosz, Anna Lise Kianzad, Anna Stepanova, Camilla Jensen, Christen Sørensen, Dorrit Andersen-Alstrup, Hanne Bille, Jan Guldager Jørgensen, Jesper Fredborg Larsen, Jørgen Drud Hansen, Lars Mathiessen, Lene Nielsen, Morten Skak, Niels Nannerup, Rabah Amir, Susanne Storm, Tanja Nissen and Zygmunt Tkocz, have helped me to keep things in perspective. What really matters in life is not economics, but kids, chatting, sitting in a café with a glass of cold beer in the hand, cracking jokes, and football.

Finally, I want to thank my family – my wife Vibeke, my son Johannes and my daughter Frida. At this moment, the time is 2.03 a.m. and I really should be at home with them. Johannes and Frida both arrived in the years when this book was in the melting pot. They have definitely made everything much more fun.

This book is dedicated to my father, Finn Jeppesen.

1. Introduction

1. BACKGROUND

This book is motivated by my own confusion about the prospects for environmental policy in the European Community. Its outline was sketched in the repercussions of the two Danish referenda in 1992 and 1993, first rejecting and then approving the Maastricht Treaty, and the narrow victory of the 'yes' vote in the French referendum. At that time the Community was mired in one of its most severe crises, and environmental policy was no exception. Environmental policy became a political football, used by the 'yes' wing to promote the advantages of Community action and by the 'no' wing as providing clear-cut examples of superfluous Community action. The year 1992 should have been the year when European integration reached its maximum, with the completion of the internal market and the launching of the European Union. Instead it became clear that further European integration was being met by unexpectedly strong resistance at national levels. One of the main questions was to decide which policy tasks should be undertaken by the Community and which should be delegated to the national governments. The subsidiarity principle appeared as a concept which could help strike a balance between Community powers and Member States' powers and to help the Community to steer a new course.

Environmental policy played a significant role in the subsidiarity debate. Harmonization of environmental policy measures was one of the major concerns of the Community's internal market project because the number of those measures had increased rapidly during the 1980s. Moreover, the growing concern about transboundary environmental problems further stimulated Community action. This 'Europeanization' of environmental policy, however, was not seen only through rose-coloured spectacles. Fears were expressed that Community action would lead to 'lowest-common-denominator' policies inadequate to deal with specific national problems and priorities. Thus, some argued that Community competences in the environment should be increased, while others felt that the present degree of cooperation was excessive (Liefferink, 1996). The reasons for the disagreement are many. One reason may lie in the complicated relationship between the internal market, subsidiarity and environmental policy. First

1

of all, the single market will increase economic activity, which will ultimately affect the environment (Task Force, 1990). How this effect will take form, however, is not clear. Second, subsidiarity was introduced in the Treaty because national governments were eager to protect their prerogatives against any undesired Community intrusion (Dehousse, 1993). How subsidiarity will affect the continued development of Community environmental policy is not clear, either.

The internal market removes border controls and technical barriers to trade, such as different technical regulations and product norms. This will affect the choice of instruments for national environmental policy. The most clear-cut examples are product norms covering mobile emission sources, such as cars or hairsprays containing chlorofluorocarbons (CFCs), or commercial products, such as consumer products containing toxic substances. The product norms set by one Member State will be environmentally ineffective in the internal market because the products cannot be prevented from being imported from other Member States, therefore undermining stricter national standards. Hence the need for Community action.

Subsidiarity was developed and included in the Treaty as a response to what was perceived by some Member States as growing and unnecessary Community competences. Subsidiarity was therefore introduced as a way of regulating the use of these competences, but it does not grant the Community additional powers. This interpretation, however, has been modified by the Community institutions, turning subsidiarity into a question of comparative efficiency. According to the Community institutions, subsidiarity should grant the Community additional powers if the Community can achieve the envisaged goal more efficiently than the Member States. This interpretation of subsidiarity involves a comparison of the costs and benefits of centralized and decentralized decision-making.

Subsidiarity is directly related to the central question in environmental federalism: should we allow local diversity in standard-setting for environmental quality or should we impose a uniform central measure? Simple economic reasoning appears to provide a straightforward answer to this question. Environmental regulations should vary across countries in accordance with national circumstances. Tietenberg (1978) discusses how to determine the optimal degree of spatial differentiation of emission charges. The optimal level of pollution is where marginal social damages equal marginal abatement costs. This is illustrated in Figure 1.1. If MAC_1 and MSD_1 are, respectively, the marginal abatement cost and the marginal social damage functions of country 1, then the optimal level of pollution in country 1 is P_1. If the MAC and MSD functions in country 2 differ from those in country 1, the optimal environmental policy in country 2 should differ from that in country 1. In the figure, country 2 should implement a more stringent environmental policy resulting in a lower level of pollution, P_2. A harmonized (uniform) environmental policy would lead to pollution level P_H and a welfare loss in country 1 as well as in country 2 (area BEF and ACD, respectively).

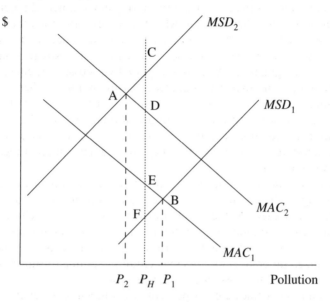

Figure 1.1   Optimal uniform and non-uniform levels of polution

Decentralized decision-making clearly has advantages. Decentralized authorities can more easily than a central authority adapt environmental policies to differences in local conditions and preferences. This means that variations in endowments, preferences and cultural traditions call for a considerable degree of decentralization of environmental policy.

There is nevertheless still a need for centralized decision-making because it has several advantages. First of all, transboundary externalities are most efficiently dealt with by a central authority because a decentralized one will tend to ignore the part of the externality outside its own jurisdiction. In this case, centralized action may be needed to ensure that the efficient abatement level is reached. Second, a central authority may also be efficient in taking advantage of economies of scale or reducing transaction costs. Third, Cumberland (1979 and 1981) has argued that in the presence of interjurisdictional competition centralized decision-making may be important. Interjurisdictional competition means that states engage in a destructive 'race to the bottom', competing for new business firms by implementing low environmental regulations. Wilson (1996) and Oates (1999), among others, have recently provided a thorough review of the literature on interjurisdictional competition. The authors find that there does not appear to be sufficient evidence of interjurisdictional competition to justify uniform environmental measures. A fourth argument for uniform measures is the cost of administering environmental regulations. Member States (and firms within Member States), and thus their abatement costs, are likely to differ. Moreover, when locational differences may lead to differing damages, it may be complicated and costly to administer decentralized regulations. As Tietenberg (1978) discusses, the consequence is that a number of environmental measures are uniform rather than spatially differentiated. This issue is dealt with in detail in Kolstad (1987), who argues that the administrative and informational costs of implementing non-uniform regulations can be large. Therefore, there may be situations where regulators may sacrifice efficiency and regulate different regions by uniform regulations.

Centralized and decentralized decision-making each has advantages and disadvantages. The optimal degree of centralization and decentralization is ultimately a matter of the comparative magnitude of welfare losses. Uniform central standards may entail allocative losses because of the failure to allow local standards to reflect local costs and benefits. Decentralized different standards may entail losses due to transboundary externalities and interjurisdictional competition.

The first time I came across aspects of environmental policy in a federal system was in 1990, while taking a course in environmental economics at Odense University. We studied the excellent book by Baumol and Oates (1988) which includes a chapter that examines whether we should choose national or local standards for environmental quality. Oates's work has since then been my greatest source of inspiration. He applies his theoretical analysis to the US experience on centralized and decentralized environmental standards. The parallel with the EU was obvious, and I sought to apply Oates's work to this area.

In doing so, two articles have been very important to me. Folmer and Howe (1991) provide an excellent study of the environmental impacts of the completion of the single market. The article is a cornucopia of research topics with respect to environmental policy in a federal system. Their analysis touches upon the relationship between subsidiarity and the internal market, but it is clear that these topics are so important from a policy perspective that they deserve additional attention. This is what Siebert (1991) does in his analysis of the options for decentralizing environmental policy in Europe. He applies economic theory to Folmer and Howes's discussion about subsidiarity and the internal market, and focuses on the choice of environmental policy instruments and transboundary character of the externality, thereby elaborating on some of the aspects identified by Folmer and Howe, while others are left unelaborated. Left unexplored were the institutional aspects in relation to subsidiarity, issues connected with relocation of firms in response to differences in environmental policies, and problems of asymmetric information. These topics are the concern of the following chapters.

2. PURPOSE

The purpose of this book is to examine the balance between the costs and benefits of centralized and decentralized environmental policies. The book consists of nine chapters which, under varying conditions, attempt to answer the question of how environmental regulatory authority can be allocated most efficiently among federal and state governments. The chapters can be divided in two parts. The first part consists of Chapters 2, 3 and 4; the second, Chapters 5 through 8.

The purpose of the first part is to examine how a political system, in this case the EU, has affected the allocation of environmental regulatory authority. This is done by examining Member States' possibilities to enact environmental regulations that are more stringent than Community measures. If this is not possible, the principles of environmental federalism are not met. Another purpose of this part is to examine the principle of subsidiarity. Subsidiarity directly affects the distribution of competences between the EU level and the Member States. The question is how it is done and what the effects are. Finally, subsidiarity is discussed in relation to public finance literature.

The purpose of the second part is to scrutinize the basic economic reasoning in determining allocation of the environmental regulatory powers presented above. The basic economic reasoning, arguing that local environmental problems should be dealt with by local governments and international environmental problems by transnational governments, is based on a number of simplifying assumptions, and the question is how robust results are to changes in these assumptions. This is examined by analysing distribution of information between different levels of government. If both the EU level and the Member States' level possess information needed to implement efficient environmental policies, what is then the optimal allocation of environmental regulatory powers? If governments engage in interjurisdictional competition to attract jobs and businesses, there may be an argument for centralizing regulatory powers to create a 'level playing-field'. Another purpose of the second part is therefore to determine whether environmental regulations do affect economic activity and whether governments engage in interjurisdictional competition. Finally, it is generally believed that the presence of transboundary externalities makes a strong case for centralized decision-making in the form of international environmental agreements. Basic economic reasoning predicts, however, that these agreements will be threatened by free-riding, perhaps thereby undermining the arguments for centralized decision-making. But this reasoning assumes that governments maximize their own welfare and ignore that of others. What if, more realistically, it is assumed that a country is also interested in the welfare of other countries and in how other countries behave in the international setting?

3. OVERVIEW

The first part of the book begins with Chapter 2, which examines the possibilities for Member States in the EU to determine a national environmental policy that differs from the environmental policy imposed by the Union. The chapter identifies the limits for national environmental sovereignty by examining the provisions in the treaties that allow Member States to maintain and enact their own national environmental measures. It thus deals with the question of allocation of powers between a central level of authority (the Union) and a decentralized level (the Member States).

Chapter 3 presents a theoretical and empirical analysis of the effects of subsidiarity on European Community legislation. The concept of 'subsidiarity' attempts to strike a balance between respect for democratic self-governance and efficiency of Community action. The chapter demonstrates, however, that the way in which subsidiarity was finally included in the Treaty favours self-governance and may inhibit Community action even in those situations where the envisaged Community action would produce clear benefits compared to action at the level of the Member States. Community institutions have implemented subsidiarity in a manner which avoids this outcome, but tends to favour Community action at the expense of respect for localities. Chapter 3 also illustrates that the effect of subsidiarity on Community legislation in the 1990s is ambiguous. On the one hand, subsidiarity has been quite successful in reducing the overall volume of Community proposals. On the other hand, it has not been able to alter adopted Community legislation from strongly binding instruments, such as regulations and decisions, to less binding instruments, such as directives.

Chapter 4 relates subsidiarity to the public finance literature. Both economic principles and the principle of subsidiarity prescribe that differences in national endowments, preferences and cultural traditions require a considerable degree of decentralization of environmental policy in the Community. However, decentralized decision-making may be inappropriate in the presence of transboundary externalities, scale economies or relatively homogeneous endowments and preferences. The chapter illustrates that subsidiarity is not a question of either centralized or decentralized decision-making, but involves a mixture of powers at different levels. An environmental regulatory system with harmonized target standards at Community level and differentiated emission standards at the level of the Member States may combine the advantages of central rules with decision-making by Member States. Community water policy legislation, which has been revised in light of subsidiarity, incorporates this system and allows Member States to choose the necessary means for achieving the harmonized standard.

The second part of the book begins with Chapter 5, which examines the proposition that central governments should let local governments control local externalities. This is examined in a model with local externalities and in a federal system, where the central and the local authorities are imperfectly informed. These respective authorities have the same goals but different information. The local authority may be better informed about the local demand for changes in environmental policy, whereas the central authority may be better informed about many scientific aspects related to changes in environmental quality. It is demonstrated that the central authority can introduce a grant-in-aid system that induces the local authority to take central authority information into account and combine it with local information. The grant-in-aid system is flexible so that the local authority is induced to use a weighted combination of local and central information. At one extreme, the central authority is highly uncertain of the environmental and health effects of a specific pollutant. In this case, the tax subsidy scheme may be designed to allow local information to play an essential role in the environmental policy. At the other extreme, the central authority is quite certain that a specific pollutant must not exceed a certain limit. In this case, the tax subsidy scheme is designed to allow local information little influence on environmental policy.

Chapter 6 examines whether environmental regulations affect international trade and capital movements. The chapter gives an overview of both theoretical and empirical studies examining this question. The general conclusion that emerges from the literature is that neither the theoretical nor the empirical analysis supports trade effects and large-scale capital flight as a response to stricter environmental policies. The implication is that there is no reason for governments to engage in interjurisdictional competition.

However, to engage in interjurisdictional competition it is enough that governments believe that they can attract capital and jobs. Therefore, the finding in Chapter 6 does not lead to a rejection of the possibility of inter-jurisdictional competition. In Chapter 7 such competition is examined when there is imperfect competition. It might be expected that imperfect competition would increase the scope for environmental capital flight, and thereby also for ecological dumping. The general conclusion is that the literature on imperfect competition provides a range of predictions about ecological dumping from the literature on perfect competition. There may be incentives for governments to loosen their environmental policy in order either to attract firms to their country or to capture market shares in international markets. This result, however, is not robust. It may also be rational for a government to implement an environmental policy which is too strict.

Chapter 8 challenges the basic economic reasoning that International Environmental Agreements (IEAs) are undermined by free-riding. Game theory argues that the number of countries in an IEA is usually very small, while such agreements do not give any additional benefits compared to the situation where they did not exist. However, cooperation does take place, and the chapter introduces two factors that may enhance the chance of forming IEAs. It is illustrated, first, that a very simple form of commitment may easily expand the stable agreement and, in the end, induce full cooperation. Second, the concept of fairness is introduced. When fairness is introduced, the countries not only maximize their own welfare, but are affected by the welfare of others as well. It is demonstrated that fairness may reduce free-riding behaviour, thereby increasing the relevance of IEAs.

2. Framing environmental policy in the EU

1. INTRODUCTION

Concern for the environment has become an important dimension of cooperation within the European Union. The introductory articles of both the EU and the EC Treaty set forth the principles of cooperation. Article 2 EC emphasizes that the objective of the Community is 'to promote . . . a harmonious, balanced and sustainable development of economic activities'. Article 3 EC cites the duties of the Community, which include the introduction of 'a policy in the sphere of the environment'. Compared to the Treaty of Rome and the Single European Act (SEA), where environmental protection is not mentioned in the introductory articles, the EC Treaty clearly attaches considerable importance to the environment.

Even though environmental protection is recognized as an important objective in the EC Treaty, it is, however, equally clear that environmental concern does not allow for national measures with an environmental aim *ad infinitum* (Krämer, 1992, p. 78). Member States' possibilities of implementing national environmental measures that differ from EU measures are restrained by several provisions in the Treaties. The internal market, in particular, imposes several restrictions on national environmental policies. Article 14 EC determines that the internal market 'shall comprise an area without internal frontiers in which the free movement of goods, persons, services and capital is ensured'. A well-functioning internal market requires in addition that equal conditions of competition for firms in the Community are maintained.

The potential conflict is most distinct when environmental regulations are imposed in the form of product standards. In the extreme, a product standard imposed as a product ban most clearly affects the free movement of goods. Is it acceptable for one country to ban a specific product because it believes the related environmental consequences are too severe? In this case, a balance has to be found between national environmental priorities and the free movement of goods.

Another source of potential conflict is where the Community has implemented an environmental policy, but where some Member States consider

9

the level of protection too low. Is it acceptable for one country to believe that the level of protection the other 14 countries agree on is too low and therefore to apply more protective measures? Again a balance between national environmental priorities and Community regulations has to be found.

The EU has up to the present adopted more than 250 pieces of environmental legislation (Jordan et al., 1999). Nevertheless, EU environmental policy measures are by no means exhaustive. There are still many environmental matters left unregulated. Whether the EU has legislated, and thereby harmonized, in a specific area has consequences for a Member State deciding to introduce new, or change existing, environmental regulations. The free movement of goods is one essential cornerstone of the internal market. Equal conditions of competition for firms in the internal market represent another.

This chapter examines the possibilities for Member States in the EU to determine a national environmental policy that differs from the environmental policy imposed by the Community. The chapter will identify the limits for national environmental sovereignty by examining the provisions in the Treaty that allow Member States to maintain and enact their own measures. The underlying premise is that a uniform harmonized Community standard imposes a welfare loss for the countries where the optimal level of environmental quality differs from the harmonized level. Figure 1.1 in the previous chapter showed that both countries suffer a welfare loss by the harmonized measure. But the size of the welfare loss depends upon Member States' possibilities to derogate from the harmonized measure and implement environmental standards that achieve the optimal level of environmental quality. If, for instance, country 2 in Figure 1.1 is free to derogate from the harmonized measure it can implement an environmental policy that achieves pollution level P_2.

Whether or not a Member State is allowed to do this is related to the complex question of allocation of powers between a centralized level of authority (the Community) and a decentralized level (the Member States). This question has several aspects, but by focusing on how the Community regulates environmental sovereignty, the chapter deals with just one of these aspects. Moreover, the question of allocation of power between a central and local level has a positive and a normative dimension. Analysis in the positive dimension deals with the questions of how the allocation of powers is made, the determinants of this allocation, and the consequences thereof. The normative analysis deals with the question of how the allocation of powers should be made. This chapter deals with the positive analysis, leaving the normative analysis to Chapters 3–5.

The chapter is organized as follows. Section 2 examines how the legal base for environmental policy has developed from the Treaty of Rome to the Amsterdam Treaty. Section 3 provides a taxonomy of Member States' possibilities to determine their own level of environmental protection. Section 4 examines how Member States' possibilities to determine their own level of environmental protection is limited by concerns for the free movement of goods in the Community. Section 5 examines Member States' possibilities to determine their own level of environmental protection when the Community has implemented harmonized measures in the area. Section 6 discusses issues of environmental federalism. Section 7 concludes.

2. FROM ROME TO AMSTERDAM

This section describes the development of the legal base on which EU environmental policy has been founded from the beginning in 1957 up to the present (see, for instance, Hildebrand, 1992; Johnson and Corcelle, 1989; and Liefferink, 1996 for more elaborate analyses). In this chapter the legal base comprises articles from three different places in the Treaty: (1) articles in the introductory part of the Treaty, defining objectives and principles; (2) the article concerning the internal market, on which, for instance, process standards are based (Article 95 EC); and (3) articles specifically relating to environmental policy, on which, for instance, process standards are based (Article 175 EC).

2.1. The Treaty of Rome

The Treaty of Rome of 1957 did not mention environmental protection. Its main goal was to establish a common market between the six founding members – Belgium, the Federal Republic of Germany, France, Italy, Luxembourg, and the Netherlands. From the very beginning, however, the shift of substantial economic competences was a continuous source of controversy (Liefferink, 1996). Consequently, unanimous voting in the Council was the rule rather than the exception.

Despite the lack of a legal base from which to pursue environmental policy, measures were nevertheless adopted for the preservation and protection of nature. The motivation behind the Community's efforts was to ensure that different national environmental measures did not become an obstacle to the common market, business competition, and the free movement of goods. The legal base consisted of Articles 100 and 235, and the measures can be divided into two categories on the basis of their legal base.

The measures in the first category were based on Article 100 of the Treaty of Rome and were directly related to the functioning of the internal market. Article 100 prescribes that the Council shall issue directives for the approximation of the laws, regulations and administrative provisions in the Member States which directly affect the establishment or functioning of the internal market. The argument for quoting Article 100 as justification for issuing environmental regulations is that differences in such regulations in the Member States may distort competition. Thus the first environmentally related directives were designed to remove barriers to trade caused by different national environmental regulations. Examples of such measures are the directives regulating permissible sound level and exhaust systems in motor vehicles (70/157/EEC), motor vehicle emissions (70/220/EEC), the composition of detergents (73/404/EEC) and sulphur content of gas oil (75/716/EEC) (Hildebrand, 1992; Liefferink, 1996).

The measures in the second category, based on Article 235 of the Treaty of Rome, were not motivated by the internal market. Rather, they were the first attempts to create a new policy. Article 235 applied whenever the Treaty did not specify a justification for carrying through a necessary action. If that was the case, the Council, acting unanimously, should take the appropriate measures. Article 235 was a 'safety valve' which enabled the institutions to react to incidents which had not been foreseen at the drafting of the Treaty. Since environmental protection was not included in the Treaty of Rome, measures such as environmental quality standards regarding surface water and air (76/160/EEC, 78/659/EEC, 79/923/EEC, 80/779/EEC) and framework provisions in the fields of water pollution and waste (75/442/EEC, 76/464/EEC, 78/319/EEC) had to be adopted on the basis of Article 235 (Liefferink, 1996).

2.2.   The Single European Act

Before the SEA came into force in 1987, it was agreed among most Member States that the EC should figure prominently in the area of environmental protection. But the SEA, which formally brought environmental issues into the Treaty, was not path-breaking, and did not produce any change in environmental policy. On the contrary, the SEA was mainly a formal confirmation of politically established practices (Johnson and Corcelle, 1989, p. 342).

The SEA included a new section (section VII, Articles 130R to 130T) that defined the Community's competence to act in the environmental sphere. Article 100 was amended by Article 100A. In this way EU environmental policy continued to have two different sources. This duality is not unique in the EU, but it illustrates the close relations between environmental policy and the internal market.

Analogous with Article 100, Article 100A of the SEA aims at complete harmonization and places responsibility on the Commission for harmonizing the laws of the Member States. In addition, the most important elements in Article 100A are:

- The article has to ensure the establishment of the internal market.
- Unanimity is no longer demanded; the Commission can now make decisions with qualified majority.
- The Commission, in its proposals concerning the environment, will take as a base a high level of protection.
- A Member State, after having notified the Commission, may apply national provisions which may restrict the free movements of goods; these national provisions shall be justified by the provisions of Article 36 or relating to environmental protection or the working environment and must not constitute a means of arbitrary discrimination on trade between Member States.

Article 130R of the SEA mentions the objectives for the activities of the EC in the environmental field, and the considerations to be borne in mind, as well as the principles for the environmental measures. It also states that environmental protection requirements shall be a component of the Community's other policies. This provision is unique. In no other policy does the Treaty specify such a requirement (Krämer, 1992, p. 10). Furthermore, Article 130R sets out guidelines for activities of the Community by establishing that the Community shall take action relating to the environment to the extent to which the objectives can be better attained at the Community level than at the level of the individual Member States. Thus the principle of subsidiarity was being applied to environmental measures before it was included as a general principle by the Maastricht Treaty.

Article 130S stipulates that the Council unanimously decides what actions are to be taken. The actions are put forward by the Commission, and the European Parliament is heard according to a consulting procedure. The Council can decide unanimously that some decisions are to be made by qualified majority.

According to Article 130T, the Member States may introduce or maintain more stringent measures. However, these must be compatible with the Treaty. Contrary to Articles 100 and Article 100A, where the objective is complete harmonization, the objective of Articles 130R–130T is minimum harmonization. Article 130T enables Member States to define their own more strict ambient or process requirements and can be viewed as an expression of balancing of Community and Member States' interests (Rehbinder, 1996).

2.3. The Maastricht Treaty

The entry into force of the Maastricht Treaty on 7 February 1992 meant a continuation of the course of action laid down by the SEA. The Maastricht Treaty did not add many new articles to the environmental field, but it developed the institutional and legal base for environmental policy previously introduced by the SEA. In the preamble to the EU Treaty, in Article 2 – which lays down the aim of the EC – as well as in Article 3, which defines the means of implementation, environment takes an important position.[1] Hence the Maastricht Treaty sharpened the focus on environmental questions in the daily work of the EC and gave environmental policy an increasingly high priority in the legal base.

As in the SEA, the key environmental policy articles in the Maastricht Treaty were Articles 100A and 130R–130T.

Article 100A was amended in only one essential respect. The Council should take decisions according to the co-decision procedure (Article 189B). The important consequence of this was that under certain circumstances the European Parliament could veto the adoption of a proposal from the Council.

The amendments of Articles 130R–130T were more comprehensive. In Article 130R the most important amendments were as follows:

- The new formulation referred to 'Community policy', instead of the previous 'Community action', in the environmental field.
- EC regional and global environmental problems were added to the objectives of EC environmental policy.
- It was added that environmental protection requirements should be integrated into the definition and implementation of other Community policies.
- Community environmental policy should aim at a high level of protection.

Further, the clause that the Community should take action only to the extent to which the objectives could be attained better at Community level than at the level of the individual Member States was dropped. The reason was that the Maastricht Treaty adopted the principle of subsidiarity as a general principle laid down in Article 3B.

Article 130S was also amended and expanded in a number of respects:

- The Council should adopt measures according to the cooperation procedure (Article 189C).[2]
- Decisions made under the provisions in Article 130S were to be coordinated with the implementation of the actions in Article 130R.

- In some cases the Council may make decisions unanimously.[3]
- In other fields the Council should adopt general action programmes setting out priority objectives. These should be adopted according to the co-decison procedure (Article 189B).[4]
- Actions should be financed by the Member States.
- The Council may make provisional exceptions and decide on financial support if the expenditures are estimated to be out of proportion to the authorities of a Member State, without prejudice to the 'polluter pays principle'.

Article 130T was unamended.

2.4. The Amsterdam Treaty

On 17 June 1997, the Heads of State and Government of the EU agreed on a new treaty. The Amsterdam Treaty was signed on 2 October 1997 and amends both the TEU and the TEC.[5] Following the Single European Act and the Maastricht Treaty, the Amsterdam Treaty was the third revision of the treaties. This has made the treaties increasingly complex. Therefore the Amsterdam Treaty has simplified and consolidated the treaties through merging and renumbering of the provisions. The new treaty was mainly sought to prepare the European Union for enlargement and to increase its democratic aspect.

In the run-up to the Amsterdam Treaty none of the large EU countries mentioned environmental policy in their government memoranda (Liefferink and Andersen, 1997). Only Denmark and Sweden, and to a lesser extent, Finland and Austria, were determined to put the environment on the agenda. It is therefore quite remarkable that the Amsterdam Treaty amended the framework for environmental policy on three points: (1) the opening articles of both the TEC and the TEU; (2) the environmental policy chapter, Title XVI (Articles 130R–130T); and (3) the environmental guarantee. The amendments in (3) will be examined in section 4.

With respect to the opening articles, only the TEC mentioned the environment before the Amsterdam Treaty. In the Amsterdam Treaty, environment appears in the opening articles of both the TEC and the TEU. The preamble to the TEU states that the EU is established 'taking into account the principle of sustainable development'.

Article 2 EU states that the Union shall set itself the objective to 'achieve balanced and sustainable development'.

In Article 2 EC the word 'sustainable' has been inserted. It is now stated that 'The Community shall have as its task . . . to promote throughout the Community a harmonious, balanced and sustainable development'.

Furthermore, a new Article 6 has been included in the principles, stating that 'Environmental protection requirements must be integrated into the definition and implementation of Community policies and activities referred to in Article 3, in particular with a view to promoting sustainable development'. Article 6 'promotes' the last sentence in 130S(2) of the Maastricht Treaty from being a principle mentioned only in Title XVI into one of the basic principles in the opening parts of the Treaty.

The amendments to the opening articles have the consequence that any new legal act in the EU can be justified only if it accords with sustainable development. Moreover, any new act must promote a high level of environmental protection and quality. The amendments stress a strong commitment to protect and preserve the environment and thus follow up on the Maastricht Treaty.

One of the official arguments for incorporating sustainable development in both the EU Treaty and the EC Treaty was that the EU thereby reaffirms its commitment with respect to the Earth Summit on Environment and Development in Rio in 1992. There may be other reasons as well, and it is difficult to evaluate the reasons for and the effect of including a concept such as 'sustainable development' in the objectives of the EU. In addition to a general interest in 'greening' the treaties, an equally important reason to include sustainable development was that to do so sends the right signals. The EU is emerging as a leading actor in negotiations over international environmental problems. At the third Conference of the Parties to the Framework Convention on Climate Change (FCCC) in Kyoto, in December 1997, the EU proposed the largest reduction in emissions of greenhouse gases (15 per cent reduction compared to the 1990 level) and stressed the need for a strong response to the risk of climate change. In this respect, to emphasize sustainable development in the opening articles of the treaties is a natural step if the EU intends to play a leading role in negotiations over international environmental problems in the future.

Article 174 (ex Article 130R) has been changed by the 'promotion' of the requirement to integrate environmental protection into the definition and implementation of other Community policies (cf. Article 6 above). Consequently, the final sentence of Article 130R has been deleted.

Article 175 (ex Article 130S) has been changed in two respects. First, the legal basis on which the Council shall decide what actions are to be taken has been changed from the cooperation procedure, Article 252 (ex Article 189C), to the co-decision procedure, Article 251 (ex Article 189B). This has the consequence that under certain circumstances the Parliament may veto the adoption of a proposal. In the Maastricht Treaty the Council should adopt decisions based on Article 189B according to that stated in Article 100B, and Article 130S stated that decisions should be adopted based on

Article 189C. Consequently, the Parliament had more influence on the environmental acts based on Article 100A than on the acts based on Article 130S. This is changed by the Amsterdam Treaty, which ensures that Articles 100A and 130S have the same decision-making procedure. Thus the Amsterdam Treaty increases the Parliament's influence over environmental policy. Furthermore, Article 189B has also been amended by the Amsterdam Treaty. In the new Article 251 it has become easier for the Parliament to reject a proposal. According to Article 189B of the Maastricht Treaty, the Council could convene a meeting in the Conciliation Committee for further negotiations if the Parliament intended to reject the proposal. This possibility is not present in the Amsterdam Treaty. According to the new Article 251, the Parliament can reject a proposal without further negotiations with the Council, thus making it easier for the Parliament to reject a proposal. It should be noted, however, that the Council continues to act by unanimity in provisions primarily of a fiscal nature. Thus a possible CO_2 tax still has to be decided by unanimity. The second change in Article 175 is that the Council must now consult the Committee of the Regions in addition to the European Parliament and the Economic and Social Committee.

Article 176 (ex Article 130T) is unamended by the Amsterdam Treaty.

2.5.　From Rome to Amsterdam: Milestones on the Way

Hildebrand (1992) and Liefferink (1996) distinguish between three phases in the history of EU environmental policy. The first phase in Hildebrand is from 1956 to 1972. In this period the overriding objective of the Community was to abolish trade impediments between Member States. Therefore environmental policy initiatives were incidental to the overriding economic objectives. In the second phase, from 1973 to 1987, a Community environmental policy begins to emerge, partly as a response to increased public pressure. The third phase, from 1987 onwards, Hildebrand labels the 'initiative phase' because Community environmental policy now rests on a solid legal base, both in terms of treaty provisions and because of the increasingly comprehensive Environmental Action Programmes (EAPs). Liefferink (1996) operates with approximately the same three phases, but defines them as: (1) the 1970s; (2) the 1980s; and (3) post-SEA.

Both Hildebrand and Liefferink stress the importance of the EAPs and political leadership by some Member States. The First EAP drafted by the Commission (Com (73)530), in particular, is identified as a milestone. That EAP defined the Community objectives, principles, priorities and measures in Community environmental efforts. By this means it formally paved the way for a new field not mentioned in the original treaties.

Hildebrand and Liefferink both argue that the third phase starts with the SEA. The SEA is another milestone in EU environmental policy because it had three important effects. First of all, it introduced the formal legal provisions that define EU environmental policy (Article 130R–T SEA). These provisions required that environmental protection should be integrated in all Community policies, incorporate the principle of subsidiarity, and define minimum harmonization by which Member States can maintain or introduce more protective measures as the rule. Second, the SEA made it clear that realization of the internal market and environmental protection are closely connected. Third, the SEA started a process of institutional changes with respect to majority voting and the Parliament's influence. The amended Article 100A prescribed a new cooperation procedure characterized by qualified majority voting and limited formal powers by the Parliament. Hence Article 130R–T was a much more explicit legal base for environmental measures than Article 235. Moreover, Article 100A was more directly related to the internal market than Article 100 (see, for example, Krämer, 1987; Koppen, 1993).

The Maastricht Treaty and the Amsterdam Treaty intensified the process of institutional change. After the adoption of the Maastricht Treaty all decisions were taken by qualified majority. Moreover, a co-decision procedure was introduced into Article 100A according to which the Parliament under some circumstances can veto Council decisions. With the Amsterdam Treaty the co-decision procedure also applies in the environmental articles.

It is difficult to assess the importance of the emphasis in the Amsterdam Treaty on sustainable development. The introductory parts of the Treaty do not directly influence Community activities. The importance should not be underestimated, though, because they are a guidance to Community activities in the medium or long term. Bär and Krämer (1998) argue that the greatest achievements of the Amsterdam Treaty in the environmental field are that the two principles of sustainable development and the integration principle have been given particular prominence.

The increased influence by the Parliament in the decision-making procedures is undoubtedly one of the most important changes in the Amsterdam Treaty. The Parliament has a reputation as the most pro-environment of the EC institutions. In an analysis of the Environment Committee in the Parliament, Judge (1992) shows that the Parliament has a considerable commitment to environmental protection and that it has been successful in its efforts to influence EU environmental policy. This last finding is important because the co-decision procedure not only allows the Parliament to veto proposals; it also provides an opportunity to involve a conciliation committee with the specific task to reach agreement. In this way, the

Parliament not only has a 'blocking' role, but also has a facilitating role in seeking to obtain agreement to environmental policy measures. Earnshaw and Judge (1996), for instance, show how the Parliament through the Conciliation Committee improved the possibilities for Member States to use national environmental taxes with respect to packaging.

Even though the Commission 'in its proposals . . . concerning environmental protection . . . will take as a base a high level of protection' (Article 95 EC), and 'Community policy on the environment shall aim at a high level of protection' (Article 174 EC), there may still be Member States that wish to implement environmental measures that deviate from those established by the EU. This depends upon whether the measures that the Member States wish to deviate from aim at minimum harmonization (Article 175 EC) or complete harmonization (Article 95 EC). These two possibilities are examined in the following two sections.

3. COMMUNITY VS MEMBER STATE COMPETENCES – A TAXONOMY

Community environmental legislation is rapidly expanding and is required to 'aim at a high level of protection'. There are still, however, a number of areas that are unregulated by the Community. When a Member State implements or enacts environmental measures in such an unregulated area, it may interfere with Community measures in regulated areas, such as Community trade. Therefore, Member States cannot freely implement or enact national measures in areas unregulated by the Community. In the regulated areas, Member States may wish to implement national measures different from Community measures. A Member State may, for instance, believe that the level of environmental protection prescribed by the Community measure is too low. Also, in this situation Member States cannot freely determine their own national measures.

Member States' possibilities to enact national measures differ in these two situations. If, on the one hand, the EU has not introduced any harmonized measures in the area, a Member State's environmental regulations, like any other national regulations, must be compatible with the Treaty and, in particular, must not constitute an obstacle to the free movement of goods. If, on the other hand, the area is one in which the EU has already introduced harmonized measures, it is important to determine whether the envisaged regulation is a product regulation or a process regulation.

If it is a product regulation, the EU environmental regulations are based on Article 95 EC, which principally requires complete harmonization. There is, however, a very limited possibility of maintaining or introducing national measures as described in Article 95 (4–10) EC. This possibility is called the environmental guarantee.

In case of process regulation, the EU environmental regulations are based on Article 175 EC, which requires partial (or minimum) harmonization which could, for instance, be a minimum standard. In this case the Member States are allowed to enact more (but not less) stringent measures. These more stringent measures are, however, subject to the same requirement as any other national regulations: they must not constitute an obstacle to free trade.

Hence, when the Community has either not harmonized, or has regulated by minimum harmonization, Member States' competences to enact more protective measures are restrained by the same requirement: they must not constitute an obstacle to the internal market and the free movement of goods. When the Community has implemented total harmonization, Member States' competences to enact more protective measures are restrained by the environmental guarantee. These two situations will be examined in the next two sections.

4.   FREE MOVEMENT OF GOODS AND ENVIRONMENTAL PROTECTION

4.1.   Minimum Harmonization

In so far as the Community enjoys concurrent competence under Article 175 EC, it does so only to enact minimum harmonization measures. According to Article 176 EC, Member States are in such a situation free to maintain or adopt more (but not less) stringent measures as long as these are compatible with the Treaty. Such measures are to be notified to the Commission (Scott, 1998, p. 40). Minimum harmonization thus means that Community legislation defines the 'floor' of rights and duties below which national measures may not sink. The 'ceiling' beyond which neither the Community nor the Member States are entitled to regulate is defined by the Treaty (Weatherill, 1994). The room left for Member States to enact measures that deviate from the EU measures is between the 'floor' and the 'ceiling'. This room defines how competence is distributed between the Community and the Member States.

When an EU environmental measure is adopted under Article 175 EC, national environmental measures deviating from the EU measures do not exceed the 'ceiling' as long as the measures are 'compatible with the Treaty'. It is, however, not particularly clear when national measures are not compatible with the Treaty. Taken literally, 'compatible with the Treaty' means that national measures must be compatible with any of the provisions and principles in the Treaty. There are many such provisions. For example, the freedom to provide services is defined in Article 49 EC, free movement of workers in Article 39 EC, free movement of capital in Article 56 EC, prohibition of state aid in Article 87 EC, the prohibition on taxing foreign products differently from domestic in Article 90 EC. A meaningful definition of the room for national competences would be difficult to obtain if all these provisions and principles were to be observed.

National environmental measures deviating from EU measures are unlikely to affect all of these provisions and principles. A process-based measure, such as the directive on the combating of air pollution from industrial plants (84/360/EC), is unlikely to affect, for instance, the free movement of workers. The room for national competences must therefore be characterized only by the provisions they affect.

Many of the national environmental measures are likely to affect the free movement of goods. Scott (1998) and Weatherill (1994) argue that a meaningful characterization has to take its point of departure in the Community policies for the free movement of goods as defined in Articles 23–31 EC. The free movement of goods is a cornerstone of the internal market. Consequently, the elimination of any obstacles to this is crucial for the smooth functioning of the internal market which, in turn, is a necessary condition for the ongoing process of European economic integration (Temmink, 2000).

Articles 28 and 29 EC prohibit all quantitative restrictions on imports and exports and all measures having equivalent effect. In this way, minimum harmonization means that the EU environmental measures provide the 'floor' and Articles 28–30 the 'ceiling', thus defining the room for national environmental competences. According to Article 28, import bans and quotas are obviously prohibited. Moreover, following the Dassonville case (Case 8/74, *Procureur du Roi* v. *Dassonville*), there is a ban on 'all trading rules enacted by Member States which are capable of hindering, directly or indirectly, actually or potentially, intra-Community trade' (Case 8/74, para. 5). This definition has a wide scope. It is hard to find any trade-related measure that does not potentially influence Community trade.

There are, however, certain limited possibilities for Member States to enact measures that restrict the free movement of goods. Article 30 EC contains a list of public concerns that may justify such restrictions. Among these concerns are, for instance, public morality, public policy or public security, the protection of health and the life of humans, animals and plants. Environmental concerns are not mentioned directly and environmental measures are thus only justified if they have a direct influence on humans, animals or plants. Such restrictions may not, however, be used as a means of arbitrary discrimination or a disguised restriction on trade.

The European Court of Justice (ECJ) has interpreted Article 30 in a restrictive way. The list of grounds which could justify trade restriction in Article 30 EC is considered as being exhaustive and cannot be enlarged. However, in the Cassis de Dijon case (case 120/78 *Rewe* v. *Zentralverwaltung*) the court interpreted Article 30 EC so as to reach practically the same result as an enlargement of the grounds of Article 30 (Krämer, 1993). The Cassis de Dijon case concerned different provisions for the marketing of products. Dissimilarities in the marketing provisions are likely to lead to a number of conflicts with Article 28 EC in cases where Community legislation is lacking. The Court declared that a Member State measure that restricted the free movement of goods had to be accepted to the extent that it was justified by mandatory requirements. Such a measure was, however, subject to two requirements. First, it had be non-discriminating between Member States. A measure must apply indistinctly to domestic as well as foreign products. Second, the restrictive measure must observe the principle of proportionality. A restriction must be based on a real need. If the same result might be obtained with measures less restrictive for the free movement of goods, these are preferred.

Mandatory requirements were defined as the necessity of fiscal controls, fair trading practices, and consumer protection. More important, though, the Court opened the way for the existence of other mandatory requirements. In the Danish Bottles case (case 302/86 *Commission* v. *Denmark*) the Court recognized that the protection of the environment was a mandatory requirement that could justify restrictions on the free movement of goods.

4.2. The Danish Bottles Case

The case against Denmark was brought to the ECJ by the Commission, claiming that the Danish regulation that introduced a deposit-and-return system for drink containers was incompatible with Article 28 EC.

Denmark has a long tradition of paying a deposit on empty beer and soft drinks bottles. This system has demonstrated its efficiency, as a great many empties are returned and deposits refunded. In 1978, 1981 and 1984 the Danish deposit system was amended in several respects which made the system more efficient. The amendments resulted in a number of limitations on the containers of these beverages. First, only beverages in containers which could be returned to the distributor were allowed to be marketed. Second, only beverages which could enter into a container collection and recycling system were allowed to be marketed. Third, the beverage containers had to be approved by the Environmental Protection Agency, although non-approved containers were allowed to be marketed in Denmark in a quantity of no more than 3000 hectolitres per year, or if the purpose was to test the container on the Danish market.

Producers of beverages and containers in other Member States complained to the Commission, asserting that the Danish system imposed upon them unnecessary additional costs. After Denmark had been heard in the case, the Commission decided in December 1986 to try to test the legality of the Danish system at the ECJ.

The Commission recognized that a returnable bottles system was a legal means of reducing packaging in society, but found that the Danish system in practice imposed a heavier burden on imported goods than on home production. Moreover, it went further than required and was in contradiction with the principle of proportionality. The opinion of the Commission in this matter was that the environmental policy objectives with a deposit system could be attained in a less restrictive form than was the case with the Danish system.

An additional problem with the Danish system was that the Environmental Protection Agency should approve new containers for beverages which might hamper the marketing of foreign products in Denmark. It was the opinion of the Commission that the specific design of the Danish deposit system gave rise to a quantitative restriction on how much non-approved packaging was allowed to be marketed in Denmark, and, thus, Article 28 EC was violated.

The Danish authorities stated that the Danish returnable packaging system was introduced out of legitimate concern for environmental protection in general, that is, concern for preservation of resources, and out of a desire to limit waste. The Commission did not contest the validity of this consideration. As regards any restrictions on the free movement of goods, the Danish authorities acknowledged that the Danish returnable bottles system had a negative effect on trade within the Community. However, they stated that the Commission itself had acknowledged that environmental protection considerations could carry more weight than considerations of free movement of goods, and that the negative effects had limited importance. The Danish authorities found that the principle of proportionality was violated only if there had been measures which were just as effective and to a lesser degree hampered trade within the EC. The Danish government was of the opinion that no such measures were to be found. As to the quantitative restriction of 3000 hectolitres per year of non-approved packaging, the attitude of the Danish authorities was that a delimitation of the derogation was necessary for the functioning of the system and, consequently, in accordance with the Treaty.

The Court stated that obstacles to the free movement of goods had to be accepted when there are no common regulations in a field, if such obstacles are needed to safeguard necessary considerations and are acknowledged by the EC. It argued that environmental protection was indeed such a consideration. However, these obstacles must not be discriminatory toward any Member State and must observe the principle of proportionality. The Court thus acknowledges that a compulsory deposit system can be accepted in order to attain legitimate environmental objectives.

Following this decision, the Court took a position on the specific design of the Danish system. It paid particular attention to the Danish demand for the Environmental Protection Agency's approval of marketed packaging. This demand was a problem because it imposed heavy additional costs on foreign producers and made it very difficult to export to Denmark. It was decided that Denmark could maintain the claim, stipulating that the packaging must enter into a compulsory deposit-and-return system with the purpose of guaranteeing recycling. On the other hand, Denmark was not allowed to maintain import restrictions on non-approved packaging of up to 3000 hectolitres per year. Denmark therefore had to withdraw the claim, saying that the Environmental Protection Agency should approve the marketed packaging. In this way the Commission's claim was sustained.

The connection between the level of environmental protection and the free movements of goods is well illustrated in the conclusion of the Advocate General's motion for resolution in the returnable-bottles case. The Advocate General said that 'there has to be a balancing of interests between the free movement of goods and environmental protection, even if in achieving the balance, the high standard of the protection sought has to be reduced' (Common Market Law Reports, 21 March 1989, p. 629).

On the one hand, the judgment shows that there is no doubt that environmental protection is a legitimate objective that can justify certain obstacles to the free movement of goods. On the other hand, the national measures cannot be applied to ensure the highest level of protection. The Commission's and the Court's chief argument that Denmark did not observe its obligations to the internal market was that the Danish system was too far-reaching. Denmark's choice of the highest level of environmental protection violated the principles of non-discrimination (indistinctly applicable) and proportionality. If the Danish authorities had chosen a returnable-bottles system that protected the environment to a lesser extent (where the Environmental Protection Agency should not approve of the packaging which, according to both the Danish authorities and the Commission, reduces the protection of the environment), it would have been much more difficult for the Commission to be (partly) upheld.

In summary, when the Community has implemented an environmental directive prescribing minimum harmonization, Member States are allowed to maintain or introduce more protective measures provided these are compatible with the Treaty. 'Compatible with the Treaty' means that the national measures must not restrict the free movement of goods, directly or indirectly, actual or potential. There are, however, two situations where national environmental measures may be allowed to restrict the free movement of goods.

The first situation is where the restrictions on the free movement of goods is justified by mandatory requirements. These measures must, however, apply indistinctly and must be proportional. In the Danish Bottles Case the Danish requirement for a returnable-bottles system had to be changed because the measures were not indistinctly applicable. The second situation is where restrictions on the free movements are justified on the basis of the explicit Treaty-based exceptions laid down by Article 30 EC. This article is more restrictive than mandatory requirements and gives less residual competence to the Member States. The mandatory requirements exception is, for instance, permitted only in the case of indistinctly applicable measures. Distinctly applicable measures may, however, be permitted by the exceptions in Article 30 EC (Scott, 1998). Mandatory requirements and Article 30 EC are nevertheless two sides of the same coin. They both express the residual competence of Member States to enact environmental measures that restrict the free movement of goods. Moreover, the freedom to enact restrictive national measures is in both situations given, provided such measures are proportional and do not constitute an arbitrary discrimination or a disguised restriction of trade.

5. THE ENVIRONMENTAL GUARANTEE

The environmental guarantee was introduced at the Intergovernmental Conference (IGC) in 1985. The reason for introducing the environmental guarantee was that there was a political will to change the decision-making procedure in Article 100 EEC (now Article 95 EC) from unanimity to qualified majority voting. Some Member States were very reluctant to accept qualified majority voting because it could lead to situations where a Member State had to implement a measure it had actually voted against in the Council. Qualified majority voting in the internal market was perceived as an attack on national sovereignty.

The Danish and German governments, for instance, feared that qualified majority voting would reduce national environmental sovereignty and that it would reduce the level of environmental protection (Krämer, 1987). Before the IGC in 1985, Denmark had threatened to vote against a directive regulating car emissions. This directive was a compromise between the different interests in the EU, but the Danish government was of the opinion that the compromise prescribed standards that were too low. It wanted the EU standards to be the same as the US standards (Holzinger, 1994). By introducing qualified majority voting in Article 100 EEC Denmark was no longer in a position to prevent the adoption of such a directive.

Therefore it was difficult to reach an agreement on how the new Article 100A should be formulated. Article 100A was a cornerstone of the Single European Act, so the Heads of State and Government were keen to reach an agreement. To do that, they finally asked all advisers to leave the room. The idea was that it would thereby be easier to reach a political agreement on a formulation of Article 100A and a possibility for Member States to opt out. An agreement was reached, and the possibility to opt out was subsequently named 'the environmental guarantee' by the Danish government.

Given this background, it should be no surprise that the environmental guarantee gave rise to a significant amount of confusion (see, for example, Krämer, 1987; Flynn, 1987; Gulmann, 1987). The confusion arose from the fact that the environmental guarantee provided for derogation after harmonization based on a Treaty article. This was rather unusual since according to established case law there are no other ways of derogating from the harmonization measure other than those included in the measure itself (Sevenster, 2000). The environmental guarantee must therefore be clarified through case law. There are, however, only a few examples where the provision has been applied in practice.

The Amsterdam Treaty clarified the environmental guarantee in several respects. In order to explain fully the provision after Amsterdam, however, we shall also examine debate about the different interpretations and the applications of the provision before Amsterdam.

5.1. In the Haze: The Environmental Guarantee Before the Amsterdam Treaty

In the SEA, the environmental guarantee was defined in Article 100A(4) EEC:

> If, after the adoption of a harmonization measure by the Council acting by a qualified majority, a Member State deems it necessary to apply national provisions on grounds of major needs referred to in Article 36, or relating to protection of the environment or the working environment, it shall notify the Commission of these provisions.

> The Commission shall confirm the provisions involved after having verified that they are not a means of arbitrary discrimination or a disguised restriction on trade between Member States.

By way of derogation from the procedure laid down in Articles 169 and 170, the Commission or any Member State may bring the matter directly before the Court of Justice if it considers that another Member State is making improper use of the powers provided for in this Article.

This formulation gave rise to several questions that had to be clarified. First, did the word 'apply' allow Member States to introduced new measures? Second, the word 'confirm' raised some uncertainties about the Commission's role. Did the Commission have to conduct a thorough investigation and a formal approval of the national measures or was the Commission just a 'rubber stamp'? Third, what were the consequences of the Commission's role? Could Member States apply national measures before the Commission had confirmed them? Fourth, did the Member States have to have voted against the measure? The phrase 'qualified majority' has been interpreted by, for instance, Craig and de Búrca (1995) as a requirement that a Member State had to have voted against the directive. Fifth, did the environmental guarantee only apply to harmonization measures adopted by the Council? The first sentence did not mention, for instance, Commission directives.

These questions had to be clarified through the legal documents. Before the Amsterdam Treaty, Germany and Denmark used the environmental guarantee to ban the use of pentachlorophenol (PCP). Following Sevenster (2000), Sloan (1995) and Somsen (1994), these two cases will be used to examine how some of the questions above were clarified by the case law before the Amsterdam Treaty.

The PCP case (Case C-41/93) was brought to Court by the French government with the claim for an annulment of the Commission's confirmation of the German regulations concerning PCP.[6] The background was that in 1987 the German government notified the Commission that it was preparing a regulation restricting the concentration of PCP in wood-treatment preparations to 0.5 per cent. The Commission replied by asking the German government to defer the adoption of the regulation because the Commission was itself preparing a directive on the subject. This directive was submitted in April 1988 and was an amendment to Directive 76/769, which restricted the marketing and use of certain dangerous substances. The proposal limited the PCP concentration in substances and preparations to 0.1 per cent and provided for derogations in three cases.

Despite this, in December 1989 Germany adopted a regulation limiting the concentration of PCP in substances and preparations to 0.01 per cent. Furthermore, the manufacture, marketing or use of the substance was prohibited, and the exemptions were rather limited. When the Council finalized the Commission's proposal for a PCP directive (Directive 91/173/EEC,

Official Journal 1991 L 85, p. 34), Germany voted against the adoption because the German government felt that the proposal was not far-reaching enough. Nevertheless, the directive was adopted in March 1991 on the basis of Article 100A and limited the PCP concentration in substances and preparations to 0.1 per cent. It provided exemptions for products intended for use in the treatment of wood, impregnation of fibres and heavy-duty textiles, as a synthesizing and/or processing agent in industrial processes and in specific treatment of buildings.

In August 1991, the German government notified the Commission that, based on the environmental guarantee, it intended to continue to apply its national provisions concerning PCP. In December 1992, the Commission confirmed the German provisions. The French government was of the opinion that the confirmation should not have been given. It brought the Commission to court, claiming that: (1) the German government did not demonstrate that the PCP regulations were justified based on the needs mentioned in Article 36, or relating to protection of the environment or workplace, or that the regulation was proportionate; (2) more restrictive national regulations can be justified only under Article 100A(4) if the circumstances are specific to that State, which was not the case here; (3) the Commission's confirmation did not observe the requisite legal standard prescribed in Article 190.[7]

The judgment of the Court considered only the latter point because this was enough for annulment. The Court decided that the Commission's confirmation of the German regulation 'did not satisfy the obligation to state reasons laid down in Article 190 of the Treaty and must be annulled for infringement of essential procedural requirements. There is therefore no need to consider the other pleas put forward by the applicant' (Case 41/93, para. 37). In the arguments for annulment, however, the Court also dealt with some of the ambiguities of Article 100a(4), and the two other claims from the French government.

The PCP case showed that if a Member State intended to continue to apply national provisions derogating from the harmonized measure, at least three conditions must be met: (1) the Member State shall notify the Commission; (2) the Commission shall confirm the derogation; and (3) the Commission or the Member State shall provide for satisfactory documentation for the derogation.

With respect to the notification procedure, the PCP case demonstrated that the Member State must notify the Commission, but it is not clear when this should occur. Paragraph 26 stated that if a Member State desires to continue to apply national provisions after the expiration of the time allowed for transposing, or after the entry into force of a harmonization measure, it is required to notify the Commission. Somsen (1994) observes that it thus appears that a Member State may notify the Commission even after expiry of the deadline for application. Paragraph 30, however, stated that a Member State is not allowed to apply the national provisions until after the Commission has confirmed them. Pagh (1996) thus argues that the logical result of paragraph 30 is that a Member State must notify the Commission during the period between the adoption of the directive and the expiration of the time allowed for transposing.

This issue is more clearly dealt with in the Commission's confirmation of the Danish provisions regarding PCP (Decision 96/211/EC). In this decision, the Commission confirmed that Denmark could apply more far-reaching measures regarding PCP. The PCP directive was adopted in March 1991, and the Member States thus had to comply with the directive by July 1992. During 1992, the Danish government informed the Commission several times that they had transposed the PCP directive. The Danish measures were stricter than the provisions of the PCP directive, but the Danish government did not wish to use the environmental guarantee because it was of the opinion that the PCP directive represented a minimum harmonization in which case the Danish government was free to implement more protective measures. This legal point of view was not shared by the Commission, which argued that the PCP directive aimed at complete harmonization. This was then accepted by the Danish government, which by 31 January 1995 notified the Commission that it wanted to use the environmental guarantee and apply its existing national measures.

In its confirmation of the Danish measures, the Commission stressed two conditions. First, that 'Denmark . . . duly communicated those provisions of its national regulations that it intends to continue to apply after the expiry of the deadline for transposing Directive 91/173/EEC. The first notification of these measures was made before expiry of the said deadline for transposition . . .' (Decision 96/211/EC, para. 5). Second, the Commission stated that 'although the formal request to apply Article 100A(4) was not presented before expiry of the deadline in June 1992, the Commission considers that in this case this should not prevent it from being examined. The Danish authorities announced their intention to make formal notification under Article 100A(4) as soon as they were convinced [that the PCP directive aimed at complete harmonization]' (Decision 96/211/EC, para. 5). From these two points, it appears that the Commission accepted the Danish notification even though it was given after the deadline, because the Danish government had acted 'in good faith' (Decision 96/211/EC, para. 5). Hence, if a Member State seeks to apply national provisions after the expiry of the deadline for transposing a directive, it must notify the Commission before the deadline. Only exceptionally can a Member State apply national provisions if they are notified after the expiry of the deadline for transposition.

With respect to the confirmation, the word 'confirm' in Article 100A(4) does not indicate a thorough evaluation of the national measures. Neither is it obvious what status the confirmation has. The PCP case makes it clear that the Commission's confirmation should be a comprehensive administrative examination of the documentation produced by the Member State. In fact, the Court and the Commission understand 'confirm' as a question of approval or denial. In this way a more precise word would have been 'authorize'. When a Member State notifies the Commission that it will apply rules derogating from the harmonized measure, the Commission must satisfy itself that all conditions are fulfilled. In particular, it must ensure that the national provisions are justified on the grounds mentioned in Article 100A(4), and that they are not a means of arbitrary discrimination or a disguised restriction on trade between Member States. This procedure shall ensure that they do not 'apply national rules derogating from the harmonized rules without obtaining confirmation from the Commission' (Case C-41/93, para. 28). Hence a Member State is not permitted to apply the national provisions until after it has obtained confirmation from the Commission (Case C-41/93, para. 30). The Commission argues that if this were not the case, the harmonization measures 'would be rendered ineffective if the Member States retained the right to apply unilaterally national rules derogating from those measures' (Case C-41/93, para. 29).

This interpretation was not, however, reflected in the actual behaviour of the Member States. Between the introduction of the environmental guarantee in the Single European Act in 1987 and the signing of the Amsterdam Treaty in 1997, there were ten cases in which a Member State has declared that it would apply Article 100A(4). The ten cases are shown in Table 2.1

From 1997 up to the Amsterdam Treaty, the Commission had confirmed only two out of ten notifications. Thus in some cases it had not replied after six years. In reality, all Member States considered their measures to be valid until they received a reply from the Commission and thus maintained their national provisions during the confirmation procedure. The main argument was that if the Commission's passivity in effect was not an approval, then the Commission would be in a position to prevent the Member States from applying their national provisions by doing nothing.

The Commission's and the ECJ's interpretation gave the harmonized measure precedence over the national measures because until the Commission authorizes the national measures, the harmonized measure remains in effect. The Member States' interpretation gave the national measures precedence over the harmonized measure because the national measures were valid until the Commission replied. These two opposing views created a situation whereby the Member States had no interest in pushing the Commission to make a decision, and the Commission did not

Table 2.1 The applications of the environmental guarantee between 1987 and 1997

Directive to be derogated from	Denmark	Germany	The Netherlands	Sweden
91/338/EEC Cadmium			Notified 1991 No reply by 1997	Notified 1995 No reply by 1997
91/173/EC PCP	Notified 1995 Confirmed 1996	Notified 1991 Confirmed 1994	Notified 1991 No reply by 1997	Notified 1995 No reply by 1997
94/60/EC Creosote	Notified 1995 No reply by 1997	Notified No reply by 1997	Notified 1991 No reply by 1997	
94/35/EC Sweeteners in foodstuffs 94/36/EC Colours in foodstuffs				
95/2/EC Food additives	Notified 1996 No reply by 1997			

Source: The Danish Environmental Protection Agency.

challenge the Member States' view at court. Consequently, in the case of, for instance, the three Dutch applications of the environmental guarantee, the confirmation procedure lasted for more than six years.

As concerns the demand for documentation, the PCP case showed that the Commission shall provide sufficient documentation for confirmation in order to challenge – at the ECJ – whether or not the conditions for confirmation are met. The Commission shall explain the reasons of fact and law on account of which it considers that the conditions in Article 100A(4) are fulfilled. It is not enough for the Commission to describe in general terms the content and aim of the national provisions and just state that those provisions are compatible with Article 100A(4).

As illustrated in section 3, it is a general principle that any derogations from the fundamental principle of the free movement of goods must be narrowly construed. This principle is consistently applied by the ECJ when interpreting Article 30 EC. Sloan (1995) and Pagh (1996) argue that this principle should also be applied to the environmental guarantee. The consequence is that if the Commission refuses to confirm the national provisions, the burden of proof lies with the Member State to show that the provisions are not a disguised restriction of trade between Member States. In particular, it should be determined whether the national measures apply indistinctly and whether they are proportional. With respect to the latter, this implies that it should be determined whether the measure was necessary for the objective and whether less restrictive measures could have been adopted.

The two decisions where the Commission has confirmed national provisions demonstrate that a very important part of the documentation is to show that there are circumstances which are specific to health protection and the environment in the Member State. This issue was raised by the French government in the PCP case, but it was not necessary for the Court to deal with it in this case because the confirmation was annulled, as it did not observe the requisite legal standard prescribed in Article 190.

On 14 September 1994, however, the Commission confirmed the German provisions regarding PCP after new and improved documentation had been produced (Decision 94/783/EC). An important part of the new documentation was that it could be shown that PCP posed a special health problem for Germany. Three major arguments were given: (1) because Germany had been a major producer and user of PCP in the past, the German population was still exposed to abnormally high doses of PCP; (2) PCP may be found in relatively high concentrations in groundwater used for consumption. As much as 72 per cent of German drinking water is groundwater; (3) dioxins are secondary products in the production of PCP, and they are viewed as a particularly serious problem in Germany.

In the Commission's confirmation of the Danish provisions regarding PCP in 1996 (Decision 96/211/EC), great importance was also attached to the specific circumstances in Denmark. The Commission noted that high concentrations of PCP had been observed in Danish groundwater, and that drinking water in Denmark contains a significant amount of unpurified groundwater. The high concentration of PCP in drinking water is due to poor absorption by the alkaline soils in Denmark. PCP therefore passes rapidly from the surface to the groundwater. Moreover, due to the low temperatures in Denmark, PCP does not easily degrade but instead tends to accumulate.

In addition to the obligation to show that there are circumstances which are specific to health protection and the environment in the Member State, the Commission's confirmation must be verified by independent experts. In its confirmation of the German provisions, the Commission decided to seek the scientific assistance of an internationally recognized expert, who presented a report to the Commission. Moreover, the Commission referred to a World Health Organization study which documented that Germany has particularly serious problems with dioxins. In its confirmation of the Danish provisions, the Commission requested the assistance of the same internationally recognized expert as in the German case. The expert was to assess whether there were specific circumstances concerning the environmental and health protection in Denmark and whether the Danish provisions had any commercial effects. The report from the expert plays a decisive role in the Commission's decision.

The PCP case does not clarify whether or not a government's desire to have a higher level of environmental protection than the overall EC harmonized level can be achieved by applying the environmental guarantee. In the first round of confirmation, the Court said that the Commission 'confines itself in the fourth paragraph to indicating the content of the German regulation and the dangers of PCP and then noting in the following paragraph that the limit laid down by the regulation is higher and that the safety margin is justified by the needs specified in Article 100A(4)' (Case C-41/93, para. 35). Hence the Court found that the Commission argued in a very general way that the national provisions were justified by the needs specified in Article 100A(4), which was not enough to justify the application of the environmental guarantee. Consequently, in the second authorization of the German provisions the arguments were much more specific. It was said, for instance, that 'the request by the German authorities to continue to apply the national provisions . . . is justified by the specific circumstances relating to health protection and the environment in Germany' (Decision 94/783/EC, para. 7). This is followed by six examples showing the specific circumstances in Germany. In the confirmation of the

Danish provisions, it was stated that the Danish provisions 'may be justified on grounds of major needs, given the specific situation in that Member State' (Decision 96/211/EC, para. 6), followed by the arguments mentioned above.

Apparently, a general ambition to have a higher level of environmental protection cannot stand alone but must be supported by documentation showing that there are specific circumstances relating to the health protection or the environment in that Member State. In both confirmations, however, the Commission stated that it found it reasonable that a Member State should wish to reduce the exposure levels of certain populations at risk (Decisions 94/783/EC, para. 7, and 96/211/EC, para. 6). The average rate of absorption of dioxins by babies in Germany is 140 times greater than the absorption of an adult man. More stringent German control on sources of dioxin emissions is therefore considered justified because it is a means by which the exposure level of babies is reduced. In the Danish case, Nordic experts have stated that for the populations in the Nordic countries a daily dose of dioxin of five pg/kg of body weight would be acceptable. The Danish authorities mention that babies being breast-fed receive a dose 50 times higher. According to the experts, additional exposure of dioxins should therefore be limited as much as possible. In this respect, the Commission considered the Danish provisions to be reasonable and 'does not have any experts' findings that would enable it to conclude that less stringent measures are available which would achieve the same level of protection' (Decision 96/211/EC, para. 6).

Hence it appears that a general ambition to have a higher level of environmental protection does not justify more stringent national environmental measures. More stringent measures may be justified, however, if a Member State can demonstrate that they must be applied because (1) there are specific circumstances related to health or environmental protection in the Member State, and/or (2) the Member State desires to reduce exposure levels among certain high-risk groups.

In summary, the German and the Danish PCP cases have clarified some, but not all, of the ambiguities in the environmental guarantee. The ECJ's annulment of the Commission's first authorization indicated that the environmental guarantee may only be used after the Commission has been notified of and approved the national measures. This has subsequently been confirmed in the Kortas case (Case 319/97 ECJ). This shows that the Danish government made a mistake in 1987 by naming Article 100A(4) as the 'environmental guarantee'. It is in fact not a guarantee that a Member State can continue to determine its own level of environmental protection. Rather, it is a 'rule of exception'. The rule is that the Community defines the level of environmental protection in the Member States and only by exception may a Member State apply a higher level of environmental protection, and only after permission to do so. Member States cannot use the environmental guarantee generally to set their own level of environmental protection. On the contrary, Member States can only be permitted to apply the environmental guarantee to implement measures that deal with environmental problems specific to that Member State and these measures must be based on thorough scientific documentation.

The main point that was not clarified by the PCP case was whether environmental guarantee could be used to introduce new measures or whether it could be used only to apply existing measures. This last point was clarified by the Amsterdam Treaty.

5.2. The Amsterdam Clarification

The Amsterdam Treaty clarified the environmental guarantee in several respects which at the same time added new ambiguities (see Bär and Krämer, 1998 for a discussion of the environmental consequences of the Amsterdam Treaty as a whole, and Sevenster, 2000 for a discussion of the changes in the environmental guarantee in particular).

In the Amsterdam Treaty Article 100A was renumbered as Article 95 EC. Paragraphs 3, 4 and 5 were replaced by the following paragraphs:

3. The Commission, in its proposals envisaged in paragraph 1 concerning health, safety, environmental protection and consumer protection, will take as a base a high level of protection, taking account in particular of any new development based on scientific facts. Within their respective powers, the European Parliament and the Council will also seek to achieve this objective.

4. If, after the adoption by the Council or by the Commission of a harmonisation measure, a Member State deems it necessary to maintain national provisions on grounds of major needs referred to in Article 36, or relating to the protection of the environment or the working environment, it shall notify the Commission of these provisions as well as the grounds for maintaining them.

5. Moreover, without prejudice to paragraph 4, if, after the adoption by the Council or by the Commission of a harmonisation measure, a Member State deems it necessary to introduce national provisions based on new scientific evidence relating to the protection of the environment or the working environment on grounds of a problem specific to that Member State arising after the adoption of the harmonisation measure, it shall notify the Commission of the envisaged provisions as well as the grounds for introducing them.

6. The Commission shall, within six months of the notifications as referred to in paragraphs 4 and 5, approve or reject the national provisions involved after having verified whether or not they are a means of arbitrary discrimination or a disguised restriction on trade between Member States and whether or not they shall constitute an obstacle to the functioning of the internal market.

In the absence of a decision by the Commission within this period, the national provisions referred to in paragraphs 4 and 5 shall be deemed to have been approved.

When justified by the complexity of the matter and in the absence of danger for human health, the Commission may notify the Member State concerned that the period referred to in this paragraph may be extended for a further period of up to six months.

7. When, pursuant to paragraph 6, a Member State is authorised to maintain or introduce national provisions derogating from a harmonisation measure, the Commission shall immediately examine whether to propose an adaptation to that measure.

8. When a Member State raises a specific problem on public health in a field which has been the subject of prior harmonisation measures, it shall bring it to the attention of the Commission which shall immediately examine whether to propose appropriate measures to the Council.

9. By way of derogation from the procedure laid down in Articles 169 and 170, the Commission and any Member State may bring the matter directly before the Court of Justice if it considers that another Member State is making improper use of the powers provided for in this Article.

10. The harmonisation measures referred to above shall, in appropriate cases, include a safeguard clause authorising the Member States to take, for one or more of the non-economic reasons referred to in Article 36, provisional measures subject to a Community control procedure.

These amendments provided the following clarifications. The first arose from the fact that the phrase 'qualified majority' in the first sentence in Article 100A(4) was deleted. A Member State is thus not required to have voted against the directive. This issue is not explicitly dealt with in the PCP case. However, in the case itself, in the opinion of the Advocate General, and in the confirmation of the Danish provisions, it is mentioned that the respective countries voted against the harmonization proposal. In fact, there has never been a situation where this requirement could be tested. The countries in Table 2.1 all voted against the five harmonization proposals. The Amsterdam clarification is thus a widening of the use of the environmental guarantee. Now it can be used even if the harmonization measure was reached unanimously.

The second clarification was that the introduction of national measures is now permitted. Paragraph 4 of Article 95 EC defines how Member States may maintain existing measures, while paragraph 5 defines in which circumstances new measures may be introduced. Paragraph 5 does not mention that new national measures may be based on the grounds referred to in Article 30 EC, as stated in paragraph 4. Instead, paragraph 5 allows national measures to be based only on grounds relating to the protection of the environment or the working environment. This is the first indication that the grounds upon which Member States can introduce measures after harmonization are more limited than the grounds on which existing measures can be maintained. Bär and Krämer (1998) argue that this contradicts the whole idea of Community environmental policy as defined in Article 174 EC, and speculate whether the reference to Article 30 EC was simply forgotten.

A second indication that the possibilities of introducing new measures are more limited than the possibility of maintaining existing measures is that new, but not existing, measures must be based on 'new scientific evidence' and must be 'specific to that Member State'. The first requirement incorporates one of the Commission's main arguments for its confirmation of the German and Danish PCP regulations. However, the requirement also incorporates some ambiguities. The definition of 'evidence' is unclear. Sevenster (2000) notices that the term 'proof' was used in earlier versions of the Treaty. Bär and Krämer (1998) argue that there is an important difference between 'evidence' and 'proof'. 'Evidence' may be contradicted by other evidence, whereas 'proof' requires both supporting evidence and lack of contradictory evidence. The fact that 'proof' was replaced by 'evidence' in the final verison suggests that Member States are not required to prove the causes of environmental damage. Instead, both Sevenster and Bär and Krämer argue that it is probably sufficient to demonstrate that there could be an environmental problem. This interpretation does not, however, appear to be consistent with the Commission's heavy emphasis on documentation and external experts in the PCP case. It is generally difficult to 'prove' causes and effect of environmental damage, but an unchallenged external expert with a high degree of scientific integrity is close to being a 'proof'.

The definition of 'specific to that Member State' is also unclear. On the one hand it is a quite meaningful requirement that a Member State must demonstrate specifically why it should wish to depart from Community standards. On the other hand, it is not meaningful at all if the requirement means that the environmental problem must occur only in one Member State. If this were the case, the result would be that the more Member States are affected, the more difficult it is to get derogations authorized. This is clearly inappropriate; it is also illustrated in the PCP case where the Commission authorized derogations in Germany and Denmark because of a specific problem in both countries.

Another reason for a Member State's wish to depart from the harmonized measure could be that it simply wants a higher level of protection. This option is no longer possible with the formulation of paragraph 5. Such a wish does not constitute an environmental problem specific for that state

(Sevenster, 2000). Hence paragraph 5 seems to incorporate formally what the PCP case indicated on this point.

The third clarification regarded the confirmation procedure. Paragraph 6 replaced the word 'confirm' with 'approve or reject'. The Commission shall approve or reject the national provisions within six months (or 12 months if the matter is particularly complex). Thus the confirmation is not simply a 'rubber stamp'; it has in fact a legal effect. If the Commission does not reply by the deadline, the national provisions are approved. This requirement prevents the very long confirmation procedures as illustrated in Table 2.1 above.

Derogations are only approved if they (1) are not a means of arbitrary discrimination or a disguised restriction on trade between Member States, and (2) do not constitute an obstacle to the functioning of the internal market. The first requirement is simply a restatement of the requirements in the old Article 100A(4) and Article 30 EC. What the second requirement adds to the first requirement is unclear. Derogations authorized under paragraphs 4 and 5 must necessarily 'affect the internal market'. A strict interpretation would thus make exceptions in paragraphs 4 and 5 unnecessary. It is generally agreed that 'obstacle' means restriction to trade. If so, it is questionable whether the second requirement adds anything to the first. If it adds anything new, it might be a proportionality test. In this way only derogations that have a disproportionate influence on the internal market would be rejected.

The fourth clarification regarded the effect of notification. It is stated in both paragraphs 4 and 5 that Member States must notify the Commission. Hence existing measures cannot be maintained and new measures cannot be applied unless they are notified. Given that the Commission approves or rejects derogations, Member States are not allowed to apply existing measures after expiry of the implementation period without approval. For the same reason, without approval, Member States are not allowed to apply new measures, even before the expiry of the implementation deadline.

The fifth clarification regarded the coverage of the environmental guarantee. Paragraphs 4 and 5 have been extended and now also include Commission measures. Commission directives may be adopted under the system set out in the comitology decision (Decision 87/373/EEC). Under this system, the Council typically adopts a framework regulation which will be followed by detailed regulations or directives by the Commission (Kent, 1996, p. 20). The practical importance of this amendment is unclear because it was not certain whether or not Commission directives were covered by Article 100A(4) EC. It could be argued that when a Commission directive is based on a Council regulation, the harmonization measure from which the Member State intends to derogate is basically a Council measure.

If this interpretation is correct, the Amsterdam Treaty amendment was no more than a clarification and a formal confirmation of established practices. If this interpretation is not correct, Table 2.2 shows that the amendment by the Amsterdam Treaty is a widening of the environmental guarantee since a growing amount of the environmental and internal market regulation is implemented via Commission directives. In 1987–92 approximately 30 per cent of the internal market and environmental directives came from the Commission, whereas it has grown to more than 50 per cent in 1993–97.

Table 2.2   Number of environmental and internal market directives adopted or signed between 1987 and 1997

	Internal market directives[a]		Environmental directives[b]	
	All directives	Of which Commission directives	All directives	Of which Commission directives
1997[c]	28	19 (68%)	10	6 (60%)
1996	41	23 (56%)	10	4 (40%)
1995	19	13 (68%)	1	0
1994	27	11 (41%)	13	2 (15%)
1993	56	31 (55%)	8	4 (50%)
1992	41	14 (34%)	6	0
1991	32	18 (56%)	13	2 (15%)
1990	26	9 (35%)	7	1 (14%)
1989	44	13 (30%)	15	2 (13%)
1988	32	15 (47%)	7	0
1987	22	11 (50%)	6	1 (17%)

Notes:
[a] Classification 13.30 in CELEX, 'Internal Market: Approximation of laws'.
[b] Classification 15.10 in CELEX, 'Environment'.
[c] Directives in 1997 appearing in CELEX by January 1998.

Source: CELEX.

The Amsterdam Treaty not only clarified the environmental guarantee but also added new ambiguities. One ambiguity is the requirement that derogations must be based on an environmental problem 'specific to that Member State' (para. 5). One obvious reason why a Member State wants to derogate from the harmonized Union measure is that the environmental problems concerned are more severe in that Member State than elsewhere. If this is the case, it is a natural requirement that a Member State must demonstrate specifically why it wishes to derogate from Union standards. If the problems were the same all over the EU there would be no need for derogations. One of the main arguments for the Commission in the PCP case to approve derogations in Germany and Denmark was that a large share of drinking water in these two Member States is groundwater on which PCP has a negative impact. The fact that both Germany and Denmark were allowed to derogate indicates that the requirement to show that specific circumstances occur does not imply that national measures are excluded once the same problem occurs in another Member State.

In summary, it is difficult to assess whether the Amsterdam Treaty has expanded or narrowed the environmental guarantee. On the one hand, it has brought clarifications and enlarged the environmental guarantee. It is now possible to introduce new measures derogating from the harmonized measure, the environmental guarantee now also applies to Commission directives and does not only apply to directives decided unanimously. On the other hand it has brought new ambiguities and narrowed the application. It is not clear what kind of documentation a Member State is required to present to get the derogations approved. Moreover, the potential grounds for introducing new measures appear to be limited compared with the former environmental guarantee.

6.   'RESIDUAL COMPETENCE' AND ENVIRONMENTAL FEDERALISM

The basic issue in environmental federalism is whether environmental regulation should be centralized or decentralized. When environmental regulation is centralized the focus is on uniform measures, which must be satisfied in all locations. When environmental regulation is decentralized the focus is on local choice, leading to non-uniform environmental regulations.

Simple economic reasoning says that environmental regulations should vary across jurisdictions in accordance with local circumstances. But as argued in Chapter 1, under certain circumstances central decision-making also has a role to play. Whether to use centralized uniform or decentralized non-uniform regulations essentially boils down to a comparison of welfare losses. The advantages of central uniform measures are low administration and information costs, no interjurisdictional competition, and internalization of any transboundary externalities. The disadvantage is the loss of efficiency by regulating different regions as though they are the same and vice versa for decentralized non-uniform regulations. Kolstad (1987) analyses the welfare loss of uniform regulation of differentiated regions from a theoretical perspective. He finds that the welfare loss is smallest with perfectly elastic marginal cost and benefit functions and that it increases when these functions become more steeply sloping. From an empirical perspective Tietenberg (1985) discusses eight case studies and identifies factors that affected the inefficiencies of uniform air pollutant emission charges. Dinan et al. (1999) measure the welfare loss from uniform national drinking water standards. They find that welfare losses are very unevenly distributed between households; some households have a large welfare loss from uniform measures.

Concerns about environmental federalism are reflected in the environmental policy in the EU and the USA. In the USA, air quality standards are uniform while water quality standards are state-specific. Under the Clean Air Act, the EPA is instructed to set minimum standards for ambient air quality. This is done by uniform maximum levels of concentration for criteria air pollutants applicable to all states. States are allowed to implement more stringent standards. In contrast, under the Clean Water Act, states are responsible for implementing water quality standards, and the role of the EPA is to specify abatement technology and issue permits. Even though Congress can take over a field and regulate to the exclusion of state law, it rarely does so. Instead, virtually every federal environmental initiative preserves a role for state standard-setting and state enforcement. Federal statutes and agencies often issue detailed regulations, but these regulations typically permit states to implement a higher level of environmental protection (Pfander, 1996).

How EU environmental policy reflects concerns about environmental federalism can be examined in at least three different ways. The first is the way in which it is determined whether the EU should regulate a specific area at all or leave it to the Member States. This question is governed by the principle of subsidiarity as laid down in Article 5 EC. Golub (1996), Bermann (1994), and the following chapter in this book, amongst others, examine this question in detail. Subsidiarity was introduced as a concept to curb the centralist tendencies of the EU. The basic results are, however, that the principle of subsidiarity is a vaguely defined concept and its application is subject to some ambiguity. Consequently, subsidiarity has not been effective in arbitrating disputes over the allocation of competence between the EU and the Member States.

The second way to examine environmental federalism in the EU is to look at the degree of specificity in uniform harmonized EU measures. The question is whether the use of directives in the EU provides for so much flexibility that environmental policies can differ between Member States. A directive is implemented centrally by the EU but leaves it for the Member States to choose the means and the enforcement efforts.

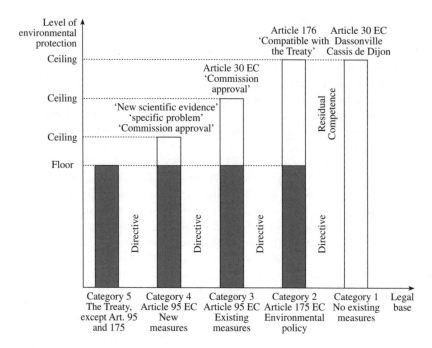

Figure 2.1   Member States' residual competence

The third way to examine environmental federalism in the EU would be to look at Member States' possibilities to establish more stringent standards than the uniform harmonized EU standards. If Member States can determine a higher level of environmental protection, it is possible to tailor state environmental policies to state environmental preferences, as Oates (1998, 1999) advocates. This was examined earlier in this chapter. It has been illustrated that Member States' possibilities to implement or enact national environmental measures fall into five categories, as illustrated in Figure 2.1. The first of these five categories applies when the Community has not implemented any harmonized regulations. Starting to the right of Figure 2.1, it is illustrated that even in this situation Member States are restricted in their possibilities to implement or enact national environmental measures. These restrictions are basically the same as the restrictions a Member State faces in the second of the five categories: where the Community has implemented environmental measures (based on Article 175 EC) aiming at minimum harmonization. In both of these categories national measures must not be means of arbitrary discrimination or disguised restrictions on trade.

The third and fourth category is where the Community has implemented environmental measures based on Article 95 EC. Even though the aim is complete harmonization, the environmental guarantee nevertheless ensures that there are certain possibilities for Member States to determine a higher level of environmental protection by introducing or maintaining more stringent national measures. These possibilities are, however, more restrictive than the possibilities in the second category. The possibilities to determine a higher level of environmental protection are more limited when a Member State wishes to introduce new stringent measures (category 4) than when it wishes to maintain existing measures (category 3).

The fifth category to the left of Figure 2.1 shows that when the Community has introduced environmental measures with a legal base other than that relating to the environment or the internal market, Member States are highly restricted in their level of environmental protection. There are basically no possibilities to implement stricter or less strict measures than the harmonized measures except if the directive itself specifies such possibilities. An example of environmental legislation in this category is the directive regarding the transportation of dangerous goods by road (Directive 94/55/EC), which is based on Article 75 (transport).

Hence, whether or not EU environmental policy reflects a sufficient degree of concern for environmental federalism by allowing Member States to establish more stringent regulations than the EU regulations is ambiguous. Two factors indicate a high degree of environmental federalism. First, it is possible for Member States to use the environmental guarantee and implement more stringent standards even where the aim is complete harmonization. Second, the extensive use of minimum harmonization in the EU environmental policy increases the possibilities for environmental regulations to vary according to national circumstances. There are, however, two factors that indicate a low degree of environmental federalism. First, even in areas where the EU has not implemented any environmental measures Member States are not free to vary regulations in light of national circumstances. In fact, in this situation Member States face the same restrictions as if the EU had already introduced minimum harmonization. Second, it appears that the environmental guarantee only provides very limited possibilities for Member States to derogate from harmonized measures. The very limited use of the environmental guarantee supports this conclusion.

7.   CONCLUSION

A high degree of national environmental sovereignty and a well-functioning internal market are two potentially conflicting goals. The EU has expressed its willingness to pursue both goals and thus faces the risk of falling between two stools.

Economics was the main motivation for the first revision of the EU treaties in 1987. The amended treaty should deepen economic integration and accelerate the establishment of the internal market. In the later revisions in 1992 and 1997 economic integration was also one of the main motivators, but other aspects such as democracy, political integration and enlargement were, however, also important.

Environmental policy was nevertheless formally introduced by the SEA in 1987, which illustrates that environmental policy, the internal market and economic integration are closely related. EU environmental measures are based either on Article 175 EC, relating to EU environmental policy, or Article 95 EC, relating to the internal market. The treaty revisions changed the legal basis for environmental measures. The importance of environmental protection has been increased by all treaty revisions. It is now determined that the EU's economic activities should promote sustainable development. Moreover, that environmental protection has a unique role is illustrated by the requirement that it should be a component of the Community's other policies. This does not apply to other Community policies. Finally, environmental policy has developed from unanimity and limited influence by the Parliament to qualified majority voting in all matters and significant influence by the Parliament.

Community environmental legislation reflects that different concerns must be balanced. Environmental protection and the internal market must be balanced and a high level of environmental protection in EU environmental policy measures must be balanced with national environmental sovereignty. This balance is reflected in the legal base for environmental measures where there are certain possibilities for Member States to derogate from the EU measures and decide their own higher level of environmental protection. These derogations must not, however, have a disproportionate influence on the internal market.

When a Member State decides to implement or enact environmental measures in a specific area, it must first be determined whether or not the Community has already adopted harmonized measures in that area. If not, Member States are free to determine their level of environmental protection and enact the appropriate measures. However, Member States have committed themselves to the Community and thus are not allowed to implement measures that are not compatible with the Treaty. This means that the national measures must not have a negative effect on the internal market and the free movement of goods. There are, however, exceptions. These exceptions are defined in Article 30 EC, which mentions possible justifications for derogations, but does not directly mention the environment.

Established case law (Dassonville and Cassis de Dijon), however, expands the justifications to include the environment. Hence Article 30 EC and the existing case law represent the ceiling above which the Member States are not entitled to regulate.

When the Community has already adopted a harmonized measure, Member States' possibilities to derogate from that measure (residual competence) depends upon the legal base of the harmonized measure. There are three different legal bases. The first is Article 176 EC concerning EU environmental policy. The second is Article 95 EC concerning the internal market. The third is all other articles in the Treaty except Articles 176 EC and 95 EC. Two examples of directives in the latter category are the directive regarding the transport of dangerous goods by road (Directive 94/55/EC), which is based on Article 37 (agriculture), and the directive regarding packaging and packaging waste (Directive 94/62/EC), which is based on Article 71 (transport). As shown in Figure 2.1, in this case Member States have no residual competence. Hence the directive is a uniform measure leaving no room for Member States to determine a higher (or lower) level of environmental protection than the level prescribed by the harmonized EU measure. The directive itself does, however, allow some flexibility. A directive is implemented centrally by the EU but is binding only as to the result to be achieved. A directive must be transposed into Member State law and thus leaves it to Member States to choose the form and methods. In this way a 'level playing-field' is created, avoiding the 'race to the bottom'.

When the Community has adopted a harmonized measure based on Articles 95 or 175 EC (in Figure 2.1 exemplified by a directive), Member States have some possibilities to determine a higher level of environmental protection than the level specified in the directive. This 'residual competence' is defined as the room between the floor, specified by the harmonized measure, and the ceiling, specified by the Treaty provisions.

When the Community bases a directive on Article 175 EC, it is typically a minimum directive allowing Member States to maintain and introduce more protective measures. These must, however, be 'compatible with the Treaty'. This means for all practical purposes that any such measures must be compatible with the internal market and the free movement of goods. Hence, as illustrated in Figure 2.1, the highest level of environmental protection achievable is the same level as if there were no harmonized measure.

When the Community has implemented a harmonized measure based on Article 95 EC, the measure in principle requires total harmonization. The environmental guarantee, however, gives the Member States certain possibilities to derogate from that harmonized measure and implement or maintain measures achieving a higher level of environmental protection. These possibilities are, however, more limited than under Article 176 EC.

Article 95 EC prescribes a strict scrutiny procedure where the Member States must notify the Commission, which then approves or rejects the derogations. When a Member State wishes to maintain (as opposed to introduce) national measures, it must notify the Commission. The Commission will approve if the national measures are not a means of arbitrary discrimination or a disguised restriction on trade, and do not constitute an obstacle to the functioning of the internal market. The scrutiny procedure is even more strict when a Member State wants to introduce new measures. In this it is not enough to verify that the derogations are not a means of arbitrary discrimination or a disguised restriction on trade and that they do not constitute an obstacle to the functioning of the internal market. Introduction of new measures is only allowed if they are based on new scientific evidence and if the circumstances are specific to that Member State.

In this chapter Member States' possibilities to implement more protective measures than the harmonized Community measures have been examined. Hence the chapter has discussed Member States' 'room for manœuvre' *given* that the Community has implemented measures in the specific area. The question of *whether* the Community should implement environmental measures in that area is not discussed. This question is essentially one of distribution of powers between the Community and the Member States. The principle of subsidiarity provides some guidelines on this issue, which is the topic of the following two chapters.

NOTES

1. The Maastricht meeting established a new treaty, the Treaty of the European Union (TEU), comprising Articles A–S, and consolidated the Treaty establishing the European Community (TEC), comprising Articles 1–248. For the sake of convenience, these two treaties will be referred to as 'The Maastricht Treaty'.
2. The cooperation procedure set out in Article 189C determines that the Council shall hear the opinion of the Parliament twice. The Council can, nevertheless, pass on a proposal against the will of the European Parliament. Consequently, the European Parliament does not have the right of veto.
3. One of the fields is 'provisions primarily of a fiscal nature'; for example a possible CO_2 tax is to be adopted unanimously by the Council.
4. The co-decision procedure set out in Article 189B determines that under certain circumstances the Parliament may veto the adoption of a proposal.
5. Again, 'Amsterdam Treaty' will refer to both the TEU and the TEC.
6. Pentachlorophenol (PCP) is a chemical used for treating wood, impregnating textiles, and sterilizing soil. It is also used as a bactericide in the dressing of skins and in the paper and pulp industry. PCP is toxic to humans and has a highly toxic effect on the aquatic environment.
7. Article 190 reads: 'Regulations, directives and decisions adopted jointly by the European Parliament and the Council, and such acts adopted by the Council or the Commission, shall state the reasons on which they are based and shall refer to any proposals or opinions which were required to be obtained pursuant to this Treaty.'

3. Subsidiarity and EU environmental policy*

1. INTRODUCTION

The Danes' rejection by referendum of the Maastricht Treaty in 1992, the narrow victory of the 'yes' vote in the French referendum, and the political and judicial challenges in the UK and Germany showed that further European integration was met with stronger resistance at national levels at the beginning of the 1990s. Member State populations felt an aversion to what was seen as the Community's inexorable march towards greater integration, which would trample claims of democratic self-governance and cultural diversity. In this delicate situation, the Maastricht Treaty drafters turned to 'subsidiarity' as a concept which would build confidence in the new Treaty. Immediately after the adoption of the Maastricht Treaty, however, it became clear that the actual scope of subsidiarity and the way in which it could be used by the Community institutions was uncertain.

The Treaty drafters were in a delicate situation in which, on the one hand, they wanted to complete eight years of hard work with the consolidation of the internal market by deepening European integration. On the other hand, Member States' confidence was to be maintained through a guarantee of the proximity of government. Subsidiarity was envisaged as a concept that should strike the balance between integration and proximity. Hence subsidiarity was included in a way that 'should help to assure the citizen that decisions will be taken as closely as possible to the citizen himself, without damaging the advantages which he gains from common action at the level of the whole Community'.[1]

This chapter is organized as follows. Section 2 defines subsidiarity. The subsidiarity test is examined and we discuss how subsidiarity relates to proportionality. Section 3 analyses how the Commission has worked with the implementation of subsidiarity. This is done by examining annual reports from the Commission. Section 4 is an empirical analysis of how subsidiarity has affected Community legislation, achieved by analysing the number and type of adopted pieces of Community legislation. Conclusions are in section 5.

47

2. WHAT IS SUBSIDIARITY?

2.1. Sources and Definition

The very idea of vertical power sharing between levels of government can be traced back to philosophers such as Aristotle, Aquinas, Proudhon and Tocqueville. However, subsidiarity has become a more explicit part of the political and philosophical thought of Western Europe since the middle the nineteenth century, finding expression in both political liberalism (for example John Stuart Mill), and Catholic social theory. Cass (1992) and Green (1994) refer to the 1931 papal encyclical 'Quadregesimo Anno', which sets out the basis of subsidiarity by stating that 'it is an injustice, a grave evil and a disturbance of right order, for a larger and higher association to arrogate to itself functions which can be performed efficiently by smaller and lower societies' (Cass, 1992, p. 1111). According to political liberalism, subsidiarity was a 'single-edged sword' used to justify non-intervention by the state in order to protect the rights of the individual. In Catholic social theory, however, subsidiarity was adopted as a 'double-edged sword', since the term may justify state intervention if it was efficient and non-intervention by the state if state intervention was inefficient.

The term 'subsidiarity' entered the Community with the conclusion of the Treaty on the European Union at Maastricht in December 1991 (the Maastricht Treaty). However, the principle of subsidiarity had been formally introduced in Article 130r(4) of the Single European Act (SEA) which came into force in 1987. Article 130r(4) reads as follows:

> The Community shall take action relating to the environment to the extent to which the objectives referred to in paragraph 2 can be attained better at Community level than at the level of individual Member States.

With the conclusion of the Maastricht Treaty, it was decided that this principle should apply not only to environmental policy but to all Community matters. Therefore, Article 130r(4) was replaced by Article 3b which is contained in the EC Treaty's part on 'Principles' and consequently establishes a general rule for all Community activity. Article 3b reads:

> The Community shall act within the limits of the powers conferred upon it by this Treaty and the objectives assigned to it therein.
>
> In areas which do not fall within its exclusive competence, the Community shall take action, in accordance with the principle of subsidiarity, only if and in so far as the objectives of the proposed action cannot be sufficiently achieved by the Member States and can therefore, by reason of the scale or effects of the proposed action, be better achieved by the Community.

Any action by the Community shall not go beyond what is necessary to achieve the objectives of this Treaty.

The replacement of Article 130r(4) by Article 3b was not just a matter of 'cut and paste'. There are substantial differences. Article 130r(4) prescribes an enquiry into the efficiency of Community and Member State action. The Community may take action relating to the environment to the extent to which objectives can be better attained at Community level than at the level of the Member States. If, however, the Member States can attain the objective more efficiently than the Community, the Member State should take action. Consequently, Article 130r(4) does not lay down any requirements which limit the scope for Community action. On the contrary, the Community is obliged to act if it can obtain the environmental objective most efficiently.[2] In this respect, Article 130r(4) is closer to the definition of subsidiarity formulated by the Catholic social theory than by the political liberalism of the nineteenth century since subsidiarity may justify Community intervention. Brinkhorst (1993) sees Article 130r(4) as a requirement for the Community to bring about a specific improvement as a whole (the net benefit should be positive). It is not necessarily required to produce better results in all Member States separately.

Article 3b sets out different requirements for Community action and contains three legal concepts. Article 3b(1) is the principle of attribution of powers, which has long been an integral part of the Community and is expressed in Article 4(1) as 'Each institution shall act within the limits of the powers conferred upon it by this Treaty.' Article 3b(2) is the principle of subsidiarity itself, and involves an assessment of the need for Community action: 'the Community shall take action, only if . . .' (the necessity test). Article 3b(3) incorporates the principle of proportionality into the Treaty and involves an assessment of the intensity of Community action (the intensity test).[3]

2.2. The Subsidiarity Tests

The necessity test in Article 3b(2) must be applied in order to justify Community action. However, the necessity test actually embraces two tests. The first is an effectiveness test, which determines if the means available to the Member States suffice to attain the objectives of the measure envisaged at Community level. This is stipulated as the requirement that 'the Community shall take action . . . only if and so far as the objectives of the proposed action cannot be sufficiently achieved by the Member States . . .'. The second is an efficiency test, which determines whether the envisioned action can be better achieved at Community level due to the scale or the effects of the proposed action. This is specified by the phrase 'and can therefore, by reason of the scale or effects of the proposed action, be better achieved by the Community'.

A literal reading of Article 3b leads to the result that if the means at the disposal of the Member States are perfectly effective in order to achieve the objectives of the proposed action, the Community is prevented from acting even though it is more efficient in achieving these objectives. This is clearly unsatisfactory because Community action is abandoned even in the situation where the envisaged action would produce clear benefits from economies of scale when undertaken at the Community level. In other words, the effectiveness test and the efficiency test may point in opposite directions.

The wording of Article 3b(2) may be the result of a compromise, whereby the Treaty authors intended to comply with different views. On one hand, the efficiency test embraces the same aspects as Article 130r(4) and the drafts of the Maastricht Treaty that were circulated before the adoption of the final document.[4] This involves a comparative assessment of national and Community measures, which can only be made by an evaluation of their respective efficiency. On the other hand the authors strengthened the wording by indicating that efficiency should come into play 'only if' the Member States cannot sufficiently achieve the objectives of the envisioned action. This is a guarantee of the proximity of government, which requires that the Community abstains from acting if the Member States can sufficiently achieve the objectives of the envisaged action. Dehousse (1993) warns against a mechanical combination of the two tests, noting that if action at Member State level is ineffective, 'adding a separate efficiency condition does not really make sense: provided it itself is effective, Community action is likely to be more efficient than ineffective national measures'.

2.3. Subsidiarity and Proportionality

Article 3b(3) incorporates the principle of proportionality, developed in the jurisprudence of the ECJ, and adds another test for the envisaged Community measure. According to Bermann (1994), proportionality requires every Community measure to satisfy three related criteria: (1) the measure must bear a reasonable relationship to the objective that the measure is intended to serve; (2) the costs of the measure must not manifestly outweigh its benefits; and (3) the measure chosen must represent the solution that is the least burdensome. By incorporating the principle of proportionality into the principle of subsidiarity, proportionality is no longer only a judicial doctrine to be applied by the ECJ in its revision of Community action. Rather, it becomes a legislative doctrine to be followed by the political branches in policy-making.

The Court and the Commission consider subsidiarity and proportionality to be in perfect harmony and to follow in a logical sequence. The Commission says that 'If it were concluded that a proposal passes the test of comparative efficiency, it would still be necessary to respond to the question: What should be the intensity and the nature of the Community action?'[5] Bermann (1994), however, argues that the two concepts are not necessarily in harmony, and may even work at cross-purposes. The relationship between subsidiarity and the 'least drastic means' aspect of proportionality is especially problematic. Suppose, for example, that a Community measure passes all three proportionality tests. The Community measure is then reasonably related to its stated purpose, producing net benefits, and Community action would be the least burdensome. This measure may nevertheless not have been necessary because action at the Member State level would have been effective in achieving the goals of the envisaged action. In this example, proportionality has dictated an action that fails the test of subsidiarity. The Council and the Commission avoid this problem by deciding that the proportionality test should not be undertaken until the subsidiarity test is settled. However, this solution may be criticized as 'sacrificing proportionality at the altar of subsidiarity and, in the process, forsaking many of the efficiency advantages of Community-level action' (Bermann, 1994, p. 389). Bermann identifies a tradeoff between proportionality and subsidiarity. A Member State action may do more harm from a proportionality point of view than it does good from a subsidiarity point of view. Conversely, a Community measure may do more harm from a subsidiarity point of view than it does good from a proportionality point of view. Whether to emphasize subsidiarity (and give preference to localism) or proportionality (and give preference to efficiency gains) is ultimately a political judgement and can be made only by the political institutions themselves.

2.4. Clarification at the Edinburgh Meeting?

At its meeting in Edinburgh, December 1992, the European Council established some guidelines to be used in examining whether a proposal for a Community measure conforms to the provisions of Article 3b, that is, whether the objectives of the proposed action cannot be sufficiently achieved by Member States' action and can therefore be better achieved by action on the part of the Community. These guidelines are:

- the issue under consideration has transnational aspects which cannot be satisfactorily regulated via action by Member States; and/or

- actions by Member States alone or lack of Community action would conflict with the requirements of the Treaty (such as the need to correct distortion of competition or avoid disguised restrictions on trade or strengthen economic and social cohesion) or would otherwise significantly damage Member States' interests; and /or
- the Council must be satisfied that action at Community level would produce clear benefits by reason of its scale or effects compared with action at the level of the Member States.

The three criteria are connected by the term 'and/or', indicating that the need for Community action exists when one or more of the three criteria are met. The first two criteria refer to the effectiveness test, where Member States cannot achieve the objective effectively. If this is the case, Community action may be justified. The third criterion simply restates the efficiency test, although it is stipulated that the comparative advantage of the Community measure over the Member State measure must be 'clear'. Presumably, this indicates that the measure envisaged must be significantly superior to the Member State measure and not just slightly better. Apparently, the Council understands the wording 'and can therefore' of Article 3b as 'and/or'. This means that Community action may be justified on the basis of the efficiency test alone. If the third criterion is fulfilled, the two others do not have to be examined and the effectiveness test does not have to be passed. In this way the Council reads Article 3b as if it were equal to the former Article 130r(4) (Lenaerts, 1994). This result is also indicated by the Commission. Even though the Commission describes the two-step procedure in Article 3b(2) (the effectiveness test and the efficiency test), it refers to Article 3b(2) as one test: 'The test of comparative efficiency between Community action and that of Member States'.[6]

At the Edinburgh Meeting, the Council declared that Article 3b should affect the nature of Community lawmaking in several respects: (1) Community measures should leave as much scope for national decision-making as possible; (2) care should be taken to respect well-established national arrangements (mutual recognition); (3) consideration should be given to setting minimum standards, with freedom for Member States to set higher national standards; and (4) the Community should legislate only to the extent necessary, and directives should be preferred to regulations and framework directives to detailed measures.

The Commission acknowledges the directive as an instrument which typifies subsidiarity because it sets the result to be achieved but leaves it to the Member States to reach the result. The directive differs from the regulation, which applies directly to the Member States and, where necessary, supersedes national legislation. Therefore preference should be given to the directive, and the use of regulations should be limited to those cases where there is an urgent need for uniform rules. However, the Commission notes that the distinction between a directive and a regulation has become blurred because directives are often as detailed as regulations. Consequently, if subsidiarity is to produce any results, the directive must revert to the original concept 'as a framework of general rules or even simply of objectives for the attainment of which the Member States have sole responsibility'.[7]

These declarations clearly serve the purposes of proportionality (Article 3b(3)) to a greater degree than subsidiarity (Article 3b(2)). Therefore, the Conclusions from the Edinburgh Meeting also contain a section with procedures and practices to be applied in the framework of the basic principles set out under Article 3b(2). The Council states that the Commission shall play a crucial role in the implementation of subsidiarity. The Commission is instructed to make more systematic use of consultation documents (for example, Green Papers) before proposing legislation. Moreover, the Commission must formally justify the relevance of its initiatives with regard to the principle of subsidiarity. Finally, it must submit an annual report to the Council and the Parliament on the subsidiarity principle. At the Lisbon Meeting, in June 1992, the Council called for a re-examination of certain EC rules, and the Presidency Conclusions from the Edinburgh Meeting therefore contain an appendix (Annex II) comprising a list of examples of pending proposals and existing legislation which should be reviewed. This list had a decisive influence on the Commission's work on subsidiarity in the following two years. It is stated that the Commission has withdrawn three pending proposals which were not warranted in light of subsidiarity, and that it considered withdrawing 11 other proposals. Furthermore, six proposals were identified which were considered to be excessively detailed. With respect to existing legislation, families of existing rules were identified for further scrutiny. The Commission sought to streamline the directives relating to technical standards and replace them with minimum requirements. The environmental regulations were to be simplified, consolidated and updated. Some of the agricultural regulations were to be reviewed in order to expand the possibilities of negotiating settlements between individuals and Member States. In addition, certain planned initiatives would be abandoned.

Thus the Edinburgh Meeting laid down the structure of the Commission's work with the subsidiarity principle in the following years. First, the Commission was instructed to find a method to justify Community legislation with regard to the subsidiarity principle. Second, the Commission was instructed to publish an annual report summarizing work done on the subsidiarity principle. The report would summarize the review of new and pending proposals, as well as existing legislation.

3.   THE ANNUAL REPORTS

Before the Edinburgh Meeting, some Member States developed lists of EC legislation to be repealed or repatriated. Even though some of these lists became public, none was officially submitted to the Commission. During 1993, however, the governments of France and the UK submitted to the Commission a list containing 24 items which they considered should be examined with a view to their repeal, withdrawal or amendment. The list contained 13 pieces of existing legislation, nine proposals, and two proposals not yet adopted by the Commission. In addition, the two governments also developed a list of eight items on which the UK and French officials proposed to undertake further discussions between departmental experts.

In November 1993, a month before the European Council Meeting in Brussels, the Commission finalized the first of the annual reports on the subsidiarity principle.[8] The introduction to the report discusses the scope and the application of the subsidiarity principle, and reviews the measures taken by the Commission. The report reaffirms the relationship between subsidiarity and proportionality, according to which subsidiarity embraces both the principle of subsidiarity itself (the necessity test) and proportionality (the intensity test). The main part of the report contains a programme of work which in some details reports the Commission's intentions for recasting, simplifying and repealing legislation. Several hundred enactments are identified, demonstrating the Commission's high ambitions. The legislation to be recast is characterized by a large number of rules and regulations, with sufficient maturity, which can be brought together in a single instrument.[9] The legislation to be simplified contains excessive detail which could be covered by a national instrument. This applies to the families of rules referred to in the Conclusions of the Edinburgh Meeting, as well as to additional rules and regulations identified by the Commission.[10] The suggestion to repeal the rules and regulations was a consequence of the recasting and simplification, a result of their being superseded by the development of other techniques such as mutual recognition. In contrast to the Franco-British list, which covers both existing legislation and proposals, the first annual report relates only to the adaptation of existing legislation to the principle of subsidiarity. Moreover, the clear emphasis on recasting and simplification shows that the report fails to return very many matters to governance by the Member States (Bermann, 1994, p. 378). The Commission included a number of the items on the Franco–British list. In a memo attached to the report, the Commission agreed that 16 out of the 22 items on the Franco-British list should be withdrawn or amended and later incorporated them in its implementation of subsidiarity.

In order to concretize the first report, the Commission presented at the

Brussels Meeting 'the 30-point Brussels programme', listing 19 specific rules and regulations to be simplified and a further 11 rules and regulations to be recast.[11] The list, which comprised more legislation to be revised than required at the Edinburgh Meeting, goes beyond mere compliance with the subsidiarity principle because some of the issues relate to the internal market, competition, transport and fishery, that is, areas lying within the Community's exclusive powers. In contrast to the report, the conclusions from the Council's December 1993 Meeting in Brussels were rather brief. The Council, recognizing the work being done by the Commission, asked the Commission 'to submit formal proposals . . . for adoption as speedily as possible'. Moreover, the Commission was asked to 'report back regularly on the application of the principle of subsidiarity. The next Commission report on the subject will be submitted in December 1994.'

The report requested by the Brussels Meeting was the second of the annual reports and falls into two parts.[12] The first part deals with how subsidiarity is taken into account in the legislative process; that is, how subsidiarity affects new Commission initiatives and the withdrawal or revision of pending proposals. The Commission states that it has exercised greater selectivity and has in some cases opted for other approaches than Community legislation. This has resulted in a decline in new proposals from 48 in 1993 to 38 in 1994. The second part of the report deals with the Commission's modification of existing legislation and shows that the Commission has concentrated on the 30-point Brussels Programme, where about half the 30 issues have been either revised or simplified.[13]

After the first two reports, the Commission took the view that the report's scope should be extended to cover all action aimed at improving the quality of legislation in the Community ('Better Lawmaking'). As a result, the annual reports on subsidiarity were retitled in 1995 to become 'Better Lawmaking' reports. The first 'Better Lawmaking' report, in 1995, follows up on the Edinburgh Meeting and sets out the structure for the Commission's future work to improve lawmaking in the Community.[14] The report was the last to refer to the 30-point Brussels Programme. By the end of 1995, almost all 30 pieces of legislation had been simplified or recast. Therefore, the report concentrated on implementing what the Commission calls the 'new legislative culture', which continues the process of reviewing Community legislation in light of the subsidiarity discussion initiated at the Edinburgh Meeting. The Commission also stated that it intended to maintain the structure laid down at the Edinburgh Meeting, where both new proposals and existing legislation were to be reviewed. The Commission determined that the 'new legislative culture' implied that new legislative proposals should meet a 'test of rigour, clarity and transparency', and that the Commission would continue to review existing legislation.[15]

Consequently, most of the revised legislation presented in the 1995 'Better Lawmaking' report goes beyond what was requested at the Edinburgh Meeting. For example, the Commission's report states that only one of the 61 pending proposals they withdrew in 1995 was on the Edinburgh list.

The 'Better Lawmaking' report in 1996 continues the implementation of the 'new legislative culture'. Proposals are reviewed and 48 pending proposals are withdrawn. The report recommends increased use of framework directives and common minimum standards. Moreover, initiatives to prompt debate are strongly emphasized. In 1996 the Commission published 15 Green Papers, 3 White Papers, and a significant number of reports, communications and action plans. The Commission continued to review the existing legislation. However, the review was no longer guided by the 30-point Brussels Programme, but 'with a view to lighten the burden'.[16]

The preparation of legislative proposals and the revision of existing legislation continues in the 1997 'Better Lawmaking' report. The Commission foresees that it will withdraw 30 proposals that are unnecessary or no longer relevant. Furthermore, the Commission states that it has produced a large number of initiatives to prompt debate. In 1997 the Commission issued six Green and White Papers, seven working papers, 103 communications and 116 reports.

The 1998 'Better Lawmaking' report is the first report after the Amsterdam Treaty. Even though the Amsterdam Treaty only codifies already established procedures, and only adds the Edinburgh Annex details as a protocol, the Commission states that 'there are now clear rules on subsidiarity and proportionality, which are to be found in the Protocol annexed to the Treaty of Amsterdam'.[17] The report is subtitled 'A Shared Responsibility', stressing the Commission's particular emphasis in the report that year. The Commission argues that it has been successful in reducing the overall number of proposals and that it has improved the consultation procedures. But it emphasizes several areas in which implementing subsidiarity is a shared responsibility. It is noted that the other institutions cannot shirk their share of the responsibility and that the Member States have an important role to play in complementing the efforts of the institutions, for instance by simplifying national legislation and transposing directives correctly.

4.   CHANGES IN COMMUNITY LEGISLATION

A wide range of legal acts of the Community is available on the CELEX database, produced and managed by the Office for Official Publications of the European Communities. Table 3.1 presents the development in the volume and the composition of Commission legislation since 1990 in three

Table 3.1 Adopted and proposed Community legislation

	All Community legislation					Internal market[a]				Environment[b]			
	Commission proposals[c]	Proposals for new legislation[d]	Adopted decisions	Adopted directives	Adopted regulations	Commission proposals	Adopted decisions	Adopted directives	Adopted regulations	Commission proposals	Adopted decisions	Adopted directives	Adopted regulations
1990	787	61	524	95	1518	61	4	26	4	41	4	6	4
1991	704	52	636	103	1461	51	1	32	2	35	6	13	5
1992	702	51	616	122	1516	63	5	42	4	36	4	6	6
1993	667	48	734	118	1376	47	7	55	2	30	56	8	10
1994	596	38	935	79	1263	26	9	26	3	25	19	13	8
1995	622	25	760	72	1119	39	13	19	8	29	8	1	7
1996	528	11[e]	787	95	1006	41	34	41	4	33	24	10	5
1997	549	7[f]	960	81	997	37	92	29	2	40	24	11	12
1998	491[g]	34[g]	875	101	1002	48	28	38	4	55	22	9	6

Notes:

[a] Defined as CELEX classification 13.30: 'Internal market: approximation of laws'.

[b] Defined as CELEX classification 15.10: 'Environment', i.e. excluding consumers' health protection and protection of animals.

[c] Source: COM (98) 715.

[d] Source: CSE (95) 580.

[e] At 27.11.1996, six proposals were presented and a further five might be presented before 1997 (CSE (96) 7 final, p. 2).

[f] As set out in the Commission's annual work programme (CSE (97) 626 final, annex II).

[g] Situation at 20/11/1998. Source: COM (98) 715.

Source: CELEX database.

categories: (1) all Community legislation; (2) the internal market, which is an area where the Community has exclusive competence; and (3) the environment, where the Community and Member States share competence. The CELEX database imposes some limitations on the analysis. First, it does not distinguish proposals for new legislation from other proposals. Therefore, proposals for new legislation are taken from the annual reports.

The Commission has stated that subsidiarity means that 'Europe must do less, so as to do it better'.[18] From Table 3.1 it is not possible to say whether the Commission has succeeded in doing better, but it is evident that it has succeeded in doing less. First, the number of proposals for new legislation has been in steep decline in the period 1990–97, from 61 to 7. This decline has not, however, continued in 1998 where 34 proposals for new legislation were presented. Second, Figure 3.1a shows that the overall volume of Commission proposals has also declined, albeit on a relatively smaller scale.[19] The 1998 level is around 62 per cent of the 1990 level. If the Commission intends to 'do less, but better', one would have expected a decrease in the number of proposals after 1994, but Figure 3.1a shows that the decline in proposals after 1994 has not been as rapid as before 1994. This is most likely because the Commission, in the 'Better Lawmaking' reports, strongly promotes the use of reports, communications and pro-

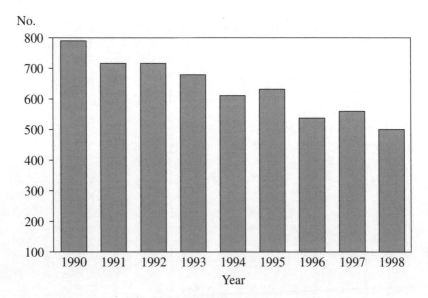

Source: Table 3.1.

Figure 3.1a   The number of Commission proposals in the Community

grammes to prompt debate as a part of the 'new legislative culture'. A reduction in the number of proposed decisions, directives and regulations may have been outweighed by an increase in the number of adopted reports, communications and programmes.

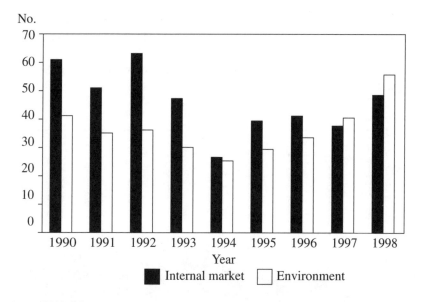

Source: Table 3.1

Figure 3.1b   The number of Commission proposals in the areas of the internal market and the environment

Figure 3.1b shows that the number of Commission proposals in the internal market decreased rapidly in 1993–94. After 1994 the number of proposals increased again to a 1998 level just slightly lower than the 1990–92 level. Commission proposals in the area of the environment decreased between 1990 and 1994, but increased rapidly after 1994 and in 1998 reached a level above the 1990 level. Thus, contrary to the total number of Commission proposals, and the number of proposals in the internal market, the number of Commission proposals in the area of the environment has not decreased compared to 1990–92. One explanation might be a stronger need for consultation initiatives in an area with shared competence where subsidiarity applies.

If it takes a year or two from the time a directive is proposed until it is adopted, one would expect a drop in the number of adopted instruments in 1995–96 as a result of the drop in proposals in 1993–94. Figures

3.2a–3.2c provide some support for this expectation. Figure 3.2a shows that in the Community as a whole the number of adopted instruments increased from 1990 to 1994, but decreased rapidly in 1995–96. After 1994, the number of adopted instruments stayed at a relatively constant level, approximately 10 per cent lower than the 1990–92 level. Compared to Figure 3.1a, this corresponds quite well to a period of two years from when the instrument is proposed until it is adopted. Hence the decrease in the number of adopted instruments in 1995–96 shown in Figure 3.2a corresponds to the decrease in the number of Commission proposals in 1993–94 shown in Figure 3.1a.

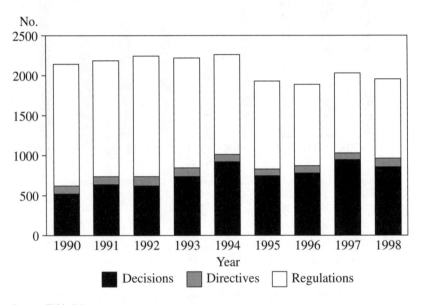

Source: Table 3.1.

Figure 3.2a   The number of adopted instruments in the Community

So, the Commission has been successful in doing less. The question now remains whether it has been successful in emphasizing less binding instruments. The type of adopted instrument is also shown in Figures 3.2a–3.2c. It is evident that the composition of adopted legislation changed in the 1990s. In the Community as a whole, the number of adopted directives remained constant at 5 per cent of the adopted instruments. More importantly, the proportion of decisions increased from around 25 per cent to almost 50 per cent, at the expense of regulations, which decreased from around 70 per cent to 50 per cent. In other words, the type of instruments adopted in the Community has changed from a situation where the majority of such instruments were regulations to one where regulations and decisions are equally important. In relation to subsidiarity, however, it is more important that the nature of Community legislation has not changed from adopting the most binding instruments to adopting the less binding directives. It seems as if the Community's hand has not changed from being a heavy hand to a lighter one.

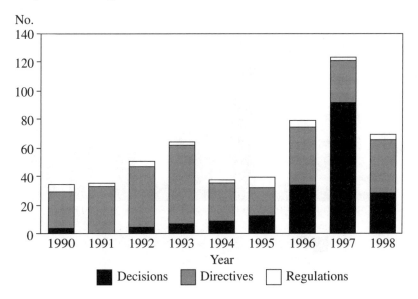

Source: Table 3.1.

Figure 3.2b   The number of adopted instruments in the area of the internal market

The number of adopted instruments in the internal market is depicted in Figure 3.2b. As in the Community as a whole, the number increased in the early 1990s and subsequently dropped. However, the decline appeared in 1994, one year earlier than in the Community as a whole. Another difference is the large increase in adopted instruments in 1996–97. In this period the number of adopted instruments reached a higher level than at the beginning of the 1990s.

The composition of the adopted instruments in the internal market differs from that of those adopted in the Community as a whole. Until 1994, the internal market was dominated by the use of directives, which accounted for more than 80 per cent of the adopted instruments. Since

1995, however, the relative importance of directives has decreased and the relative importance of decisions has increased. In 1997, decisions accounted for about 75 per cent of the adopted instruments and directives for only 25 per cent. The proportion of adopted regulations was in general less than 10 per cent.

No.

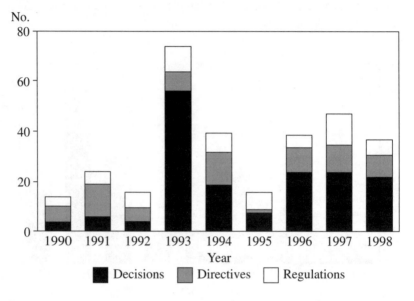

Source: Table 3.1.

Figure 3.2c   The number of adopted instruments in the area of the environment

Compared to the internal market, it is more difficult to identify a trend in the development of adopted instruments in the area of the environment (Figure 3.2c). A comparison of Figures 3.2b and 3.2c shows that there are some similarities between the internal market and the environment, although the increase in the number of adopted instruments in 1993 was much larger in the area of the environment, and the increase in 1996–97 somewhat smaller. Still, as with the internal market, the level of adopted instruments is higher in 1996–98 than at the beginning of the 1990s. The composition of the adopted instruments differs from that of both the Community as a whole and the internal market. Decisions in the area of the environment have also increased in relative importance, but the environmental area is characterized by a greater variety of instruments (except from 1993, when a very large number of decisions were adopted). It should be noted, however, that the conclusions in the area of the environment rest on a weaker foundation than those for the Community as a whole or the internal market. Fewer instruments have been adopted, and perhaps more important, the environment is a relatively new policy area which only since the 1987 Single European Act has had an explicit legal basis in the Treaty.

5.   CONCLUSION

This chapter has examined what subsidiarity is and how it has affected Community legislation. It can be concluded that the way in which subsidiarity was formulated in Article 3b of the Treaty produced an ambiguous balance between respect for local conditions and efficiency of Community action. On the one hand, if Community objectives can be achieved efficiently by the Member States, a literal reading of Article 3b results in Community action being abandoned even where such action would produce clear benefits compared to action at the level of the Member States. On the other hand, the Community institutions have interpreted subsidiarity as a test of comparative efficiency; who would achieve the goal most efficiently, the Community or the Member States? This interpretation differs from the literal reading of Article 3b but may be criticized for sacrificing respect for local conditions to the altar of efficiency. (See, for instance, Jordan and Jeppesen, 2000; Lenaerts, 1994; Bermann, 1994; O'Keeffe and Twomey, 1994.)

The Commission has played a central role in implementing the principle of subsidiarity. Its revision of Community legislation was structured by the guidelines decided at the Edinburgh Meeting. In 1993–95 this process focused on revising the legislation identified by the Commission up to the Edinburgh Meeting and the Franco-British list. Much emphasis was put on recasting and simplification, and did not refer very many matters to governance by the Member States. Since 1995 the process has turned into 'Better Lawmaking' reports, in which emphasis is on the Commission's role of making extensive use of initiatives, such as reports, communications, working papers, and Green/White Papers, to prompt debate.

The way in which the Commission has implemented subsidiarity means that two effects of subsidiarity on Community legislation should be expected. First, fewer instruments would be adopted. Second, less binding instruments would be preferred to more binding ones. This chapter has shown that the Commission has been more successful with respect to the first than the second effect.

The analysis of the composition of Community legislation in the 1990s reveals that the number of Commission proposals, and particularly proposals for new legislation, has decreased since 1990 and especially after 1992. This result, however, was not found in environmental policy and internal market legislation. Here the number of adopted instruments decreased after 1994 but has increased since then. This may indicate that after a 'subsidiarity shock' in 1992–94 the Community is returning to 'business as usual'. This development is most profound in environmental policy, where the number of proposed and adopted instruments is larger in the late 1990s than in the early 1990s.

Since CELEX does not divide proposals for new legislation into categories, such as the environment and the internal market, it is not possible to obtain information about the number of new pieces of legislation in these areas. However, Jordan et al. (1999) show that there was no difference in the average number of major new environmental policy items adopted in the period 1987–93 and 1994–95.

The Community has not been successful in preferring the directive to the regulation. Compared to regulations and decisions, the relative importance of directives has decreased. In the environmental policy area and the internal market, the relative importance of directives was in 1996–98 about half of the 1990–92 level.

The changes in the composition of legislation identified here are not due to subsidiarity alone. First, the EEC Treaty suggested from the outset that harmonization measures were to be curbed once the internal market was functioning properly.[20] Moreover, the directive has already been envisioned as the main harmonization instrument in the Treaty of Rome. Furthermore, the Commission and the Council often use legislative instruments designed to avoid unnecessary Community actions. The principle of mutual recognition, for instance, means that the Community is satisfied that the regulatory regime in the Member States meets certain minimum criteria and can therefore leave the Member States' regimes in place (Bermann, 1994, p. 372). A second example is the 'new approach to technical harmonization' announced in 1985, the purpose of which was to limit harmonization to those aspects of a regulatory problem deemed to be 'essential'. In practice, this would mean that the quantity and the detail of issues that a directive needs to address should be limited. Another explanation for the downward trend in adopted legislation and proposals could be the new decision-making procedure in the Maastricht Treaty. These new procedures may have increased the period in which a proposal is in the process of being adopted, which might then have reduced the volume of adopted legislation in the years following the Maastricht Treaty.

Golub (1996) finds that subsidiarity has caused the number of EC environment proposals to decrease in 1992–95. He concludes that 'subsidiarity has already returned a significant amount of sovereignty to the states by curtailing the number of new EU proposals from the agenda, and amending others to allow greater national leeway' (Golub, 1996, p. 703). This chapter has presented an empirical analysis of how subsidiarity has affected the development of Community legislation in the period 1990–98. It concludes that the effect of subsidiarity is ambiguous. Subsidiarity has led to a reduction in the number of new Community initiatives. It has not, however, led the Community to adopt fewer strongly binding instruments, such as recommendations and decisions, and has turned to less binding instruments, such as directives. On the contrary, in the internal market and in environmental policy, the relative importance of directives has decreased. Hence, in contrast to Golub (1996), it is concluded that subsidiarity has not allowed greater national leeway.

Subsidiarity was introduced as a concept that should strike the balance between integration and proximity. Essentially, this involves a comparison of the advantages of centralized and decentralized decision-making. Subsidiarity clearly involves economic efficiency as an instrument to achieve this balance. But how does economic theory strike this balance? And how does EU environmental legislation reflect this balance? These issues will be examined in the following chapter.

NOTES

* This Chapter was previously published as Jeppesen, T. (2000), 'EU environmental policy in the 1990s: allowing greater national leeway?', *European Environment*, **10**: 96–105. Reprinted with kind permission from John Wiley & Sons, UK.

1. SEC (92) 1990 final, p. 1.
2. This formulation was used by Jacques Delors in his speech 'The Principle of Subsidiarity: Contribution to the Debate', *Proceedings of the Jacques Delors Colloquium*, European Institute of Public Administration, Maastricht, 21–22 March 1991.
3. Lenaerts (1994) argues that Article 3b(2) also involves the assessment of the intensity of Community action because it says that 'the Community shall take action, only if and in so far as . . .'. This chapter will follow the structure laid down in most papers on subsidiarity and refer to Article 3b(2) as the necessity test and Article 3b(3) as the intensity test.
4. Dehousse (1993) quotes a draft circulated during the Luxembourg Presidency which referred to 'objectives . . . better achieved by the Community than by the Member States acting separately' (p. 8).
5. Ibid.
6. SEC (92) 1990 final, p. 2.
7. Ibid., p. 15.
8. Com (93) 545 final.
9. Areas of rules and regulations to be recast are customs, right of residence, pharmaceutical products, competition, and trade mechanisms for agricultural products. As an example, the Community customs code includes several hundred regulations and directives which the recasting brings together in two regulations.
10. Rules identified at the Edinburgh Meeting cover technical standards, professional qualifications, environment, recognition of the possibility of Member States negotiating

settlements with individuals, animal welfare and social policy. Rules identified by the Commission included indirect taxation, company law, common organization of agricultural markets, transport policy, common fisheries policy, energy policy and consumer protection.

11. See, for instance, CSE (95) 580.
12. Com (94) 533 final. The report states that it is the first annual report. However, the following annual reports all refer to the report as the second.
13. The Commission now uses the word 'revision' and not 'recasting' as they did in the first annual report. Presumably it means the same.
14. CSE (95) 580.
15. CSE (96) 7 final, p. 1. In the Commission interim report on the application of the subsidiarity and proportionality principles presented to the European Council at its meeting in Florence 1996, the 'new legislative culture' is described as Community legislation 'based on strictness, coherence and openness' (CSE (96) 2 final, p. 1). Presumably these two descriptions of the 'new legislative culture' complement each other, so all six words jointly reflect the 'new legislative culture'.
16. CSE (96) 7 final, p. 7.
17. Com (1998) 715, p. 2.
18. Com (96) 90 final.
19. The overall volume of Commission proposals includes programmes, reports and communications in addition to decisions, directives and regulations.
20. Article 3h of the EEC Treaty suggested that Member State laws should only be harmonized 'to the extent required for the proper functioning of the internal market'.

4. Centralized or decentralized European environmental policy?

1. INTRODUCTION

The creation of the internal market in the Community at the beginning of the 1990s has affected the national choice of environmental policy instruments. Product standards covering mobile emission sources, such as cosmetics containing CFCs, or commercial products containing polluting substances, will be environmentally ineffective due to the principle of mutual recognition. To the extent that this principle applies in the Community, the result is that products which fail to meet the standards set by one Member State cannot be prevented from being imported from other Member States, thereby undermining stricter national environmental standards. However, at the beginning of the 1990s the principle of subsidiarity entered the political agenda in the Community as an instrument of decentralization and a guarantee that the decisions were to be taken as close as possible to the citizen. Thus a balance has to be found between, on the one hand, the economic advantages of further European integration and, on the other, the advantages of giving Member States the possibility of setting their own national standards.

This chapter examines how this balance is found. The process involves a choice between a centralized and a decentralized system of environmental decision-making. Which level of government should be responsible for environmental regulation in the Community? Should environmental standards and other regulatory instruments be decided by the Community, resulting in uniform measures to be satisfied in all Member States, or should they be decided by the Member States themselves? The economic literature on this question was rather limited until the late 1980s. The economics of (de)centralization was first discussed by Tiebout (1956), by the literature on public finance (Musgrave, 1959), and by the literature on fiscal federalism (Oates, 1972). Building upon this tradition, the number of works on the economics of (de)centralization increased rapidly in the 1990s. These works examine the (environmental) economics of a federal system and have to a great extent been initiated by revisions of the EC Treaty in 1987 and 1992 and by the decentralization of environmental regulation in the USA during the

Reagan/Bush administrations (Folmer and Howe, 1991; Howe, 1993; van den Bergh et al., 1996; van den Bergh, 1994; Faure and Lefevere, 1999; Shapiro and Petchey, 1995; CEC, 1993; Oates and Schwab, 1988, 1989. For textbook examples, see Braden et al., 1996; Braden and Proost, 1997).

This chapter examines the balance between the economic advantages of further European integration and the advantages of giving Member States the possibility of setting their own national standards from both an economic and from an institutional perspective. Section 2 examines the first elements of an economic theory of the costs and benefits of centralization and decentralization in a federal system. Even though these seminal contributions need some refinements in order to explain modern federal structures, they are nevertheless useful in providing a basic understanding of the elements of the economics of (de)centralization. Braden et al. (1996) offer several refinements of this basic model. Section 3 examines how subsidiarity is defined and implemented by Community institutions, and the arguments used by the institutions to justify Community action are compared to the arguments for central action identified by the economic model in section 2. Section 4 examines how subsidiarity has affected Community legislation on water policy. Directives on Community water policy are examined in order to see how they comply with subsidiarity and what arguments for Community action are used. Section 5 describes European preferences for environmental protection by using opinion polls on environmental policy questions. The results are then applied to the economic analysis in section 2 and show that there do not appear to be significant differences in national preferences for environmental protection in the Community; nor does there appear to be strong empirical evidence to support a renationalization of Community environmental policies. The conclusions are presented in section 6.

2. THE ECONOMICS OF CENTRALIZATION AND DECENTRALIZATION

2.1. Interjurisdictional Competition

A competitive market obtains allocative efficiency when the free choice of buyers and sellers produces an efficient outcome. This can also be obtained by a multi-level government which imitates the structure of the market. In such a system, governments are sellers of legislation, and consumers are buyers according to their preferences. This system is the framework for Tiebout's classic article on the optimal provision of public goods (Tiebout, 1956).

In Tiebout's model, individuals with heterogeneous preferences can buy and consume different bundles of purely private goods and still live side by side. Public goods, however, cannot be consumed by people with heterogeneous preferences if these persons live side by side. This is illustrated by the following example. If there are two groups of people: (1) those who value clean air very highly; and (2) those who do not value clean air especially, then it will be impossible for the two groups to live side by side and at the same time have their preferences satisfied. In this case, it would be better if people who value clean air highly could cluster together in communities with others who have similar preferences.

This is the basic point in Tiebout's analysis: the optimal provision of local public goods is offered in a decentralized society where people with the same preferences can cluster together in small communities. Hence, allocative efficiency is obtained if people can move freely between a large number of communities which offer differing bundles of local public goods. The decentralized provision of local public goods is superior to the central solution because local authorities are assumed to have an information advantage. It is assumed that they can better adjust the provision of the public good to the different preferences.

Tiebout makes an analogy between legislators and firms. A law, legal rule, or institution also has the characteristics of public goods. A legal rule is indivisible and non-excludable. States may offer individuals and firms a varying set of legal rules and institutions. In a perfectly mobile world, every state faces competition from other states to which the (human) capital may flow. The states will avoid (human) capital flight by offering the policy which best satisfies citizens' preferences. The legal rules will therefore reflect the preferences of citizens and firms in a given locality because firms and citizens are free to move to the jurisdiction in which the laws are best adapted to their preferences. Thus states are engaged in interjurisdictional competition which ensures allocative efficiency. Citizens and firms 'vote with their feet'.

Tiebout's analysis has some very strong underlying assumptions which may restrict the application. The conditions that must be fulfilled are that there be: (1) a sufficiently large number of legislators; (2) perfect mobility; (3) perfect information; (4) no interregional externalities; and (5) no economies of scale or transaction cost savings which require large jurisdictions. Moreover, legislators must maximize their size in a competitive way.

It is clear that many of these conditions will not be fulfilled in the real world. First, it will not always be possible for a state or a citizen to find a state with the legal arrangement which best fits their preferences. Second, even though the single market has been working for some years now, there are still barriers to the free movement of goods, capital and persons. Third, firms may have an information advantage relative to the legislators, and information may be so costly as to prevent firms from choosing the best legal system. Fourth, many environmental problems are transboundary. Fifth, scale economies exist and will often necessitate large legal areas. Large legal areas might also be optimal due to high information costs. Finally, legal orders may compete under prisoner's dilemma conditions.

All six conditions do not always hold in reality. Moreover, when the last three points do not hold, each of them carries with it an argument in favour of centralization. For example, international environmental problems like the increased CO_2 level are best solved at a central level; large legal areas minimize costs if economies of scale are present; and prisoner's dilemma situations may require a central authority to enforce the Pareto-dominant outcome.

2.2. Fiscal Federalism

The public sector comprises several layers of government which address matters of national, regional and local concern. Each layer of government has fiscal responsibilities for its own geographical jurisdiction. This federal structure of the public sector opens up a large array of important issues: the proper allocation of fiscal functions among the different levels of government; assignment of specific instruments to the various levels; and the vertical assignment of regulatory responsibilities (Oates, 1994).

Musgrave's (1959) tripartite division of functions for the public sector serves as a benchmark for allocating fiscal functions among levels of government. The three government functions defined are stabilization, distribution and allocation.

Stabilization refers to the general macroeconomic stabilization, for example, monetary and fiscal policy, where it is only a centralized government that is in a position to make use of monetary and fiscal instruments at the same time. Hence, when macroeconomic stabilization is desired, the public finance literature argues that this is best obtained by a central government because the actions of the decentralized governments are constrained due to their limited availability of instruments.

Distribution refers to the distribution of income and offers equally strong arguments for centralization. This is because if one region wants a more equal income distribution than others, the poorest people will immigrate, and the richest people will migrate. Hence regional redistributive programmes are limited by the potential mobility of the residents. The degree of mobility can be questioned, but it seems reasonable to assume that mobility is inversely dependent upon the size of the regions. Thus migration between countries is less likely than migration between municipalities.

Therefore the distributive government function also calls for a high degree of centralization.

Allocation refers to the establishment of an efficient pattern of resource use and is less clear-cut than the first two functions. The allocation of some public goods provides convincing arguments for centralization, but others provide equally convincing arguments for decentralization. Thus it is much more likely that a system of decentralized decision-making will be efficient in the allocation branch than in the two other branches. Musgrave (1959) concludes his section on fiscal federalism by stating that 'The heart of fiscal federalism thus lies in the proposition that the policies of the Allocation Branch should be permitted to differ between states, depending upon the preferences of their citizens. The objectives of the Distribution and Stabilization Branches, however, require primary responsibility at the central level' (Musgrave, 1959, pp. 181–2). Hence the gains from decentralization are to be realized in the tailoring of outputs of local public goods to the particular tastes and circumstances of the different regions. The Tiebout model is an extreme example of this proposition.

Oates (1972) shows that the distribution of the benefits is important in deciding whether a system of centralized or decentralized government will be most efficient. An example is a pure public good like air quality. Assume that air quality may be improved either by local and individual measures, or by centralized common measures. The necessary condition for efficient measures taken to improve air quality is that the marginal cost of the measure equals the sum of the value placed on clean air of all the individual regions. This is not likely to be obtained by the decentralized solution. The individual regions consider only the benefits which their own residents will receive. The regions therefore maximize their own welfare, disregarding the aggregate welfare. The result is that the measure is set too low; for example, air quality will be lower for decentralized compared to centralized measures. Hence, when the public goods confer benefits to members of all or several regions, a central government is superior to a decentralized government.

However, it is also possible that the allocation function requires a decentralized government. Here it is necessary to recognize the shortcomings of a central government. Oates assumes that the central authority has a uniformity constraint because it can only impose uniform quantities of the public good. Uniform quantities can only be efficient if benefits are distributed equally in the regions. If we have a public good whose benefits are limited to subsets of the regions, a decentralized government is more efficient than a central government because it does not take into consideration the varying preferences between the regions. Thus, in the case of the uniformity constraint on central measures, where preferences differ between subsets of population and the benefits of the public good distributed unequally, there is a need for variations in the provision of the public good and, thus, a need for a decentralized government.[1]

Oates captures the basic arguments by formulating the principle of perfect correspondence and the decentralization theorem. He assumes that the public good is a Samuelsonian-like public good where the level of consumption of the good is independent of the number of consumers. Moreover, Oates assumes that the geographical distribution of the good is fixed, and that the costs of providing the good in each region are the same for central and regional governments. In this set-up, the principle of perfect correspondence implies that there should exist a government for each subset of the population to supply the public good. An example is bathing water quality in the EU. Benefits of improved bathing water quality will certainly be unequally distributed among the various Member States. According to the principle of perfect correspondence, bathing water quality should therefore be regulated decentrally by the individual Member States. In order to satisfy the preferences of their own citizens, each Member State should regulate its own bathing water quality. Naturally, if a central government could identify the different demands in the different Member States, it could, in principle, provide efficient quantities of the public good. As noted above, however, Oates imposes a uniformity constraint, implying that governments are limited to providing uniform quantities. Now, if preferences differ between the regions, the central government is unable to achieve perfect correspondence. The decentralization theorem follows directly from this. Given the assumptions above, the theorem asserts that it will be more efficient for local governments to provide the efficient quantities of the public goods.[2] This is equivalent to Tiebout's result and is in fact an expansion of it. Even in the absence of consumer mobility there will still exist welfare gains from varying local outputs with local tastes and costs. The decentralization theorem leads to a federal system with many layers of government of different geographical size. Each regional government is responsible for the provision of the public good consumed by the individuals in that region.

Even though the decentralization principle rests on some quite restrictive assumptions, it provides some valuable insights into the economics of centralized or decentralized decision-making. However, as Walsh (1993) notes, the decentralization theorem holds true only when comparing a first-best decentralized solution with a second-best centralized solution. When the restrictive assumptions are relaxed, and the model becomes more realistic, it becomes much more complicated to design the federal system. Four assumptions have to be relaxed:

1. *Impure public goods.* If the condition that the level of consumption of the good is independent of the number of consumers is not met, the number of consumers becomes a variable. The problem is now to determine the optimal-sized group of consumers. Basically, optimization weighs the welfare gain from greater decentralization against the welfare gains from increased centralization.
2. *The cost of collective decision-making.* It is more realistic to assume that governments are formed at a cost (administration, elections, information). If these costs are included there will be an incentive to reduce the number of government layers. Again the benefits from establishing a level of government must be weighed against the increased costs of collective decision-making.
3. *Consumer mobility.* Naturally, the geographical position of individuals is not fixed. As in the Tiebout model, we would expect that mobility increases the gains from decentralization due to the formation of more homogeneous groups. On the other hand, unrestricted mobility may carry a congestion cost.
4. *Interjurisdictional externalities.* The decentralization theorem assumes that the spatial distribution of costs and benefits of consumption includes only the persons in the region. Perfect correspondence implies internalization of all costs and benefits. The air pollution example given earlier is an example of a transboundary externality where all costs and benefits are not internalized in the case of a system with decentralized decision-making. In the presence of interjurisdictional externalities, potential gains accrue from cooperation, thus making a case for centralization.

Fiscal federalism thus suggests that a central government should be responsible for stabilization and distribution problems and for providing efficient outputs of those public goods that significantly affect welfare in all regions. On the other hand, a decentralized government may be superior to a central government if we have a public good whose benefits are limited to subsets of the regions. However, when the ideal and restricted model is extended in a more realistic way, the best division of responsibilities between different layers of government will no longer result in perfect correspondence. In some cases, the government will not include all those who benefit from the good or who are not affected by the good at all.

3. SUBSIDIARITY COMES INTO PLAY

The subsidiarity principle regulates the exercise of powers and not the conferment of powers. This is a matter of the Treaty. The subsidiarity principle nevertheless prescribes an enquiry into the efficiency of Community action compared to action by the Member States. In this process, arguments in favour of Community action and action by the Member States are identified. This section compares the efficiency analysis of Community action prescribed by subsidiarity with the efficiency analysis of central decision-making discussed in the previous section.

3.1.   Arguments for Community Action

At first glance it appears that the way in which subsidiarity is defined[3] implies a very low threshold with regard to the assessment of the need for Community action in the environmental area. As argued in Chapter 3, the Community should take action if the issue under consideration has transnational aspects which cannot be satisfactorily regulated via action by Member States or if actions by Member States alone or lack of Community action would conflict with competition and trade. Clearly, many environmental problems are transnational. As Chapter 2 showed, the fact that many environmental regulations potentially restrict trade was the argument for Community action in the first environmentally related legislation in the Community in the late 1960s.

It is possible to identify four categories of arguments in favour of Community action from the way in which the Community institutions have applied the subsidiarity test and the way in which they have justified Community action in the recitals of the directives (van den Bergh et al., 1996).

1. *Transboundary externalities.* If pollution crosses the national borders of the Member States, the Member States only internalize the externality present in their own state. Community action is necessary in order to internalize fully all the externalities from transboundary pollution.
2. *Prevention of unequal competition.* Centralization should in this category establish a 'level playing-field' for industry in Europe, which is deemed necessary for the functioning of the Common Market. Disparity between national provisions on discharge of dangerous substances into the water may create unequal conditions for competition among Member States.
3. *Free movement of goods.* Harmonization of, for instance, product standards is considered necessary in order to achieve free movement of goods. This argument lay behind the first directives with an environmental objective.[4] The driving force behind these directives was not environmental concern but the removal of obstacles for market integration.

4. *General concern about the environment and human health.* In the intro-
    ductory part of the Treaty (Article 2 and 3 EU) it is stated that the
    Community is concerned about the environment and that the
    Community shall promote higher standards of living and better
    quality of life.[5] Arguably the protection of the environment is a means
    of achieving that aim. Moreover, Articles 95 EC and 174 EC state that
    Community policy on the environment shall aim for a high level of pro-
    tection. On these grounds, it could be argued that environmental stan-
    dards in the Community should be harmonized to guarantee a basic
    environmental quality.

These categories are in agreement with Stewart's (1992) classification of
environmental spillovers. Stewart defines four types of environmental spillovers. The first type consists of the well-known situations where pollution
crosses boundaries and is analogous to the first category above. Article 175
EC contains the required legal basis for Community action. The need for
Community action is justified under the first of the three categories of arguments for Community action identified at the Edinburgh Meeting. The
second type includes product spillovers created when Member States 'seek to
reduce foreign products on the ground that they are environmentally defi-
cient, creating trade barriers' (Stewart, 1992, p. 45). The appropriate legal
basis is Article 95 EC, and the need for action is found in the second of the
categories above, which argues that Community action may be justified in
order to avoid restrictions on trade. The third type includes the competitive
spillovers generated by the Member States' fear that environmental regulations may affect their competitive advantage negatively. This is avoided by
Community action. The sufficient legal basis may be found in both Articles
95 EC and 175 EC. The need for action is found in the second of the
Edinburgh categories, which calls for Community action in order to correct
distortion of competition. The fourth type includes preservation spillovers,
which Stewart defines as 'an especially scenic or ecologically significant
natural resource located in one state will be admired by citizens in other
states, who will wish to visit it or simply know that it is being preserved'.[6] As
with transboundary pollution, the state is likely to disregard out-of-state
interest and fail adequately to preserve the resource. The legal basis on which
to act may be found in Article 175 EC, and the need to act may be justified by
the 'transnational' aspect, that is, the first of the three Edinburgh categories.

3.2. Application of Subsidiarity

Since the inclusion of subsidiarity in the Maastricht Treaty, great efforts
have been made to adapt the principle to the Community legislation. As

defined, subsidiarity embodies several ambiguities. The principle of subsidiarity itself does not provide a clear answer as to how it should be applied. This has to be defined post-Maastricht by the Community institutions. In the Maastricht Treaty negotiations, subsidiarity had a prominent position. This position was further strengthened after the ratification of the Maastricht Treaty and especially after the Edinburgh Meeting, when the Commission was committed to examine the application of subsidiarity and eventually to revise Community legislation, both existing and future.

With respect to future Community legislation, the Commission developed a list of questions which all have to be answered in any justification of all new legislative proposals.[7] This list, a sort of 'subsidiarity guideline', is used throughout the Commission in its daily work. It represents the Commission's view on how subsidiarity should be applied, and asks the following questions:

1. What are the aims of the proposed action in terms of the Community's obligations?
2. Does the proposed measure fall within the Community's exclusive competence, or is competence shared with the Member States?
3. What is the Community dimension of the problem (in other words, how many Member States are involved and what solution has been applied to date)?
4. What is the most effective solution, given the means available to the Community and the Member States?
5. What is the specific added value of the proposed Community action and the cost of failing to act?
6. What is the means available to the Community (recommendation, financial support, regulation, mutual recognition and so on)?
7. Are uniform rules necessary, or would it be sufficient to adopt a directive laying down general objectives and leaving implementation to Member States?

Questions 1, 2 and 6 are natural and obvious questions to ask of all proposals. Question 7 deals with proportionality, which applies to both exclusive and shared competence.

Questions 3–5 deal directly with subsidiarity. Question 3 deals with the degree to which the problem is transboundary. In order to justify Community action, it must be proven that a number of Member States are affected by the action. It could also be argued here that the action is proposed in order to achieve one of the objectives as enshrined, for instance, in Article 2 or 3 of the Treaty. A third source of arguments for Community action is that if the envisaged Community action is not adopted, obstacles to trade may be the result.

If it is proved that there is a significant Community dimension to the problem, one can proceed to question 4. Ideally two scenarios, a Community and a Member States scenario, are constructed. In both scenarios, the means available must be identified, and the effects of the scenario quantified. Both direct and indirect effects should be included, as well as physical and 'non-physical' effects. The two scenarios can be compared, and the most effective scenario identified. Presumably, this stage stops with quantification. That is, there is no monetarization of the effects. Consequently, in cases where there are great differences in the effects of the two scenarios, they may be difficult to compare. Ideally, in order to be able to compare the two scenarios, a full cost–benefit analysis should be conducted. This is presumably what is indicated in question 5. However, it is only an indication because that question is formulated in an ambiguous way and because the relation to question 4 is not clear. The two scenarios in question 5 are not necessarily the same as those in question 4. The Community scenario is identical to the one in question 4, but the 'failing-to-act' scenario is not necessarily the same as the Member States scenario. Thus question 5 actually demands that the costs and benefits from three different scenarios be identified: (a) the costs and benefits of Community action; (b) the costs and benefits of 'no Community action'; and (c) the costs and benefits of the actions taken by the Member States in the absence of Community action.

It should be emphasized, however, that due to problems with quantification and monetarization, and due to the limited time-horizon, the Commission is presumably unable to make a full cost–benefit analysis of the three scenarios. It should also be emphasized that the terms 'costs' and 'benefits' should be given the broadest possible interpretation. The costs of the Member States scenario, for instance, might be distortions to the internal market, or negative environmental effects. These 'costs' are impossible to monetarize but may be important elements in answering question 5. Subsidiarity increases the importance of the Member States scenario compared to the 'failing-to-act' scenario. In light of subsidiarity, it is most important that the costs and benefits of the Community action can be proven to exceed the costs and benefits of the Member States scenario.

3.3. Subsidiarity and Economic Theory

Interjurisdictional competition and fiscal federalism both lead to the conclusion that a local externality calls for a decentralized approach to environmental regulation. Decentralized authorities are assumed to have an informational advantage over central authorities and will therefore be better able to adjust the provision of public goods, such as environmental quality, to the preferences of the citizens. The optimal level of environmental quality is where marginal damages of pollution are equal to marginal abatement costs. Both damages and costs may be local in character and, thus, likely to vary between jurisdictions. This result is based on a number of restrictive assumptions which, if not fulfilled, may alter the result. In the case of transboundary externalities, for example, a central solution should be preferred due to the possible existence of scale economies and/or the inabilities of the local regions fully to internalize all costs and benefits.

The theoretical analysis raises the question of whether we should set Community environmental standards applicable in all Member States, or whether we should adopt a more decentralized approach to environmental standard-setting that would allow the Member States to determine specific standards for their own jurisdictions. The theoretical analysis seems to provide a straightforward answer. Standards should vary among Member States according to local circumstances. Local pollutants should be regulated by standards specific to the Member States, and transboundary pollutants should be regulated by Community standards. Thus, in light of this basic economic reasoning, a number of Community regulations may appear problematic. For this reason, the drinking and bathing water directives (Directives 80/778/EEC and 76/160/EEC, respectively) as well as the proposed directive laying down minimal standards for keeping animals in zoos (Com (91) 177 final) have been viewed by some authors as falling outside the purview of Community powers (for example, Wils, 1994; Steinberg, 1996).

There are many similarities among the four categories of arguments in favour of Community action on the one hand and Tiebout's and Oates's theoretical results on the other. The four arguments for Community action may easily be reformulated in economic terms. Clearly, transboundary externalities and economies of scale provide strong arguments for centralization in economic theory as well as in the principle of subsidiarity.

There is a parallel in Oates's concern about the cost of collective decision-making and the arguments for transaction cost savings in the Community. Oates argues that the costs of collective decision-making may exceed the benefits of decentralization due to high costs of administration and information. Transaction costs in the Community relate to the diversity in rules, and it is clear that a harmonization (centralization) of the rules reduces the transaction costs. Under uniform Community regulation, firms do not have to inform themselves about differences in national rules and the way in which they are enforced. These transaction cost savings should thus be compared to possible costs of collective decision-making.

The argument for creating a 'level playing-field' for industry in Europe is based on a fear that the Member States will engage in 'a race to the bottom', that is, implement lax environmental standards in order to attract business investment. This argument should not be pushed too far, however. Jaffe et al. (1995), for instance, show that the effect of environmental regulation on firm location is insignificant and, hence, do not find scientific evidence to support that fear. Ulph (1997) shows that even if governments believe that they can affect the location of firms, it is not necessarily rational for a government to implement a lax environmental policy. Moreover, competition between Member States may also initiate a 'race to the top', where the states implement high environmental standards. If competition works, regulations may act as a positive driving force for the economy. High environmental standards may also protect domestic products. Finally, the states may believe that there is a 'first-mover advantage'.

Behind the arguments for free movement of goods are the scale economies and transaction cost savings which may be achieved through harmonization of product standards. These benefits from centralization may be quite substantial.

Despite the similarities between subsidiarity and economic theory, it is also clear that subsidiarity provides some further arguments for centralization which are hard to fit into an economic analysis. If it is accepted that the Community shall contribute to the protection of environmental quality and human health, and this alone provides a reason for central measures, it becomes hard to find any examples of Community environmental measures which cannot be justified. Van den Bergh et al. (1996) note that this argument for Community action can only be explained in terms of equity. In developing 'Europe for Citizens', it may be argued that environmental standards should be harmonized so as to guarantee to the Europeans a basic environmental quality.

Basic economic reasoning would require that the obligation to ensure a high standard of living and quality of life as an argument for Community competences in environmental policy should be held up against the benefits of decentralized standard-setting. In order to strike that balance, one should distinguish between quality standards and emission standards (van den Bergh et al., 1996). A quality standard (or target standard) defines the environmental quality that has to be achieved in the jurisdiction. An emission standard defines the quality and/or the quantity of the polluting substances from a specific source.

When a general concern for the environment and human health or the obligation to ensure a high standard of living and quality of life justifies Community competences, it might only justify the setting of a quality standard. It should then be the responsibility of the Member States to achieve this environmental quality by choosing emission standards. If the Member States define the emission standards, they are likely to differ according to local circumstances. In this way the EU defines the minimum environmental quality in order to ensure a high standard of living and quality of life, while at the same time it is possible to realize the benefits of differentiated emission standards. This combination of harmonized quality standards and differentiated emission standards could achieve an optimal mix of central rules and decentralized decision-making.

One advantage of this system is that it is possible to decide the optimal specificity of standards (van den Bergh et al., 1996). In a first-best world, differentiation should be carried out until all kinds of detail have been taken into account. In any other world than a first-best world this is impossible because information and monitoring costs increase with the degree of differentiation. There is a tradeoff between the benefits of differentiated standards and the information and monitoring costs. The optimal specificity of standards is where the marginal benefits of increased differentiation equal the marginal information and monitoring costs of increased differentiation. This optimization is solved in a system where the Community sets the environmental quality standards and the Member States choose the emission standards according to their site-specific circumstances. The Member States will have to monitor and enforce the differentiated standards in their jurisdictions, and the Community will have to monitor and enforce the quality standard. This system recognizes that Member States have more information on the site-specific circumstances necessary to find the optimal level of specificity than does the Community. Further, it recognizes that the Community has more information necessary to monitor and enforce overall environmental targets. The system prevents the prisoner's dilemma situation whereby Member States set too low emission standards because the Community has a fair chance of controlling environmental quality.

The proposition that the Community should harmonize quality standards is valid irrespective of the preferences for environmental protection in Europe. In light of fiscal federalism, one could argue that if the preferences for environmental protection are heterogeneous, for instance if the different Member States prefer different environmental quality, the Community should not harmonize the standards. The quality standards should then vary according to the preferences. However, the system of harmonized quality standards and differing emission standards is based solely on the fact that the Treaty directs the Community to ensure a basic environmental quality. This may or may not accord with the preferences for environmental protection in Europe.

4. EFFECTS ON EU WATER POLICY

4.1. The Development of EU Water Policy

The development of Community water policy from the beginning to the present can be divided into two periods. The first period starts with the first Environmental Action Programme (EAP) in 1973 and ends in the late 1980s. The first EAP determined that Community water policy should adopt two instruments, quality standards and emission standards. This kick-started the Community water policy and the first 'wave' of legislation was adopted shortly after the first EAP (Lefevere, 1999).

The EAP was followed by a number of directives setting quality standards for various uses, including surface water for the abstraction of drinking water, quality of drinking water, bathing water, water for freshwater fish, and water for shellfish.[8] At the same time several directives were adopted laying down emission standards for various substances. The most important were the surface water directive and the groundwater directive.[9] Together, these directives defined Community water policy.

The second period in the development of Community water policy started in the late 1980s because the directives in the first period needed a revision after ten years of operation. The directives in the first wave did not contain any regulation of water quality. Moreover, the first wave of legislation was adopted in a very piecemeal manner and daughter directives proved much more difficult to adopt than anticipated because unanimity was required. Finally, the directives in the first wave focused on industrial pollution, ignoring municipal and agricultural sources. Consequently, several new water directives were adopted at the beginning of the 1990s. Included in this second wave of water legislation were the urban wastewater directive and the nitrates directive.[10]

The inadequacy of the directives in the first wave was, however, not the only reason for revising Community water policy. The subsidiarity debate at the beginning of the 1990s also pushed for a substantive revision.

4.2. The Subsidiarity Revision

Allocation of environmental policy competence between Community level and Member States level is a central issue in the environmental policy of the Community. Transboundary and local environmental problems require different action at different levels of authorities, and uncoordinated national environmental policies may distort competition, calling for some degree of Community action.

This was recognized in the first EAP in 1973, which included subsidiarity as one of the 11 principles in the programme in these words:

> In each category of pollution, it is necessary to establish the level of action (local, regional, national, Community, international) best suited to the type of pollution and to the geographical zone to be protected. Actions likely to be most effective at Community level should be concentrated at that level; priorities should be determined with special care.[11]

The fact that subsidiarity was included in the chapter on environment in the SEA in 1987 before it was turned into a general principle in the Maastricht Treaty in 1992 also illustrates that decision-making at different levels is a central issue in Community environmental policy.

At the December 1992 European Council Meeting in Edinburgh, the environment was identified as one of the families of rules and regulations which the Commission declared it would scrutinize in light of subsidiarity. In the Conclusions from the Edinburgh Meeting, the Commission declared that it 'intends to simplify, consolidate, and update existing texts, particularly those on air and water, to take new knowledge and technical progress into account'. As illustrated in the previous chapter, it was decided that the Commission should publish an annual report on the application of subsidiarity.

In the first of the Commission's annual reports, environmental policy is the policy area which takes up the most space.[12] The report is divided into two parts: water policy and air policy, as outlined by the conclusions from the Edinburgh Meeting. The identified directives on water policy should be reoriented 'towards compliance with essential quality and health parameters, leaving Member States free to add secondary parameters if they see fit'. All the identified directives constituted the first 'wave' of water legislation mentioned above. Thus the subsidiarity revision started a process in which all the pieces of water legislation in the first wave were to be replaced by four framework directives: on drinking water; ecological quality surface water; quality of bathing water; and a directive on freshwater management and groundwater protection. These four framework directives should be supplemented by the two existing directives concerning urban wastewater treatment and nitrates from agricultural sources, which require control pollution at source. In the Commission's opinion, the two latter directives 'comply with the subsidiarity principle in that they simply define an objective, leaving Member States free to achieve it in their own way'.[13]

Air policy is regulated on a wholly sectoral basis, and there is no definition of common objectives. Therefore the Commission stated that it will work for an agreement on common objectives before the existing legislation is reviewed.

The proposal for a framework directive on the quality of bathing water was presented on 29 March 1994,[14] the proposal for a directive on the ecological quality of surface water was presented on 8 July 1994,[15] and a proposal for a drinking water directive was presented on 30 May 1995.[16] The revised drinking water directive was adopted in December 1998.[17] The proposal for a directive on the ecological quality of surface water was met with very strong criticism from a number of Member States and in particular the Parliament. The main objections were that the proposal was not sufficiently coherent and that it did not combine quality and quantity aspects. Consequently, the Commission decided to draw up a new proposal for a water framework directive which would integrate water quality and quantity management as well as surface water and groundwater management.

The result was presented on 26 February 1997, when the Commission presented a proposal for a directive establishing a framework for Community action in the field of water policy.[18] This proposal was to replace five water directives: the freshwater directive, the shellfish water directive, the surface water for drinking directive, the directive on sampling methods, and the groundwater directive. In November 1997 it was expanded to incorporate the surface water directive. Hence, if adopted, it will replace all the water legislation from the first wave. It will, however, leave intact the legislation from the second wave, the drinking water directive, and the bathing water directive (Lefevere, 1999). Thus the directives on water policy legislation identified at the Edinburgh Meeting for review have been reduced to a drinking water directive, a bathing water directive, and the framework directive for Community action in the field of water policy.

In the air policy area, the Commission has presented a framework directive to simplify air quality legislation, which establishes a framework for the harmonization and evaluation of air quality standards within the Union, while leaving it to the Member States to take specific measures to reduce levels of pollution in their respective countries.[19]

4.3. Subsidiarity in the Water Policy Directives

The way in which subsidiarity has been applied in the environmental policy directives and the arguments used to justify Community action show how the Community institutions have dealt with the questions of central and decentralized Community environmental policies. Below a few case studies will be presented to illustrate this work.

Three proposals for directives from the mid-1990s explicitly examined the seven questions in the subsidiarity guideline developed by the Commission. These include the proposals for the bathing water directive, the directive on the ecological quality of surface water, and the proposed drinking water directive. How questions 3–5 in the subsidiarity guideline are examined in these three proposals is essential to the question of central versus decentralized environmental policy. Other proposals or environmental directives in Community water policy do not explicitly deal with subsidiarity but nevertheless examine the need for Community action and thereby implicitly also subsidiarity. These proposals will also be examined.

4.3.1. Proposal for a new bathing water directive (Com (94) 36 final)

The proposed directive will replace the old bathing water directive (76/778/EEC), which was one of the directives identified after the Edinburgh Meeting to be reviewed in light of subsidiarity. The main purpose of the proposal is to continue to maintain and improve the quality of bathing water and to protect human health. Moreover, it requires that Member States measure the quality of bathing water, that they report annually to the Commission, take measures necessary to protect the quality of bathing water, and monitor all discharges which may reduce it.

The proposal deals directly with subsidiarity. The old bathing water directive has often been questioned on subsidiarity grounds, and the proposal has dealt with this by simplifying it. This is done primarily by reducing the parameters, deleting redundant parameters and making certain definitions more explicit. The Commission emphasizes that it must not weaken the protection of the bathers' health. It is argued that this is ensured because 'the basic microbiological requirements cannot differ from Member State to Member State, as they are based on scientific evidence. As regards the other parameters, they reflect minimum conditions for satisfactory water quality' (p. 5). The proposal answers the seven questions in the subsidiarity guideline. The argument for Community action is given by the answer to question 3. Here it is simply stated that all Member States are concerned by the action and that the old directive applies to more than 16 000 identified bathing areas. Other arguments for Community action are found elsewhere in the proposal. It is argued that the proposal is needed because it ensures bathers the same basic common standards of health protection all over the Community, it contributes to the solution of transboundary problems of water pollution, and it ensures that there is no distortion of competition in the tourism industry. Thus the proposal draws on three of the categories of Community action, but it is done in a very cumbersome way. It is stated, but not justified, that the old directive 'has made a significant contribution towards improving the quality of life for the citizens of Europe' (p. 7). It is not proved that distortions of competition are likely to occur if the proposal is not adopted, and it is not clear how the proposal contributes to the solution of transboundary problems with water pollution.

The answer to question 4 of the subsidiarity guideline states that two aspects related to the quality of bathing water can only be solved efficiently by central action: (1) common standards for the protection of the health of bathers throughout the Community; and (2) the transboundary dimension of water pollution.

In question 5 of the subsidiarity guideline, the benefits of central action should be compared to the costs of no action. The benefits of central action are indicated by the success of the old bathing water directive, and the Commission states that the new directive, with its technical improvements, will continue to contribute to this 'added value'. Furthermore, it is stated that the new directive will have the advantage of ensuring that established 'holiday areas' are not abandoned due to poor quality bathing water, thus preventing loss of income due to reduced tourism and the unnecessary use of unspoiled coastal resources. Moreover, it is stated that the old directive has also had health-related benefits, thus reducing public health expenditures. All these effects are difficult to quantify in financial terms, so this is not done in the proposal. Thus the benefits of the proposal are not supported by any financial analysis, and the costs of inaction not calculated.

4.3.2. Proposal for a directive on the ecological quality of water (Com (93) 680 final)

The objective of the proposal is to maintain and improve the habitat potential of surface waters and thereby improve the quality of such waters generally, increasing their potential value as sources of water for drinking and other purposes, and increasing their amenity value. The proposal requires Member States to monitor the ecological status of their surface waters, identify sources of pollution, establish 'operational targets' for the achievement of 'good ecological quality', and implement programmes in order to reach those targets.

The proposed directive deals explicitly with subsidiarity and stresses the freedom of Member States to choose means and to consider local aspects. The Commission states that the proposal 'leaves it to the Member States to decide, in accordance with regional and local conditions and with respect to the protection of any other waters affected, which action is necessary to improve water quality'. Moreover, it is stated that the directive 'fixes only the general objectives and aims to be attained by the Member States, and leaves to them the choice of appropriate means and ways to achieve these objectives. In doing so, Member States should take into account the specific conditions of each body of water concerned by this proposal' (p. 11).

Two aspects are mentioned in the answer to question 3 in the subsidiarity guideline. The first is an obligation to ensure that the water resources are available for human, economic and recreational uses. The second is an obligation to ensure that those Community surface waters not covered by national or international programmes will be covered by such systematic efforts to improve water quality. Thus the arguments for Community action are that surface waters may be transboundary, and a general concern about the environment and human health. Furthermore, a third argument for Community action is that water policies interact with other policy areas such as fisheries and agriculture, and actions taken to improve environmental quality in these policy areas may be triggered by a Community policy on surface waters.

In the discussion of the most efficient solution in question 4 in the subsidiarity guideline, it is stressed that other Community water legislation also protects surface waters. Therefore the proposal should complement the existing legislation and only add the necessary action. The Commission states that since surface waters are transboundary, action at the level of individual Member States will often not be cost-effective, if effective at all. Hence Community action is more efficient than action by the Member States.

When answering question 5 in the subsidiarity guideline, the Commission notes that some benefits (for example recreational use and nature conservation) cannot be meaningfully quantified in monetary terms and others (for example tourism and fisheries potential) can only be quantified with great difficulty. Therefore a comparison of the added value of the proposal and costs of inaction concentrates on the purely economic costs. The Commission adopts a cost–benefit approach and assumes that for surface waters abstracted for different uses the benefits of the proposal may be equated with the savings in treatment expenses as a result of implementation of the proposal. The benefits may therefore be expressed as the additional costs of providing water treatment facilities. The cost of removing pesticides in 1 per cent of the abstracted surface water would be about 5000 million ECU. The Commission notes that it is not possible to give any exact global estimate of the costs of implementing the proposal. However, by using the experience with the Rhine Action Programme, the Commission estimates that the total additional investments in Member States following the adoption of the proposal are not expected to exceed 3000 million ECU. Finally, the Commission compares the costs of not implementing the proposal with the costs of providing treatment of water which can no longer meet the necessary quality requirements. The Commission concluded that the investment costs in a scenario where the proposal is not adopted will exceed the investments necessary to implement the proposal if more than 0.5 per cent of the surface water has to be treated to remove pollution.

4.3.3. Proposal for a new drinking water directive (Com (94) 612 final)

The proposed directive is a revision of the old drinking water directive (80/778/EEC) as requested after the Edinburgh Meeting. The main purpose is to protect human health from the adverse effects of contamination of water intended for human consumption by ensuring that it is wholesome.

In the proposal it is stated that subsidiarity is met by the directive if the most essential quality objectives on drinking water are set centrally, leaving Member States free to adopt further objectives and to choose the means by which to reach the objectives set at central level. Therefore a main argument for the proposal is to 'implement the principle of subsidiarity in the Directive as agreed at the European Council in Brussels in 1993 by restricting the quality parameters to those essential to human health and by leaving Member States free to set other parameters which they find appropriate' (p. 82), and that 'only those parameters which are known to be of general importance in the Member States or which are representative of the most important groups of substances that occur in drinking water are retained in the proposal' (p. 19).

The consequence of reviewing the old directive in light of subsidiarity is a reduction of the requirements set at the Community level. Besides, it is accepted that the Community should only set objectives that are of universal relevance, that is, objectives for which the preferences do not vary between different areas since they are essential to human health and based on scientific knowledge. This is the same argument used in the proposal for a bathing water directive.

In answering question 3 of the subsidiarity guideline, the Commission has two arguments for Community action. First, water which is safe to drink is a basic requirement for protecting human health, and the Community would therefore have failed to achieve the objective of Article 2 in the Treaty if it did not pursue this goal. Second, water is used as an input factor in the production process, and clean water is necessary if the final product is not to be affected by the quality of the water. Therefore, common health-related standards applicable to it will prevent obstacles to trade.

In the fourth question of the subsidiarity guideline, the Commission notes that the old drinking water directive has been effective in improving the quality of the drinking water, and European consumers expect to receive water which they know will be safe to drink. The Commission therefore concludes that the new directive should be a framework directive which allows Member States as much freedom as possible. However, the framework is underpinned by a central pillar of requirements and standards, and the Commission claims that the directive 'provides the essential health protection for all Community citizens while at the same time allowing local circumstances to be addressed in the most efficient manner'.

Question 5 of the subsidiarity guideline is answered in a section with the title, 'What added value will the action bring to the Community and what are the costs of the actions?' This title reflects the fact that the Commission in the section says little about 'the cost of failing to act', as required by the subsidiarity guideline. Instead, the section examines the costs and benefits of the proposed directive. It is argued that the proposal sets the necessary standards at Community level and allows for sufficient national modifications to allow for a smooth and cost-effective implementation. The Commission concludes that the change in the parametric value for lead will result in a major increase in compliance costs, but that other parametric changes will result in insignificant compliance costs, mainly because compliance cost increases will be approximately offset by the increased scope for cost-effective implementation.

4.3.4. Proposal for a directive establishing a framework for Community action in the field of water policy (Com (97) 49 final)

The overall purpose of this directive is to establish a framework for the protection of surface freshwater, estuaries, coastal waters and groundwater in the Community. This includes the protection of aquatic ecosystems, promotion of sustainable water consumption based on a long-term protection of available water resources, and provision of a supply of water in the qualities and quantities needed for sustainable use of these resources. The proposed directive integrates qualitative and quantitative aspects of protection and management of both surface waters and groundwater. The proposed directive uses a 'combined approach' with regard to pollution abatement, in that it combines the control of pollution at the source with the setting of objectives for the environment.

Some of the main requirements of the proposed directive concern the establishing of various administrative procedures and structures, including coordination, monitoring and reporting procedures. The directive also obliges Member States to ensure that the price of water (to the user) reflects the economic costs involved. These costs are the full costs of the services associated with the use of water (supply of water as well as treatment of wastewater). Moreover, Member States are required to ensure that, where necessary, the price of water use also reflects environmental costs and resource depletion costs. This requirement, however, seems rather weak since it is not specified what is meant by 'where necessary'. Also, it is for the Member States to consider if, how and when to impose the charges representing the environmental and resource costs. Finally, it is stated that price differentials stemming from variations in natural conditions in different river basin districts should not be viewed as distortions to competition as long as they are genuine reflections of the environmental and resource depletion costs involved.

The proposal does not deal directly with subsidiarity. In the introduction it is simply stated that the directive is 'in accordance with the principle of subsidiarity'. Further, it is stated that diverse conditions and needs exist in the Community which require different specific solutions, that decisions should be taken as close as possible to situations where water is used or affected, and that priority should be given to action within the responsibility of Member States through the drawing up of specific measures adjusted to regional and local conditions.

The arguments for centralization are only indirectly mentioned. The Commission notes that the supply of water is a service of general interest, and that the Community is concerned with prevention and reduction of pollution, as set out in Article 174 EC. Moreover, it is stated that 'common principles are needed in order to coordinate Member States' efforts to improve water quantity and quality, to promote sustainable water consumption, to contribute to the control of transboundary pollution problems, to protect ecosystems, in particular aquatic ecosystems and to safeguard the recreational potential of Community Waters'. Finally, the Community is under an obligation to act when it has signed international conventions, such as the UNECE Convention on the protection and management of international lakes and transboundary water courses which require river basin management.

4.3.5. The urban wastewater treatment directive (91/271/EEC) and the nitrates directive (91/676/EEC)

According to the Commission, both the urban wastewater treatment directive and the nitrates directive comply with the subsidiarity principle and are therefore not revised following the Edinburgh Meeting. Consequently, the directives do not deal with subsidiarity. Nevertheless they state why the Community should take action. The purpose of the urban wastewater directive is to reduce pollution of surface waters with nutrients (particularly nitrates and phosphates) from urban wastewater, and to reduce nitrate concentrations in drinking water. The directive establishes conditions for collection, treatment and discharge of urban wastewater as well as wastewater from certain industrial sectors.

The arguments for Community action are, first of all, that a Council resolution on the protection of the North Sea and other waters in the Community requested that the Commission submit proposals for measures required at Community level for the treatment of urban wastewater. Second, the transboundary externality argument is also used. It is stated that pollution due to insufficient treatment of wastewater in one Member State often affects the waters of other Member States.

The purpose of the nitrates directive is to reduce and prevent pollution of waters caused or induced by nitrates from agricultural sources. The directive regulates agricultural nitrate pollution (diffuse source pollution), and supplements the urban wastewater directive. The directive requires Member States to produce and promote Codes of Good Agricultural Practice in order to reduce the level of nitrate loss to surface water and groundwater. It contains monitoring requirements and in areas identified as vulnerable to nitrate pollution imposes Action Programmes with legally enforceable constraints on agricultural practices.[20]

The arguments for Community action are found in the presence of trans-boundary externalities and a general concern for the environment and human health. It is stated that since pollution of water due to nitrates by one Member State can affect waters in other Member States, action at Community level in accordance with Article 175 EC is therefore necessary. Moreover, it is said that the reduction of water pollution caused by nitrates is necessary in order to protect human health and living resources and aquatic ecosystems.

5. PREFERENCES FOR EUROPEAN ENVIRONMENTAL POLICY

The preceding analysis suggests that a policy task should be undertaken at government level which allows social welfare to be maximized. This is achieved by choosing the policy level which best represents the citizens' preferences. Consequently, if preferences differ between countries, environmental policies should also differ between countries. Conversely, if preferences do not differ between Member States, a uniform environmental policy might be optimal.

In the context of the Community, the uniformity constraint implies that the central level of authority (the Community) is unable to provide for sufficient variation in environmental policies. Moreover, as argued in Chapter 2, Kolstad (1987), among others, argues that a central authority may have a cost and informational advantage because administrative and informational costs of implementing decentralized non-uniform regulations can be large. Consequently, if preferences for environmental protection differ between Member States in the Community, so should environmental policies. Conversely, the more homogeneous environmental preferences are, the more need there is for a harmonized Community environmental policy.

It is often assumed that preferences for environmental protection in the

EU are heterogeneous. It is a commonly held belief, for instance, that the Scandinavian countries value environmental protection more highly than the Mediterranean countries. This could be due to greater environmental awareness and/or because demand for environmental protection increases with level of income.

It is impossible to draw a map of the environmental preferences in the EU. However, opinion polls shed light on how environmental protection is valued by the citizens of the different Member States. Eurobarometer (EB) takes opinion polls every half-year, and some of the responses by the citizens of the EU may be of interest.[21] Inspired by the subsidiarity debate, EB has since 1990 asked whether certain policy areas should be decided jointly within the EU or by the national governments. Environmental protection is one of these policy areas, and Figure 4.1 shows the percentage of the population in Denmark, the Netherlands and all 12 Member States (EU-12) which believes that environmental protection should be decided centrally by the Community.[22] The figure indicates that in the most 'Euro-sceptical' Member State, Denmark, 45–63 per cent of the population is in favour of EU decision-making. This share varies between 79 and 84 per cent in the Netherlands, the most 'Euro-friendly' Member State. In the EU-12, on

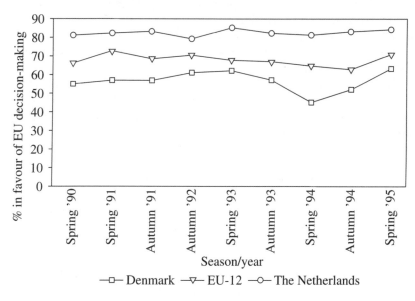

Source: Eurobarometer No. 33–42.

Figure 4.1   Share of population in favour of EU environmental decision-making

average 60–72 per cent of the citizens believe that environmental protection should be decided jointly by the Community. This share has been more constant than the share of the Danish population alone. Especially after the two Danish referenda in 1992 and 1993, the Danes were increasingly reluctant to shift competence from the national to the EU level. This may explain why less than half of the population in Denmark in 1994 was in favour of EU decision-making. The decrease in the share of population in favour of central decision-making in 1992–94 can also be found in the EU-12, but on a smaller scale. Thus, Figure 4.1 indicates that the citizens of the EU generally believe that the Community is the best decision-making level in relation to environmental policy. This has not changed significantly through time, although countries such as Denmark have experienced some fluctuations for domestic policy reasons.

The fact that the citizens of Europe think that the Community is the best decision-making level in the area of environmental protection does not necessarily say much about their environmental concerns. In 1986, 1988, 1992 and 1995, EB asked the following question: 'Many people are concerned about protecting the environment and fighting pollution. In your opinion, is this (1) an immediate and urgent problem, (2) more a problem for the future or (3) not really a problem?' In 1992 EB also asked whether the social dimension of the single market was to be considered a good or a bad thing. Comparing these two questions indicates whether or not the preferences for environmental protection differ more than preferences for the social dimension.

The share of Member State populations saying that environmental protection was an immediate and urgent problem is shown in Figure 4.2, with Member States ranked according to their welfare in 1992.[23] In 1995, an average of 82 per cent of the respondents considered environmental protection to be an immediate and urgent problem, 14 per cent saw it as a problem for future generations, and only 2 per cent saw it as no problem at all. In 1986 the figures were 72 per cent, 22 per cent and 3 per cent, respectively. The countries with the lowest share of the population viewing environmental protection as an urgent problem were Ireland and France (70 per cent), and the country with the highest share was Greece (97 per cent), which is the poorest country in the EU.

Figure 4.2 indicates that there are relatively small differences between the Member States. All 12 countries except Greece lie between 70 and 90 per cent. In 1986 on average 72 per cent of the populations stated that environmental protection was an immediate and urgent problem. Differences between countries in this year are similar to those in 1995. Thus Figure 4.2 shows that differences between countries have not changed through time. Figure 4.2 does not support the view that the richer countries in the North

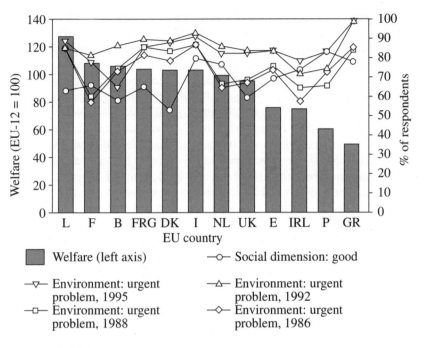

Source: CEC (1995).

Figure 4.2 Urgency of environmental protection

of Europe are more concerned about the urgency of environmental protection than the poorer countries in the South.

On average, 67 per cent of the respondents saw the social dimension of the single market as a good thing, and 8 per cent saw it as a bad thing. The highest share of the respondents seeing the social dimension as a good thing came from Portugal (81 per cent), and the lowest from Denmark (52 per cent). Comparing the two questions, the tentative conclusion is that differences in preferences for environmental protection do not appear to be greater than differences in preferences for the social dimension.

It should be noted that the fact that respondents consider environmental protection to be an urgent problem does not reflect a strong interest in environmental protection in general. That environmental protection is an urgent problem could also reflect that environmental policy has been given low priority, resulting in increased pollution and environmental degradation. Clearly, environmental protection is more urgent when environmental quality is low. Moreover, it is costless to state that environmental protection is urgent. It may well be that lower priority is given to the environment when environmental protection is traded off against economic development, especially in low-income countries. Information from the Eurobarometer surveys indicates that there are more variations between EU Member States when this tradeoff is examined.

In 1992 and 1995 Eurobarometer asked interviewees whether: (1) economic development should receive a higher priority than concerns for the environment; (2) economic development should receive a lower priority than concerns for the environment; or (3) environmental protection and economic development should be ensured at the same time. Figure 4.3 shows the share of the respondents in the Member States that gave priority to either the environment or economic development. Sixty-nine per cent of the respondents in the 12 Member States thought that environmental protection and economic development should go hand in hand. On average, five times as many citizens expressed a priority for the environment as for economic development (22 per cent and 4 per cent respectively). There was no Member State where the citizens expressed a priority for economic development rather than for the environment. Figure 4.3 indicates

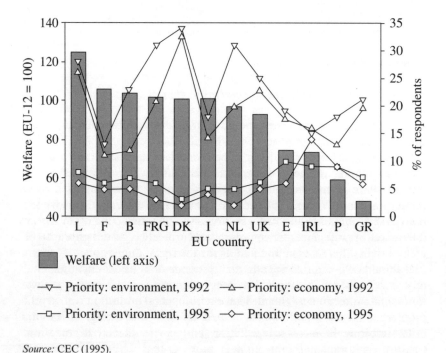

Welfare (left axis)

—▽— Priority: environment, 1992   —△— Priority: economy, 1992

—□— Priority: environment, 1995   —◇— Priority: economy, 1995

Source: CEC (1995).

Figure 4.3   Environmental protection and economic development

that there are significant differences in the share of respondents giving priority to the environment. Moreover, there appears to be no correlation with the level of welfare. There is less variation between Member States in the share giving priority to economic development. Moreover, the share of respondents giving priority to economic development appears to be inversely related to welfare. There are only minor changes between the 1992 and 1995 survey. For some Member States, however, there are some changes from 1992 to 1995. In Belgium, Germany, the Netherlands and Portugal there has been a significant drop in the share of respondents giving priority to the environment.

Another expression of citizens' environmental preferences is the different actions taken by individuals to improve environmental quality. If people have strong preferences for environmental protection they are more likely to be aware of different possibilities that they have as individuals to reduce environmental degradation.

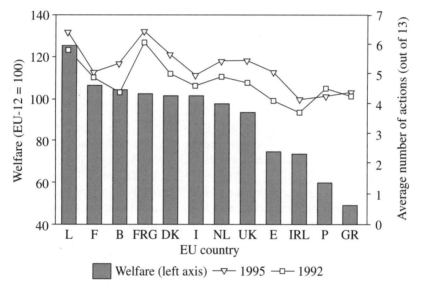

Source: CEC (1995).

Figure 4.4   Personal actions taken to protect the environment

In 1992 and 1995 Eurobarometer asked respondents which of 12 possible actions to reduce environmental degradation they have taken. Figure 4.4 shows the average number of actions taken in the 12 EU countries. Citizens in Luxembourg and Germany appear to have done the most, while citizens in Greece, Ireland, Portugal and Spain have done the least. The average number of actions taken in the Member States is clearly inversely related to the level of welfare and, hence, there are some differences between the wealthiest and the poorest Member States in the EU.

Figures 4.1 through 4.4 draw a rough picture of what Europeans think about the environment. This is done to get an indication of whether there are large differences in environmental preferences between Member States. If this is the case there is, *ceteris paribus*, more need for decentralized environmental policies by which Member States can tailor policies to national environmental preferences. It appears that there are small national differences in the expressed concern for environmental protection, but larger differences in the actions actually taken by individuals in the Member States. These differences between Member States have been fairly constant through time. It appears that high- and low-income Member States express an equal concern about environmental protection. But when it comes to a tradeoff between the environment and economic development, or actual actions taken by individuals, there is some evidence indicating that high-income Member States have stronger preferences for environmental protection.

6.   CONCLUSION

Interjurisdictional competition and fiscal federalism are based on quite restrictive assumptions. Therefore one can question the relevance of these theories for the real-world problems of choosing between centralized or decentralized elements of Community environmental policy. Even though interjurisdictional competition and fiscal federalism do not fit neatly into the complex and political decision-making procedures of the Community, it is still important to examine questions of centralization and decentralization from an economic perspective.

If the costs and benefits of a pollutant are localized and specific, due for instance to differences in assimilative capacity, an economic approach requires a balancing of control costs against damages. A decentralized authority has an advantage over a centralized authority in that it can better tailor environmental policies to the particular circumstances of individual regions. Therefore varying endowments, preferences and cultural traditions call for a considerable degree of decentralization of environmental policy in the Community. However, a decentralized approach may be inappropriate in the presence of transboundary externalities, scale economies or relatively homogeneous endowments and preferences.

Subsidiarity is an ambiguous concept and does not offer a clear rule for how powers should be exercised in the Community. However, subsidiarity demands that the Commission examine the efficiency of Community action compared to action by the Member States. In this process, arguments in favour of Community action and action by the Member States have been identified. Four groups of arguments for Community action were identified: (1) transboundary externalities; (2) prevention of unequal competition; (3) free movement of goods; and (4) general concern about the environment and human health. Thus it is clear that the economic approach and subsidiarity have many similarities in their arguments in relation to the Community. It is nevertheless also clear that there are differences.

The economic approach examines whether the powers should be placed at Community level or the level of the Member States. Subsidiarity, on the other hand, involves a mixture of powers at different levels. A regulatory system with harmonized target standards and differentiated emission standards may combine the advantages of central rules with the advantages of decision-making by Member States. In such a system, the Community can set the necessary rules in order to guarantee the citizens of Europe a certain minimum of environmental and health protection, and the differentiated emission standards may guarantee optimal specificity and at the same time avoid incomplete internalization of externalities.

Following the Edinburgh Meeting, the Commission was instructed to revise the environmental policy legislation and to develop a procedure to prove the relevance of proposals with regard to subsidiarity. The revision of Community water policy legislation in light of subsidiarity has been done in a way that corresponds quite closely to the system of Community target standards and Member States' emission standards. This is most clearly expressed in the proposed drinking water directive and bathing water directive, which state that the Community should only set objectives that are of universal relevance, that is, objectives for which the preferences do not vary between different areas, since they are essential to human health and based on scientific knowledge. This means that the Community should set minimum standards for water quality and leave it to the Member States to choose the means to reach the objectives.

The Commission has developed a list of seven questions which must be answered to justify the proposal. The Commission's answers in the Community water policy show that they contain a low threshold with regard to the assessment of the need for Community action. It has been quite easy to justify that the action involves a transboundary element, and the documentation proving that the transboundary elements are significant has been weak. Moreover, many of the benefits of Community action have been difficult to quantify, and the costs of inaction have proven to be equally difficult to estimate. Thus the degree to which a proposal is seen to comply with subsidiarity seems to depend to a larger extent on the degree to which Member States are allowed to choose the means, and to a lesser extent on the subsidiarity guideline. In the proposal for a framework directive for Community action in the field of water policy (Com (97) 49 final) and the proposal for a directive concerning the depositing of waste (Com (97) 105 final), for instance, subsidiarity is dealt with explicitly, but the seven questions in the subsidiarity guideline are not answered. Instead, it is stated that the proposals are consistent with subsidiarity because they introduce harmonized standards but leave the Member States free to choose how to fulfil the requirements.

Opinion polls conducted by Eurobarometer provide some information on whether environmental preferences in the EU are heterogeneous or homogeneous. In some dimensions there appear to be only moderate differences between Member States. In all Member States a large majority of the population are of the opinion that environmental policy should be decided jointly by the EU. Moreover, citizens of the different Member States express an equal concern for the urgency of environmental protection. This indicates that environmental preferences are more homogeneous than heterogeneous, suggesting that there is a need for central decision-making. However, when concerns for the environment are traded off against economic development, or when it comes to actions actually taken at the level of individuals, there appear to be larger differences between Member States. In these cases low-income Member States appear to have weaker environmental preferences. This indicates that environmental preferences are more heterogeneous than homogeneous, suggesting a need for decentralized environmental decision-making.

NOTES

1. Oates (1972) gives three arguments in favour of a decentralized government. First, it provides a means by which the levels of consumption can be tailored to the preferences of the society. Second, decentralization may increase both static and dynamic efficiency in the production of public goods. Third, a decentralized government may provide an institutional setting that promotes better public decision-making by compelling a more explicit recognition of the costs of public programmes (p. 13).
2. The decentralization theorem reads: 'For a public good, the consumption of which is defined over geographical subsets of the population, and for which the costs of providing each level of output of the good in each jurisdiction are the same for the central or the respective local government, it will always be more efficient (or at least as efficient) for local governments to provide the Pareto-efficient levels of output for their respective jurisdictions than for the central government to provide *any* specified and uniform level of output across all jurisdictions' (Oates, 1972, p. 35).
3. See Chapter 3.
4. Directive 67/548 concerning the packaging and labelling of dangerous substances, and Directives 70/157 and 70/220 on noise levels and pollutant emissions of motor vehicles.

5. Article 2 emphasizes that the aim of the EU is 'to promote . . . [a] sustainable and non-inflationary growth respecting the environment'. In Article 3 the duties of the EU are mentioned, among them the introduction of 'a policy in the sphere of the environment'.
6. These spillovers are also discussed by Wils (1994).
7. Com (93) 545 final, p. 3.
8. The directive on the quality required of surface water (Directive 75/449/EEC), the drinking water directive (Directive 80/778/EEC), the directives regulating the quality of shellfish waters (Directive 78/659/EEC), the quality of water for freshwater fish (Directive 79/923/EEC), and the bathing water directive (Directive 76/160/EEC).
9. The directive on pollution caused by certain dangerous substances discharged into the aquatic environment (Directive 76/464/EEC) and the directive on the protection of groundwater (Directive 80/68/EEC),
10. Directive 91/271/EEC on water treatment; Directive 91/676/EEC on nitrates.
11. Quoted in Haigh (1994).
12. Com (93) 545 final.
13. Com (93) 545 final, p. 16.
14. Com (94) 36 final.
15. Com (93) 680 final.
16. Com (94) 612 final.
17. Council Directive 98/83/EC on the quality of water intended for human consumption.
18. Com (97) 49 final.
19. Com (94) 109 final.
20. Com (96) 59 final, p. 26.
21. This section draws on Mors (1993).
22. Denmark and the Netherlands are chosen because they are the Member States where the smallest and largest part of the population are in favour of central decision-making. Finland, Austria and Sweden are not included since they joined the EU in 1995.
23. Welfare is GDP per capita measured in purchasing power standard (PPS). In this section 'Germany' refers to Federal Republic of Germany (FRG) in order to be able to compare with data before German unification.

5. Coordination of local pollution control in a federal system

1. INTRODUCTION

Analysis of the appropriate division of functions among levels of government goes back to Musgrave's (1959) treatment of the public sector. The various layers of the public sector deal with matters of (supra)national, regional and local concern. Each layer of government has fiscal and regulatory responsibilities for its own geographical jurisdiction. This federal structure of the public sector opens up a large array of important issues, including the proper allocation of fiscal functions among the different levels of government, assignment of specific instruments to the various levels, and the vertical assignment of regulatory responsibilities (Oates, 1994).

An economic approach to the assignment of environmental regulatory responsibilities involves a balancing of control costs against damages. As illustrated earlier, if costs and benefits are localized and specific, environmental policies should be tailored to the particular circumstances of localities. A local environmental problem should be regulated by a local authority. If pollution is transboundary, more centralized measures are required.

This result assumes, however, complete information. This chapter examines local pollution control in a federal system where the central and the local authorities are incompletely informed. In our analysis, both the central and the local authorities possess information which should be used in the determination of environmental policies. Consequently, a wholly decentralized approach is inappropriate, and we examine how the central authority can induce the local authority to take central information into account.

The USA and the European Union have different experiences with the development of the institutional arrangements for pollution control. The USA has exhibited an oscillation of environmental regulatory responsibilities between the states and the federal government (Vig and Kraft, 1990). In the 1960s the federal government's role was limited to management of public lands. Air and water pollution were considered local issues. This changed dramatically at the beginning of the 1970s, when rising public concern about the environment triggered the development of federal institutions such as the Environmental Protection Agency (EPA) and the Council on Environmental Quality and of federal environmental policy programmes, such as the Clean Air and Water Acts. In the 1980s the Reagan administration had a very different environmental policy agenda. 'Environmental deregulation' was part of a large policy change intended to reduce the scope of federal regulation and shift responsibilities to the states. Between 1981 and 1983 the EPA's budgets were cut by more than 50 per cent, the number of employees fell significantly, and the states were delegated enforcement responsibilities for a large amount of the emission standards (List and Gerking, 1996).

The institutional arrangements for pollution control in the EU have evolved quite differently than in the USA. Until the signing of the Single European Act (SEA) in 1987, environmental policy had no formal treaty basis. Environmental directives were nevertheless passed, either based on trade interests or restricted to general framework provisions. The driving force behind the SEA was to complete the single market in 1992. However, the SEA also brought the formal introduction of a legal basis for environmental policy. The legal basis has been strengthened and enlarged with the amendments of the 1993 Maastricht Treaty and the Amsterdam Treaty in 1997. The amendments have changed the decision-making procedure from unanimity to qualified majority, and the powers of the European Parliament have been increased, so that it is no longer just a consulting institution exercising veto powers in some situations. The EU has thus built up substantial powers previously located exclusively in the domain of the Member States. However, Liefferink (1996) shows that the increased EU competences did not necessarily pre-empt or replace national environmental policy. For countries such as the Netherlands and Germany, the EU established an additional level of governance. Only in the Mediterranean countries were environmental policy responsibilities limited by the increased EU responsibilities. Furthermore, it should be noted that the distribution of environmental policy responsibilities has been debated since the introduction of environmental policy in the SEA. The principle of subsidiarity was included in Article 130r of the SEA, that is, before it was adopted as a general principle in the Maastricht Treaty.

Even though the two systems are quite different, a common feature is that central and local authorities have 'shared responsibilities'. This means that the central authority sets environmental policy goals and leaves it to the local authorities to implement the environmental policies necessary to obtaining those goals. Examples of shared responsibility are the Clean

Water Act in the USA and the extensive use of directives in environmental policy in the EU. The Clean Water Act requires local authorities (the states) to develop and implement plans for reducing non-point source pollution to achieve the federally specific goals (see, for example, Freeman, 1990; Portney, 1990). A directive is an instrument that allows the objective in terms of minimum quality (for example, of drinking water) to be set at the Community level while leaving it to the Member States to decide the means by which to reach the objectives (see, for example, Com (93) 680 final, and Com (94) 612 final).

This chapter develops a simple model that captures the interaction between a central authority and a local authority in the regulation of local pollution problems. In our model, the local authority has the competence to determine the local environmental quality based on its private information. However, this information should ideally be transmitted to the local authority. In this way, the central authority is in a position to implement a grant-in-aid system which induces the local authority to take into account central information. Thus the central and local authorities have shared responsibilities in the sense that they both possess relevant information and both have an interest in the formulation of environmental policies. The local authority may be better informed about, say, the local demand for changes in environmental policy, whereas the central authority may be better informed about scientific aspects related to changes in environmental quality. We will argue here that the central authority can construct a grant-in-aid system that induces the local authority to choose its decision variables in such a way that the welfare function of the central authority is also maximized. The flexible grant-in-aid system induces the local authority to use a weighted combination of local and central information. At one extreme, the central authority is highly uncertain of the environmental and health effects of a specific pollutant. In this case, the grant-in-aid system is designed to allow local information to play an essential role in the environmental policy. This leaves a great deal of room for the local authority to regulate the environment. At the other extreme, the central authority is quite certain that a specific pollutant must not exceed a certain limit. Here the grant-in-aid system is designed to allow local information little influence on environmental policy, leaving little room for the local authority to regulate the environment.

This chapter is structured as follows. Section 2 provides an overview of theoretical approaches to the analysis of the distribution of environmental policy responsibilities in a federal system. Our model is presented in section 3, and in section 4 we determine the optimal mix of central and local information. The concluding remarks are presented in section 5.

2. THEORETICAL APPROACHES TO ENVIRONMENTAL POLICY IN A FEDERAL SYSTEM

At first sight, basic economic reasoning seems to offer a straightforward solution to the problem of distributing environmental regulative responsibilities between a central and a local authority: standards should vary among states according to the local circumstances. A standard should be set where marginal abatement costs equal marginal benefits. If the costs and benefits are regional or local they are likely to vary between states, a condition which clearly calls for a decentralized approach to environmental regulation. In the case of transboundary pollutants, however, a decentralized approach is inappropriate. In this case, each state will consider only the impact of pollution on the residents of the state where it is emitted. Thus the decentralized provision of public goods generating spillovers into neighbouring states is inefficient and justifies central government intervention (Oates, 1972; Baumol and Oates, 1988; Cropper and Oates, 1992). However, this basic economic reasoning ignores migration responses to unilateral actions to control pollution, and that the central and the local authority possess asymmetric information. If factor mobility and asymmetric information are included in the analysis, the derived results will differ from the basic economic reasoning.

2.1. Factor Mobility

If labour is mobile, a decentralized provision of public goods may be socially efficient. Myers (1990) shows that decentralized governments provide efficient levels of local public goods if consumers are perfectly mobile and governments can make interregional income transfers. There is no role for a central authority because it is in the local authorities' self-interest to make the transfers in order to obtain a preferred local population.[1]

Wellisch (1994) demonstrates that Myers's result also holds when local governments provide goods that generate spillovers. In Wellisch (1994), two regions generate transboundary pollution. Labour is perfectly mobile. As with Myers (1990), perfectly mobile labour (for example, a fully integrated labour market) serves as a disciplinary mechanism inducing implicit cooperation between local authorities and thus improves the quality of the environment. The fact that labour reacts to differences in environmental policy forces local authorities to take into account the welfare of non-residents due to the presence of transboundary pollution. Thus local decision-making internalizes the externalities from transboundary pollution, and the decentralized outcome is socially efficient.

Silva (1997) uses a model quite similar to that of Wellisch (1994), except that it is only one of the regions that generates a transboundary pollutant (upstream–downstream pollution). Silva also derives the result that the decentralized outcome is efficient in the case of transboundary pollution. In contrast to Wellisch (1994), this is obtained even if it is not possible for the local authorities to make interregional income transfers. This is due to the fact that the upstream region's abatement enables the downstream region to lower its abatement. In this way the abatement expenditure of the upstream region takes the role of explicit income transfers.

If capital is mobile, regions might engage in a destructive interjurisdictional competition in order to attract new business investment. Such competition may take the form of lowering environmental taxes, with low environmental quality as a likely result. Thus, in addition to transboundary pollution, tax competition may provide another argument for central government intervention. Oates and Schwab (1988, 1989) have constructed a set of models based on perfect competition. Here local officials trade off tax revenues and environmental quality for local jobs and income. In their basic model, local choices under simple majority rule will be socially optimal. It is in the interest of the local authority to select a zero tax on capital and to set a standard such that the cost of improved environmental quality at the margin equals the locals' willingness to pay. This result is also obtained if the interests of future generations are taken into account. Local officials choose an efficient environmental policy because both present and future environmental policy is capitalized into property values.

However, models based on imperfect competition and increasing returns to scale derive a different result. Markusen et al. (1995), Hoel (1994b), Rauscher (1994, 1995b), and Motta and Thisse (1994) all show that a decentralized outcome in general will not be socially efficient. However, it is not clear whether the rate of the environmental tax will be higher or lower than the socially optimal tax rate. The environmental tax may be higher than the socially optimal tax because we have the 'Not-In-My-Back-Yard' (NIMBY) case, where it is rational for a local authority to raise the environmental tax in order to drive the polluting industries out of its jurisdiction. The environmental tax may also be lower than the socially optimal tax because it could be rational for a local authority to lower the environmental tax in order to attract new business investment.

Hence the general presumption that local (transboundary) pollution problems should be solved locally (centrally) does not seem to be very robust. If capital is mobile, a local authority does not necessarily solve local environmental problems efficiently. If labour is mobile, transboundary pollution problems may be solved efficiently by local authorities.

2.2.   Asymmetric Information

The approaches with labour and capital mobility do not say much about information. Presumably, perfect and symmetric information is assumed. List (1997), Klibanoff and Poitevin (1996), Klibanoff and Morduch (1995), Rob (1989), and Farrell (1987) all deal with aspects of externalities and asymmetric information. Labour and capital are assumed to be immobile. Klibanoff and Morduch (1995) studied the efficiency of decentralization in the case of externalities. Centralization is not considered. They adopt a mechanism design approach and emphasize the crucial role of individual-rationality and incentive-compatibility constraints. Local information is superior to central information, and the autonomy of individual localities is respected. Klibanoff and Morduch show that coordination through Coasian bargaining can raise social welfare only when external effects are relatively large. When external effects are relatively small, coordination cannot yield improvements at all. Autonomy and private information can make it very difficult to internalize externalities and may result in substantial losses in social efficiency. Thus the argument that small externalities lead to small inefficiencies while large externalities give rise to large inefficiencies is not necessarily true. Individual-rationality constraints mean that agents cannot have a central project imposed upon them.

In order to study both centralization and decentralization, Klibanoff and Poitevin (1996) ignore individual-rationality constraints. They consider the decision over a project which affects the welfare of two agents. In the centralized setting, the agents have no rights over the project (agents have no participation constraints). In the decentralized setting, the central authority has no means of imposing a project size (agents have participation constraints). The result is that it is not necessarily true that large externalities justify centralization. A decentralized approach may be justified if the distribution of benefits is differently distributed between regions and the variance of the externality is large enough. Further, they demonstrate that a local authority does not necessarily take local heterogeneity into account better than a central authority. More heterogeneity in the size of the private benefits favours centralization if the expected externality is sufficiently large.

List (1997) uses a differential game approach to analyse the aspects of environmental policy in a federal system with asymmetric information. Dynamic games with symmetric information usually derive the result that central pollution control Pareto-dominates local pollution control (Dockner and van Long, 1993; Kaitala et al., 1991). List introduces asymmetries between players as well as informational advantages for localities and derives the opposite result. Now local pollution control may Pareto-dominate central control if damages from pollution are highly different across regions. More specifically, List assumes that agents across regions have different preferences for the environment and that damages are also different across regions. Local authorities can observe their constituents' tastes for environmental quality and tailor policies closely to match these preferences. The central authority, however, has imperfect information on local preferences. This means that it has to impose uniform standards across regions. List demonstrates that there exists a threshold value for one of the states' pollution costs for which the state will strictly prefer decentralization even if it receives all welfare accrued under central control. This is because a central authority, imposing uniform regulations, will restrict production of the polluting good so much that the state becomes worse off. In the limit, both regions could be better off under local control if substantial asymmetries exist.

2.3. Shared Responsibilities

It is characteristic of the literature mentioned above that environmental policy in a federation is analysed as either a fully centralized regime or a fully decentralized regime. In practice, however, environmental policies are often set at both the central and the local level. Silva and Caplan (1997) assume that neither the central nor the local authority possesses full control over the environmental policy instruments. The central authority is assumed to control pollution taxes, whereas the local authority controls the instruments to produce pollution abatement.

Two types of federal systems are examined. In the first, the central authority is assumed to be a Stackelberg leader, and the two local authorities are followers. This system features centralized leadership in environmental policy-making. The second system features decentralized leadership. Here the local authorities are the Stackelberg leaders and the central authority is the follower. In both systems the central authority can make income transfers which may influence the local authorities' pollution abatement. Moreover, it is assumed that there are regional taste differences over pollution control. Information is complete and labour is immobile. The result is that decentralization of responsibilities over pollution abatement will always generate larger than socially desirable levels of pollution in a system with centralized leadership. However, in a system of decentralized leadership, decentralized control over pollution abatement will always produce a socially efficient environmental policy. This last result, however, depends crucially on the assumption about interregional transfers, tastes and information.

Segerson et al. (1997) do not explicitly analyse the question of the appropriate division of environmental responsibilities between different levels of authorities. However, they examine the question as to which level should pay for the cost of implementing environmental policy. When a central authority imposes mandates on local authorities that require them to meet minimum standards or environmental quality goals, the mandates can either be fully funded from the central authority or not funded at all. Segerson et al. do not consider asymmetric information as such, but the central authority suffers from 'fiscal illusion', that is, it does not consider the costs incurred by the local authorities when the central authority decides upon its mandates.

Depending on the funding decision, a double moral hazard problem may exist. On the one hand, if the central authority does not fund the mandates, this creates a moral hazard problem for the central authority because it does not recognize the full cost of environmental regulation. The result is over-regulation. On the other hand, if the mandates are fully funded, this creates a moral hazard problem for the local authorities because they will not face the proper incentives for innovation and cost-minimization. In addition, in the absence of federal mandates the local authorities may implement an environmental policy which is 'too lax' due to factors such as interjurisdictional externalities. Both systems (fully funded and unfunded mandates) will thus be inefficient. Instead, the double moral hazard problem should be solved by a funding rule under which the central authority would be required to fund mandates that exceed the efficient mandate but would not be required to fund those that are less than the efficient mandate.

Both models emphasize that responsibilities may be allocated at different levels at the same time; that is, the models are characterized by neither full decentralization nor full centralization. As pointed out by Silva and Caplan (1997), it is important to model systems using a mixture of centralized and decentralized pollution control. Moreover, the models focus on transboundary externalities and assume that the local authority has no incentive to take these externalities into account unless they are given relevant incentives. In Silva and Caplan (1997) relevant incentives are created by making the central authority a Stackelberg follower. In Segerson et al. (1997) the central authority moves first by creating an efficient funding rule. This rule implies that the central authority should be required to provide full funding if it imposes a mandate exceeding the social optimum and no funding if it imposes a mandate short of the social optimum.

The model presented in section 3 is in accordance with the above-mentioned models in having shared responsibilities, but the focus is on local pollution. The model assumes that central and local authorities possess different kind of private information, which ideally should be used in formulating environmental policies. The local authority may have private information by being close to the local community, whereas the central authority may have private information obtained from technical experts placed at the central authority due to economies of scale. Like Segerson et al. (1997), we derive an efficient funding rule but for quite different reasons. In Segerson et al. (1997) the rule depends upon whether the centrally imposed mandate is above or below the socially efficient mandate. In our model, the rule depends upon the mix of central and local information.

3.   THE MODEL

We consider a model with a central authority and a local authority. The central authority maximizes the central welfare function, and the local authority maximizes the local welfare function. The two welfare functions differ from each other. Information about the welfare function is private; that is, the central authority knows its own welfare function, but not the local welfare function. The local authority knows the local, but not the central, welfare function. The two authorities have the same basic goal. The objective of the authorities is to determine the level of environmental quality, which is a function of a pure local externality.

Although the local authority has all the competences to determine the level of environmental quality, the central authority still plays a part because we assume that both central and local authorities possess information relevant to determining environmental quality. The local authority is better informed than the central authority about local demand for changes in environmental policy. Therefore it is superior to the central authority in tailoring environmental policy to local conditions and preferences. The central authority is better informed about many scientific aspects related to changes in environmental quality. Local authorities may be better informed about, say, the willingness to pay for increases in drinking water quality, whereas the central authority knows more about potential health risks of different levels of pesticides in drinking water. Hence in this model the central authority possesses important information which should be 'pooled' at the local authority level.

The solution, of course, is simply to transmit information from the central to the local authority. This process, however, is not without difficulties. Transmission of information does not necessarily mean that it is used. The local authority may not have incentives to make use of central information. Casual empiricism suggests that local authorities are not always particularly enthusiastic about following central authority advice.

It is therefore important for the central authority to construct incentive systems (for example, grant-in-aid systems) that induce the local authority to choose its decision variables in such a way that the welfare function of the central authority is maximized. This presumes that the behaviour of the local authority is known to the central authority, and that the authority has a well-defined welfare function. These assumptions are in general not ful-filled, and we show how the incentive system can be constructed to promote allocative efficiency, and how it can be used for transmission of informa-tion from the central to the local authority.

The local authority determines its level of environmental quality so that the consumers' surplus plus revenue less local costs is maximized. Con-sumers' surplus is based on a local authority estimate of the demand curve. Local authorities take into account potential grant in aid from the central authority.

Assume that

X is the level of environmental quality, X_L, and X_C is the local and central environmental quality

$D_C(X)$ is the central authority estimate of the inverse demand curve

$D_L(X)$ is the local estimate of the demand curve

$C(X)$ is the total cost curve, and $MC(X)$ the marginal cost curve

$G(X)$ is the total grant-in-aid curve, and $MG(X)$ the marginal grant-in-aid curve.

The local maximization problem is

$$\max_{X_L} W_L = \int_0^{X_L} (D_L + MG - MC)(X)\, dX, \quad X \geq 0. \tag{5.1}$$

If $(D_L + MG - MC)(0) > 0$ and $D_L + MG - MC$ is monotonously decreas-ing with respect to X, the optimal level of environmental quality is deter-mined by the first-order condition

$$\frac{\partial W_L}{\partial X_L} = (D_L + MG - MC)(X) = 0. \tag{5.2'}$$

By inversion, we obtain the optimal value of X_L:

$$X_L^* = (D_L + MG - MC)^{-1}(0). \tag{5.2''}$$

where X_L^* is the optimal level of environmental quality chosen by the local authority, ignoring the central demand curve. The central authority has an estimate of the demand curve, and finds that it should also be included when the local authority decides the level of environmental quality.

However, the central authority is uncertain about the local demand curve. This is illustrated in Figure 5.1, where the central authority does not know whether the local demand curve is below the central demand curve (D_L^1), or above (D_L^2). Thus, from the point of view of the central authority,

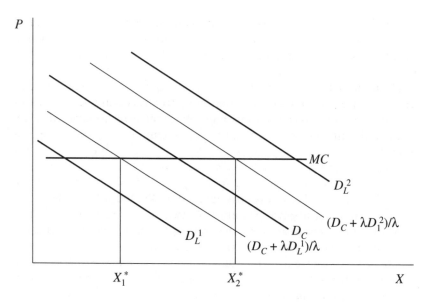

Figure 5.1   Optimal level of externality with uncertain local demand curve

the local demand curve is uncertain, such that an estimate has to be drawn from some well-behaved probability distribution as regards some parameters describing the demand curve.[2] The relative uncertainty of the estimates is a function of the good considered. Therefore, we further assume that

λ is a non-negative weighting factor expressing how much weight the central authority attaches to local information

$\varphi(\alpha)$, $\alpha\epsilon A'$ is a frequency function for the local estimate with respect to some set of parameters, A'.

In some cases, the central authority believes that it has vital information which must be taken into account when the local authority decides the environmental quality. In other cases the central authority believes that knowledge of local conditions is of decisive importance. Therefore, the central authority wants to induce the local authority to use a weighted estimate of the demand curve. The central authority decides a weight, λ, which reflects the weight the central authority attaches to local information. λ is decisive for the grant in aid that the local authority receives from the central authority. In Figure 5.1 the central authority must set λ so the weighted demand curve is between D_C and D_L^2 (or D_L^1). If $\lambda = 0$, local information is not taken into account. However, the greater the value of λ, the closer the weighted demand curve is to the local estimate D_L^2. If $\lambda \rightarrow \infty$, central information is not taken into account. Hence, the greater the value of λ, the greater the importance of local information relative to central information.

In this way, local environmental quality is decided in a two-step procedure. In Step 1, the central authority decides how much weight should be attached to central and local information and thereby the grant-in-aid schedule. In Step 2, the local authority decides the level of environmental quality, given the grant-in-aid schedule. The maximization problem for the central authority is

$$\max_{X_{C(\alpha)}} W_C = \int \varphi(\alpha) \int_{0}^{X_{C(\alpha)}} \left[\left(\frac{D_C + \lambda D_L^\alpha}{1 + \lambda} \right) - MC \right] (X) \quad dX d\alpha. \qquad (5.3)$$

The subscript $C(\alpha)$ indicates that in contrast to (5.1), the central environmental quality is a function of α. In case of linear demand curves the first integration could be over the intercepts of the ordinate axes and over the slopes of the demand curves. The second integral gives the consumers' surplus plus revenue, less total costs for every possible local estimate D_L^α.

The maximization of (5.3) implies that an optimal environmental quality should be found for each level of the local authority estimate parameterized by α. That is, for every value of α, we determine the environmental quality chosen by the central authority, by maximizing the second integral in (5.3). The first-order condition becomes

$$\frac{\partial W_C}{\partial X_{C(\alpha)}} = \int_{A'} \varphi(\alpha) \left(\frac{D_C + \lambda D_L^\alpha}{1 + \lambda} - MC \right) (X) \quad d\alpha = 0. \qquad (5.4')$$

By inversion, we obtain the optimal level of environmental quality chosen by the central authority

$$X_{C(\alpha)}^* = \left(\frac{D_C + \lambda D_L^\alpha}{1 + \lambda} - MC \right)^{-1} (0). \qquad (5.4'')$$

$X_{C(\alpha)}^*$ is the optimal level of environmental quality chosen by the local authority, taking into account the central information.

The central authority has no direct control over the local level of environmental quality, but several grant-in-aid systems can be chosen by the central authority so that the local choice of environmental quality is equal to $X_{C(\alpha)}^*$ for all functions of D_L^α. According to (5.2), the local authorities ensure that $(D_L + MG - MC)(X) = 0$. The task for the central authority is to make incentive systems that would guarantee that $X_{C(\alpha)}^*$ and X_L^* coincide for each value of α. The family of these systems is given by the function MG, which satisfies (5.5) for all functions of D_L^α.

$$k(D_L^\alpha + MG - MC)(X) = \left(\frac{D_C + \lambda D_L^\alpha}{1 + \lambda} - MC\right)(X), \tag{5.5}$$

where k is a positive constant. Thus

$$MG(X) = \left[\frac{1}{k}\left(\frac{D_C + \lambda D_L^\alpha}{1 + \lambda} + (k-1)MC\right) - D_L^\alpha\right](X). \tag{5.6}$$

The most interesting interpretations of (5.6) is if $k=1$ or $k=\lambda/(1+\lambda)$, where we get (5.7′) and (5.7″), respectively.

$$MG(X) = \left(\frac{D_C - D_L^\alpha}{1 + \lambda}\right)(X) \tag{5.7′}$$

$$MG(X) = \left(\frac{D_C - MC}{\lambda}\right)(X) \tag{5.7″}$$

Equation (5.7′) gives an incentive for the local authority to select what from the point of view of the central authority is the correct level of environmental quality. However, there are two problems with this. First, as mentioned, D_L^α is unknown to the central authority. Second, the central authority cannot expect the local authority to reveal the correct information about the demand curve estimate. Therefore (5.7′) must be replaced with (5.7″), which is independent of D_L^α.

We interpret (5.7″) graphically in Figures 5.2a and 5.2b. In Figure 5.2a we have depicted the central authority demand curve (D_C) and the marginal cost curve (MC). From these curves we have constructed two marginal grant-in-aid schedules (MG^1 and MG^2) for the weights $\lambda=1$ and $\lambda=2$ respectively. In Figure 5.2b the net marginal cost curves are depicted (MC less MG). Further, two different estimates of local demand curves (D_L^1 and D_L^2) are shown. From these curves, the level of environmental quality is determined. X_0 is the level of environmental quality based exclusively on central information (based on the weight $\lambda=0$). X_2 and X_3 are based on the weight $\lambda=1$, and X_1 and X_4 are based on the weight $\lambda=2$. Note that the lower the weight λ, the closer the levels of environmental quality are to X_0. Hence, the smaller λ, the higher grant in aid. Moreover, the marginal net gain of environmental quality according to the central authority estimate changes from positive to negative at the level X_0. Therefore, the marginal grant in aid changes in the same way at that level. Below X_0 the grant in aid is positive, but above X_0 it is negative. In this way the central authority may overcome the difficulties of transmitting information from the central to the local authority because by choosing (5.7″) the central authority gives

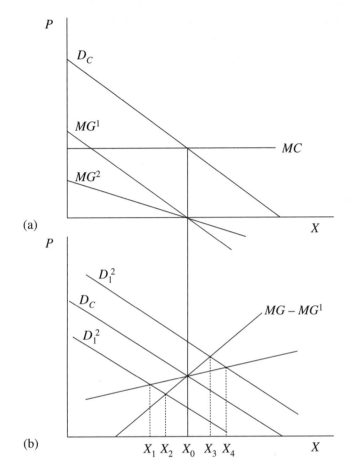

Figure 5.2   Optimal externality for different incentive systems

the local authority an incentive to take the central information into account when it decides on the level of environmental quality.

4.   THE OPTIMAL MIX OF CENTRAL AND LOCAL INFORMATION

The weight λ is of central importance to the construction of the grant-in-aid curve. Therefore it is important to discuss the considerations behind choosing a given value of λ. One argument could be that λ is simply a measure of the desired degree of autonomy of the local authority. Another argument could be that λ should reflect the relative degree of uncertainty of the central and local estimates. We choose the second approach.

The central authority can choose λ with certainty because it knows its own demand, and thus how much weight to attach to local information. We now assume that the central authority is uncertain of its own demand. From the point of view of the central authority, both demand curves are now uncertain. We assume that: (1) demand curves are linear with the same slope; (2) the uncertainty is related to the intercept on the ordinate axis; (3) the central and the local estimates are stochastically independent and have the same mean equal to the true intercept; and (4) marginal costs are constant. We assume that

$D_C - bX$ is the central estimate of the demand curve
$D_L - bX$ is the local estimate of the demand curve
MC are the constant marginal costs
$T - bX$ is the true inverse demand curve.

We choose the maximand

$$V = \int h(X_L) \int_0^{X_L} (T - bX - MC) \, dX dX_L, \tag{5.8}$$

where $h(X_L)$ is the frequency function for X_L. However, using (5.2) X_L is determined by

$$X_L = \frac{D_L + G - MC}{b - g}, \tag{5.9}$$

where $MG = G + gX$. Using (5.7″) we get

$$X_L = \frac{\dfrac{D_C + \lambda D_L}{1 + \lambda} - MC}{b} \tag{5.10}$$

Thus, we may rewrite (5.8) as

$$\max \int h_1(D_L) \int h_2(D_C) \int_0^{\frac{D_C + \lambda D_L}{1 + \lambda} - MC}{b}} (T - bX - MC) \, dX dD_C dD_L \tag{5.11}$$

where $h_1(D_L)$ and $h_2(D_C)$ are the frequency functions for D_L and D_C respectively. We then get the optimal value of λ as

$$\lambda^* = \frac{\sigma^2(D_C)}{\sigma^2(D_L)}, \tag{5.12}$$

where $\sigma^2(D_L)$ and $\sigma^2(D_C)$ denote the variances on D_L and D_C. In general it is not possible to obtain an analytical determination of λ^*, but here we have obtained a simple and sensible expression for the optimal weight.

In the discussion of centralization vs decentralization emphasis has been placed on both the results of the decision process and the decision process itself. In the model presented here we can define a decision process as over-decentralized (under-decentralized) according to whether λ is higher (lower) than λ^*.

5. CONCLUSION

Environmental policy in a federal system focuses on whether we should set national standards applicable to all areas in a state, or whether we should allow local authorities to determine specific standards for their own jurisdictions. The answers to these questions depend on the perspective. Conventional wisdom argues for decentralization in absence of spillover effects and for some degree of centralization with the presence of spillover effects. This view could be changed with an introduction of capital and labour mobility and with informational asymmetries.

In this chapter, we have focused on informational asymmetries. The central authority and the local authority have the same objective, but have different information. The local authority chooses the level of environmental quality, but its choice is influenced by the incentive system given by the central authority. In principle, the central authority could use a 'forcing contract', but since it recognizes that its information is imperfect, it will use a flexible grant-in-aid system where a weighted combination of local and central estimates is used. The weight should reflect the relative quality of the two estimates. If the central authority is weighting its estimate higher (lower) than its quality indicates, we could call the system relatively over-centralized (under-centralized), even though the competence is located at the local level.

NOTES

1. This result is also obtained in the case of imperfect mobility. Mansoorian and Myers (1993) introduce imperfect labour mobility by assuming that people derive utility from living in their native country. Their result, however, is dependent on the absence of spill-overs.
2. From the point of view of the local authority the central demand curve is uncertain. However, the local authority does not consider the central demand curve.

6. Impacts of pollution control on international trade and capital movements

1. INTRODUCTION

It is often claimed that environmental regulations have negative consequences for economic activity. Managers fear that increased environmental regulations will increase firm-level environmental compliance costs, thereby reducing firms' competitiveness. The results, it is argued, are reduced exports, reduced foreign direct investments, firm relocation and increased unemployment. Naturally, governments have been sensitive to such arguments. Consequently, a number of environmental regulations are implemented so as to minimize the burden on firms. That environmental regulations have negative impacts on economic activity was a major argument launched by opponents in the discussions about the introduction of environmental and energy taxes in, for instance, Denmark, Sweden and the Netherlands. They have also played a role in the discussion about an EU CO_2 tax. Because of possible capital flight the Dutch energy tax, and the Danish and Swedish CO_2 tax, applies only to consumers and small producers (see, for example, Komen and Peerlings, 1999). An EU CO_2 tax is still under discussion, but it is doubtful whether it will be introduced at all. Moreover, some of the larger industries in Denmark and Sweden are exempted from the CO_2 tax because of possible capital flight.

Environmentalists argue that this is unfortunate. First, to exempt large firms from pollution taxes is not in accordance with the polluter pays principle. Second, environmental improvements are reduced. Third, the relationship between environmental regulation and economic activity is ambiguous. Porter (1991) argues, for instance, that environmental regulations and economic activity may be positively related. Environmental regulations may actually be a positive driving force, motivating producers to innovate and produce more efficiently.

Another unfortunate effect is that governments may engage in a destructive 'race to the bottom'. In this race, governments will compete to attract investments and jobs by lowering environmental regulations. The unfortunate result is inefficient by lax environmental regulations and 'pollution havens'.

If this destructive 'race to the bottom' does occur, it is a good argument for the centralization of the implementation of environmental regulations. Whether or not it does occur is examined in the following chapter. But fundamental for a 'race to the bottom' is the assumption that economic activity and environmental regulations are adversely related. The purpose of this chapter is to examine this assumption.

Environmental regulations potentially affect economic activity in a number of ways. New plant location may be reduced (for example, Friedman et al., 1992; Levinson, 1996; Gray, 1997; Becker and Henderson, 2000), foreign direct investment (FDI) may decrease (Keller and Levinson, 1999; List and Co, 2000), and jobs may be lost (Duffy-Deno, 1992; List and Kunce, 2000). Finally, international trade and capital movements may also be affected. This is the focus of this chapter. It will examine the assumption that environmental regulations are negatively associated with economic activity by surveying studies focusing on the relationship between environmental regulations and international trade and capital movements. In this way, this chapter adds to a number of other studies that have surveyed these issues. Jaffe et al. (1995) and Tannenwald (1997) are relatively broad surveys encompassing all dimensions of economic activity. Jeppesen and Folmer (2001) focus on location behaviour of firms, and Jeppesen et al. (2001) focus on new plant location decisions.

It should be noted that the likelihood of capital movement and firm relocation has undoubtedly been facilitated by trade liberalization and harmonization of regulations and product norms, both regionally (the enlargement of the EU and the creation of the North American Free Trade Agreement (NAFTA)) and at the world scale (World Trade Organization (WTO)). As a consequence of these developments, firms that relocate may still have access to the market they have left. In this context international mergers are also relevant because they may make it possible to shift production without physical relocation of production facilities. Moreover, as a consequence of the opening up of new markets in developing countries and Eastern Europe, regions have emerged with environmental policies that are substantially more lax than those prevailing in most Western countries.

The remainder of this chapter is organized as follows. Section 2 summarizes the Heckscher–Ohlin model, some models of international capital mobility, and some models that combine trade and international capital mobility. These models form the framework within which the effects of environmental policy on international trade and capital flight are analysed. Section 3 deals with theoretical analyses of the impact of environmental policy, while section 4 presents an overview of empirical studies. Conclusions follow in section 5.

2. THE GENERAL THEORETICAL FRAMEWORK

In the analysis of capital flight induced by environmental policy, extensive use is made of the Heckscher–Ohlin (HO) model of international trade and the theory of international capital movements. Both theoretical frameworks are summarized below. Moreover, a model that combines both approaches is discussed.

2.1. The Heckscher–Ohlin Model

In the HO model, international trade is explained by differences among countries in terms of resources, such as land, capital and mineral resources. In the standard HO model two commodities are produced in two countries using two factors of production (that is, capital and labour). It is assumed that factors of production are mobile between sectors but immobile between countries, there are no transport costs, and there is free trade and perfect competition.

A country is abundant in a resource if it has a large supply of the resource relative to the supply of other resources. The country will tend to produce more of the commodities that use the more abundant resource intensively. In the absence of trade, capital will earn less in the capital-abundant country than in the labour-abundant country, and labour will earn more. The capital-abundant country will have a lower relative price for the capital-intensive commodity than the labour-abundant country. Further, the difference in relative prices of commodities implies an even larger difference in relative prices of factors.

In the presence of trade the country will increase its production of the product in which it has a comparative advantage. The result is the HO theorem: countries tend to export commodities that are intensive in the factors with which they are abundantly supplied. Under the assumptions that: (i) production functions are identical in both countries and homogeneous of degree one; (ii) one commodity requires a greater proportion of one factor than the other commodity at any factor price at all points on any production function; and (iii) trade does not bring about complete specialization, the relative prices of commodities converge, which leads to convergence of the relative prices of capital and labour. In the HO model, factor prices will be completely equalized. The capital-abundant country increases its production of the capital-intensive commodity and trades this commodity for the labour-intensive commodity of which the labour-abundant country has increased production. That is, more capital is embodied in the capital-abundant country's export than in its import. In this way the capital-abundant country exports some of its capital to the labour-abundant country. This is not done by a physical movement of capital (capital is assumed to be internationally immobile), but by exporting the product which embodies the abundant factor. Hence factor price equalization is obtained through international movements of commodities. The classic references are Heckscher (1919), Ohlin (1933) and Samuelson (1948, 1949). Recent references are, for instance, Krugman and Obstfeld (1997) and Gandolfo (1987).

2.2. International Capital Mobility

We now turn to capital location in a model with international mobile capital and no trade. Jasay (1960), MacDougall (1960) and Kemp (1964) (referred to as the MacDougall–Kemp model) examine the costs and benefits of foreign investment. It is assumed that there are two countries, two factors, unimpeded capital imports, perfect competition, constant returns to scale, external economies, no taxation and full employment. In each country the capital stock is owned partly by the native population and partly by foreigners. In this model, capital will flow to whichever country offers the greatest marginal return. Therefore, this model has the same property as the HO model, and factor prices will be equalized.

Important features of the model are diminishing average return on capital and the fact that capital-rich countries tie up too great a proportion of their resources in the foreign country. One argument for the latter is that there is divergence between the social and the private optimum. A capital investment in a country lowers the marginal product of capital but raises the marginal product of labour. The private investor does not consider the influence their investment has on domestic productivity; they consider only their private average rate of return. From the country's point of view, the optimum is attained when the marginal product of capital at home is equated to the marginal earnings abroad. Therefore, foreign investments tend to be excessive and should be curbed. This leads to the MacDougall–Kemp theorem (Ruffin, 1984): it pays the capital-exporting country that is large enough to influence the world interest rate to restrict incipiently its capital exports if the rest of the world does not retaliate.

For the analysis of environmental capital flight the general equilibrium neoclassical model developed by McLure (1970) is very important. He uses this model to examine the sensitivity of capital location to various taxes levied in only one country. The model assumes that two countries use two factors, capital and labour, to produce one product under perfect competition. Taxes on production, labour and capital are considered, and mobility parameters describe the degree of interstate factor mobility. They express the tendency of factors to migrate in response to differences in their earnings. The locational response of capital to a tax on production depends upon the elasticity of demand for the product. The higher the elasticity in the country that levies the tax, the higher the propensity to migrate to the non-taxing country. In addition to the elasticity of demand, the ease of substituting the untaxed for the taxed factor has to be taken into account. Thus the model implies that capital migrates more in response to taxation of capital or production: (i) the more easily labour can be substituted for capital in the taxing state; (ii) the more easily capital is absorbed in production in the non-taxing state; and (iii) the better commodities from different states are substitutes in consumption.

2.3. Trade and International Capital Mobility

The HO model is an extreme case with unrestricted trade and factor immobility. The theory of international factor movements is the opposite extreme, assuming perfect factor mobility but no trade. The real world is found in between these extreme cases. Mundell (1957) develops a theory for international factor mobility and describes the effects of introducing factor mobility into the HO model. His starting-point is the HO model, that is, two countries, two commodities and two factors. One of the countries is well endowed with labour and poorly endowed with capital relative to the other country. One of the products is labour intensive relative to the other. Under the assumption that factors are immobile and trade impediments are absent, trade will arise and commodity and factor price equalization will occur.

When we leave the classical HO model, and assume that all impediments to the movement of capital are removed and that the marginal product of capital is the same in both countries, no capital movement will take place. When the labour-abundant country under these conditions introduces a tariff on the capital-intensive commodity, the price of the capital-intensive commodity will rise relative to the labour-intensive commodity (in the labour-abundant country). Factors will move out of the labour-intensive industry into the capital-intensive industry. At constant factor prices the production shift creates an excess supply of labour and an excess demand for capital because factors are moving away from the labour-intensive industry. According to the Stolper–Samuelson tariff argument (Stolper and Samuelson, 1941), the marginal product of labour must fall and the marginal product of capital must rise. This is due to the fact that the capital-intensive sector becomes less capital intensive due to the inflow of labour from the labour-intensive sector. But since capital is assumed to be mobile, its higher marginal product in the labour-abundant country induces a capital movement into the country from the capital-abundant country. This will change the factor endowments so as to make the labour-abundant country more capital intensive. With linear, homogeneous and identical production functions, as in this model, the mobility of capital results in equalization of prices as well as marginal products of both capital and labour. The tariff has eliminated trade, but after the capital movement there is no longer any need for trade; capital movements have had the same effect as trade would have had. In this model, capital mobility is a perfect substitute for trade.[1]

3.   IMPACTS OF ENVIRONMENTAL POLICY: THEORETICAL APPROACHES

For more than 25 years the impact of environmental policy on trade and capital movement has been in the limelight of literature on environmental economics. Some important references are: Baumol (1971), D'Arge and Kneese (1972), Walter (1974), Siebert (1974, 1977, 1979, 1985), Markusen (1975), Asako (1979), Siebert et al. (1980), McGuire (1982), Rubin and Graham (1982), Merrifield (1988), Krutilla (1991), Rauscher (1991, 1992, 1995a, 1995b, 1997), Dean (1992), Zaelke et al. (1993), Cameron et al. (1994), Chichilnisky (1994), Copeland (1994), Copeland and Taylor (1994, 1995), Steininger (1994), Wang (1995), Beghin and Potier (1997) and Ulph (1997). Any of these works has its own peculiarities and there is no easy way to summarize them.

We continue the structure laid down in the preceding section. We start with a model combining international capital movements and environmental policy. This type of approach is relatively simple because international capital movements can be dealt with in a framework with only one commodity. International trade models are more complicated and include at least two commodities. Most of the work has been done in the second category, connecting environmental policy and trade. From a policy perspective, the most interesting models are the third category, which is a combination of the two extremes. It is an unrealistic description of reality when either imperfect mobility of capital or absence of trade is assumed. There are, however, relatively few approaches that include both trade and international capital mobility.

As we shall show in the sequel, when the restrictive assumptions are relaxed in the HO model or in the models of international capital movements, the results become rather ambiguous. This may go some way to explain the limited number of studies dealing with trade and international capital movements simultaneously.

3.1. International Capital Movements

Rauscher (1997) develops a two-country static general equilibrium model with only one commodity produced and consumed. The model is based on the classic MacDougall–Kemp model. Capital stocks owned by the citizens of the home and foreign country are exogenously given and fixed. Capital in both countries is a composite of domestic and imported capital. Factors are assumed to be immobile across sectors but internationally mobile. Commodities are not internationally mobile so there will be no trade and transport activities. Pollution is caused by domestic and foreign emissions and stems from production as well as consumption. Income is composed of domestic output plus the return on capital invested abroad minus interest payments made to the owners of foreign capital. Welfare is a function of consumption and environmental quality is a function of emissions.

In this model there is a direct and an indirect productivity effect of emissions. The direct effect, which relates to emissions as a production factor, increases the productivity of capital. The indirect or external effect is that emissions may reduce the productivity of capital via production losses. The fact that the direct and the indirect effects have opposite signs generates ambiguities. This can be illustrated by also considering Rauscher (1992), of which Rauscher (1997) is an extension in the sense that Rauscher (1992) does not have consumption externalities or external effects on production.

In both models the central question is: what happens when a government relaxes its environmental policy? Two situations must be distinguished: (i) the country is small, that is, the marginal productivity of capital is fixed via the world market; and (ii) the country is large, that is, the home country's environmental policy has an impact on the foreign marginal productivity of capital. In the small-country case, Rauscher (1992) derives the unambiguous result that imposing a restrictive environmental policy repels mobile capital. Rauscher (1997), however, leads to more ambiguous results. The effects of a change in environmental policy on mobile capital consist of two effects, a productivity effect and an effect dependent upon consumption externalities. If the sum of the productivity effect and the consumption externality effect is positive (negative), capital tends to be attracted (repelled). For the overall productivity effect to be positive, the direct positive productivity effect needs to be larger than the negative indirect production effect. Decisive for the sign of the consumption externality effect is the size of the elasticity of substitution between capital and emissions. The elasticity of substitution is inversely related to the external effect on the marginal productivity of capital. The smaller the external effect on production, the larger the substitution effect, and a large elasticity of substitution gives a positive consumption externality effect. Therefore, a country may either attract or repel capital by imposing a restrictive environmental policy. The overall result is highly dependent on the typical parameter configuration representing the productivity effect and the consumption externality effect. It follows that under certain parameter constellations, the pollution haven hypothesis holds, while under other parameter constellations, an 'environmental haven' hypothesis holds. In the latter situation, countries can attract capital by introducing a tight environmental policy. This may, for instance, be the case when employees are unwilling to live in pollution havens.

If the country under consideration is large, matters become even more complicated. Now we have to distinguish between the situation where the foreign emissions are given and the situation where they are variable. In the simple model without consumption externalities and external effects on production and under the assumption that foreign emissions are given, Rauscher (1992) shows that the large country can attract capital by relaxing its environmental policy. This effect is the same as in the small-country case. However, it is weaker because it influences both the domestic and the foreign rates of return on capital.

If we assume that foreign emissions are variable,[2] then the effect of implementing a lenient environmental policy is also affected by an effect from the foreign country, which is induced by a change in emissions in the large country. Also in this situation a country can attract capital by implementing a more lenient environmental policy. However, the result is amplified because the capital flight from the foreign country reduces the marginal productivity of emissions and, since it is now lower than the emission tax, the foreign firms will react by reducing their emissions.

When consumption externalities and external effects on production are included, interaction effects of the consumption externalities and the pollution effects on production are generated and a great variety of results may occur. To derive results the analysis is simplified in two ways. First, it is assumed that the foreign emissions are either given or are variable. Second, it is assumed that there is either no consumption externality, or no external effect on production.

If the foreign emissions are given and there is no consumption externality, we get the result that the effects of a change in environmental policy on mobile capital may be positive or negative. As in the small-country case, it is the direct and the indirect production effects that cause the ambiguities. The direct effect of increased emissions on marginal productivity is positive.

But the indirect effect is that increased emissions have detrimental effects on both domestic and foreign capital productivity. If the direct effect dominates, the country can attract mobile capital by imposing a lenient environmental policy. If the indirect effect dominates, it repels capital. If there are no external effects on production and foreign emissions are still given, we get the unambiguous result that a country can attract capital by imposing a lenient environmental policy. This result is similar to those obtained in the simpler model in Rauscher (1992).

If foreign emissions are variable and there is no consumption externality, all effects of a more lenient environmental policy on capital location are ambiguous. The introduction of emission taxes adds further complexities to the model and, hence, many of the effects become indeterminate.

Under the assumption that there is no external effect on production (but there are consumption externalities), a country can attract capital by implementing a more lenient environmental policy. Increased domestic emissions increase the productivity of capital and therefore foreign direct investment is increased. The foreign country now employs a smaller capital stock and if productivity is not affected by the externalities, the foreign country will experience a reduction in the marginal productivity of emissions. With a given emission tax, foreign producers will reduce their emissions.

3.2. Trade

In some early papers, D'Arge and Kneese (1972), Walter (1974) and Siebert (1974) discuss how environmental policy influences commodity prices and thereby comparative price advantages. Siebert (1974) considers a two-country, two-sector model with only one production factor (natural resources). Production generates a pollutant that affects the ambient quality of the environment. The environment is considered as a receptor of pollutants. An environmental protection agency imposes an effluent charge and maximizes its 'profit' in terms of environmental quality.[3] From this maximization an expression for the scarcity price of the environment is obtained. Siebert (1974) finds a positive relationship between the scarcity price for the environment and commodity prices. If the two countries have different scarcity prices for the environment, it follows that the commodity prices will also differ. If country 1 has a lower scarcity price for the environment, the environment is relatively abundant in that country. Moreover, if country 1 has a relative price advantage in commodity 1, it will export that commodity. This leads to the theorem: the country richly endowed with the environment will export the commodity with a high pollution content. Similar conclusions are reached in D'Arge and Kneese (1972) and Walter (1974). In summary: when environmental policy is included in trade models, relative commodity prices are not only determined by relative marginal productivities, but also depend on (i) the marginal tendency to pollute, (ii) the marginal social damage caused by one unit of pollutant, and (iii) the total supply and demand of environmental services.

Environmental policy is not explicitly taken into account in the literature quoted above. Pethig (1976) relates trade theory to environmental policy and explicitly rationalizes and qualifies environmental scarcity in a general equilibrium model. The model consists of two sectors where only one production factor (labour) is used in the production of two commodities ($X1$ and $X2$). $X1$ is relatively environment intensive and $X2$ is relatively labour intensive. Pethig assumes a fixed consumption ratio, which ensures that the international production ratio of $X1$ and $X2$ cannot change. Only the volume of production can change.

Production generates a pollutant that is released into the environment. In Pethig's model, pollution is not internationally mobile but is indirectly imported or exported in the two commodities. In this way trade affects the countries' environmental quality. Pethig (1976) first analyses a situation where the supply of environmental resources is large relative to demand, and no environmental controls are enforced in the two countries. These could be two developing countries. This situation leads to the Ricardian result as if labour were the only production factor. The countries' endowment of environmental services has no impact on trade. However, the countries' capacity in environmental services does affect the welfare in the countries. The country that specializes in the production of the environment-intensive commodity may suffer a welfare loss from trade, because additional pollution damages might offset the usual material gains from trade. The other country gains from trade. Next, Pethig considers the situation of two countries that have implemented pollution control differently; that is, pollution control is more restrictive in country 1. Then country 2 exports and specializes in the production of the environment-intensive commodity. This implies that the Ricardian case is replaced by a factor endowment basis for trade. This is the standard HO result, and is in accordance with D'Arge and Kneese (1972), Walter (1974) and Siebert (1974).

If an environmental standard is implemented, Pethig (1976) shows that the country with the lowest shadow price for pollution becomes relatively well endowed with the pollution factor. The two countries' welfare is interdependent, because a change in one country's environmental policy will affect the volume of production and hence welfare in both countries.

In summary, Pethig shows that if environmental scarcity is explicitly taken into account, it may or may not affect trade depending on the scarcity of the environment. Further, it is shown that the usual gains from trade do not always materialize. Welfare may decrease if the exported commodity is the more polluting commodity. Asako (1979) also obtains this result. Siebert et al. (1980) and McGuire (1982) extend Pethig's analysis to the case of two primary factors. Environmental policy in these models is, however, exogenous. By endogenizing environmental policy, patterns of trade are explained as a function of the underlying technology and endowments, rather than as merely reflecting exogenous environmental policy differences. This has been done in many different ways: (i) whether a country is small (for example, Copeland, 1994) or large (for example, Krutilla, 1991); (ii) whether pollution is local (for example, Copeland and Taylor, 1994; Steininger, 1994) or transboundary (for example, Markusen, 1975; Copeland and Taylor, 1995); or (iii) whether or not consumption externalities are taken into account (for example, Steininger, 1994; Rauscher, 1992). In the sequel we shall analyse aspects of environmental policy and trade following Rauscher (1997). This model can be seen as a unified framework in which the different factors can be taken into account. Furthermore, he includes transport externalities and external effects on production, which are not dealt with in the other papers.

Rauscher (1997) considers a model with trade in final consumption commodities, and internationally immobile, but intersectorally mobile, factors. A country is producing two commodities with two factors, capital and an environmental resource. Perfect competition prevails. The foreign country is the rest of the world, of which only its import demand or export supply functions are considered. Commodity one is the numéraire and its consumption does not cause any pollution. The consumption of commodity two, however, does cause pollution. Finally, environmental quality affects production, but not demand. In this model it is possible to vary the environmental policies and the pollution-impact parameters[4] and to analyse the effects on comparative price advantages and thereby competitiveness, specialization and trade. Three types of environmental policy are considered: an emission tax, a consumption tax and a trade tax. A distinction is made between the small-country case and the large-country case.

In the small-country case the country cannot affect the world market prices and cannot use its environmental policy to improve its terms of trade. The analysis is therefore reduced to the way in which environmental policy affects the volume of trade and changes in imports and exports. Since there are transport-specific externalities in the model, a trade tax becomes an environmental policy instrument as well. It is assumed that the country is a net exporter of commodity one and a net importer of commodity two, and that foreign pollution does not affect the domestic environment. In this model the effects of environmental policy on international trade are ambiguous. The reason is again the external effect on production mentioned in the preceding section. In the simpler version of the model, where external effects on production are ignored, the ambiguities are reduced but not eliminated, as the following examples show:

1. A higher emission tax in sector two increases the comparative disadvantage in the production of this commodity. The country will therefore specialize even more in the production of commodity one and import of commodity two is increased.[5] A higher emission tax may therefore increase trade and the pollution impact of transportation may dominate the effect of more strict environmental policy.
2. A tax on the consumption of commodity two reduces trade because consumers substitute towards commodity one, which may lead to an overall reduction of pollution via both the production and transportation effect. Hence, in a small open economy the impacts of changes in environmental policy are in general ambiguous because the regulation of a pollution activity has spillover effects to other pollution activities. Moreover, the effect may vary along with the policy instrument.

In the large-country case the country has an impact on world market prices and can use its environmental policy to improve its terms of trade. It is now assumed that trade interventions are restricted, for instance because the country is part of a free-trade agreement. Moreover, transport externalities are ignored and, contrary to the small-country case, pollution is assumed to be transboundary. Further, in order to avoid indeterminate results it is assumed that foreign import demand is not too inelastic. This model leads to unambiguous price effects, but ambiguous effects on pollution. If a tax is levied on the consumption of a commodity, its demand will be reduced and the world market price goes down. If emissions in one sector are taxed, the supply of the final commodity in that sector is reduced and the world market price is increased.

The ambiguous pollution effect of a change in environmental policy arises because of the transboundary externality that generates leakage effects. Leakage effects occur, for instance, if the consumption tax rate is increased. The direct effect is that pollution decreases. However, since terms of trade change,[6] the foreign country might be induced to increase its emissions. This leakage effect may outweigh the direct effect from an increasing consumption tax.

A somewhat different approach to the analysis of environmental policy and trade than the one in Rauscher (1997) can be found in the literature on trade between a rich region (North) and a poor region (South) (Copeland and Taylor, 1994, 1995; Chichilnisky, 1994; Beghin and Potier, 1997). These models assume a sufficiently asymmetric distribution of human capital endowments and absorptive capacities between North and South. These endowment differences will be translated into income differences and a lower valuation of the environment in the South than in the North. The result is that the North implements a more stringent environmental policy than the South. In Copeland and Taylor (1994), the income-induced differences in pollution taxes are the sole determinant of trade flows. The model is a static two-country general equilibrium model with a continuum of commodities differing in their pollution intensity of production. Pollution is local. The result is that free trade shifts pollution-intensive production to the human-capital-scarce South and raises world pollution. Nevertheless, there is no market failure because pollution stays within the country of origin and it is assumed that governments regulate pollution optimally. Consequently, trade always increases welfare.

In a subsequent paper, Copeland and Taylor (1995) extend their 1994 model and allow for transboundary pollution. In order to focus on income effects they maintain that income-induced differences in attitudes towards the environment are still the sole motive for trade. The result is that if the distribution of income is highly skewed, then free trade harms the global environment, but if the distribution of income is even, then free trade has no adverse effect on the environment. Because low-income countries have a strategic advantage in setting pollution levels in a free-trade regime, they have an incentive to delay international pollution negotiations until multilateral trade liberalization has been achieved.

Chichilnisky (1994) considers another reason for differences in environmental policy between North and South. She considers the difference in institutional capacity between North and South to define property rights on natural resources and the environment. The differences in institutional capacity provide a basis for trade, driven by ill-defined property rights and a tragedy of the commons. The North overconsumes underpriced resource-intensive products imported from the South. In this case the implementation of environmental taxes in the South may be inappropriate, basically because taxes reduce the price of the resource and lead to more extraction. Property right policies may be more effective.

3.3.   Trade and International Capital Movements

McGuire (1982) discusses what happens when regulation is incorporated into the standard HO model with international factor mobility. He alters the HO model to accommodate the environment by assuming that the environment is a production factor that is used in industrial processes. Being a production factor, the environment will be used up to the point where its marginal product equals its price, which, in the absence of any regulation, is equal to zero. The environment is a factor in only one of the industries, so there is a regulated and an unregulated industry. McGuire further assumes that capital, labour and emissions are equally substitutable. Thus when environmental regulation occurs, the shape of the production function is not altered. In this way environmental regulation, which constrains the allowable level of pollution to some given marginal product, is equivalent to negative neutral technological progress.

With respect to trade it is important to distinguish between coordinated and uncoordinated environmental regulation. Under coordinated environmental regulation, both countries face the same shadow price of pollution. The qualitative implications of the HO model still hold and so does the factor price equalization. However, with uncoordinated environmental policy, factor price equalization is lost. For a small country, facing given world commodity prices, environmental policy depresses the world commodity price of the regulated product and the released factors have to be absorbed by the unregulated industry. When international factor movements are possible it is clear that labour and capital will have an opportunity to relocate according to factor rewards. In the HO model with identical technologies but international mobile factors, factor price equalization cannot be restored until all of the polluting industries have left the country with the strictest environmental policy. The regulated country will be driven out of production of the regulated commodity. Thus international factor mobility and uncoordinated environmental regulation lead to complete specialization in at least one of the countries and perhaps in both.

Merrifield (1988) develops a model inspired by McGuire (1982). The general equilibrium model allows commodity and input prices to be determined endogenously. Commodities, pollution and capital are internationally mobile. He considers the economic impact of tighter abatement equipment standards. The model considers two countries (A and B) which produce one composite commodity each ($X1$ and $X2$, respectively). Country A consumes some of $X1$ and exports the balance to country B and vice versa for country B. The model incorporates a production function in which the scarcity of capital services varies directly with the pollution flow in order to capture the positive impact pollution has on input, production procedures, commodities and so on. Thus the production factors are capital, labour, emissions, pollution-abatement equipment and transboundary pollution. Two pollution-abatement strategies are analysed: (i) an equipment standard strategy (command-and-control approach); and (ii) production tax strategy (economic approach). Due to internationally mobile commodities, capital and pollution, the production tax has an ambiguous impact. The production tax may actually increase pollution because the change in pollution flows, due to a reduction in the emissions of one country, may be more than offset if capital movements increase the output and emissions of the other country. In other words, a production tax in country A may induce the polluting industries to move to country B, which reduces country A's emissions by a certain amount, but increases the emissions in country B by an even larger amount. This result is similar to the result in Rauscher (1997). The change in pollution flows, which results from the production tax, depends on which country produces the most pollution-intensive commodity. If country A's output is relatively more pollution intensive than country B's, then a production tax on country B's output will result in a net increase in pollution flows because capital movement increases country A's output and emissions. However, a production tax on A's output reduces pollution flows. In this case, the capital movement from country A (and the increased pollution in country B) is not enough to offset the emission reduction in country A. This ambiguity is not present in the case of an equipment standard.

Wang (1995) analyses the impacts of a production pollution tax on environmental capital flight and national product in a two-country static general equilibrium model with two-way foreign investment. There is only one produced commodity that is tradable and produced using labour and capital. The endowment of labour is fixed and internationally immobile. Endowment of capital is fixed but internationally mobile. Capital is a composite of domestic and imported capital, and the analysis allows for different degrees of substitutability between domestic and imported capital. Pollution is assumed to originate in the production process, and the productivity of capital can be negatively or positively affected by domestic or foreign emissions. Production pollution taxes in both countries are designed to mitigate environmental degradation optimally by reallocating capital and national product. In this way, the investment decision is influenced by the pollution tax because the equilibrium rates of return on capital and national products in both countries are affected. The result is that when a tax is levied in country A, it initially reduces the rates of return on inputs and then production. Capital tends to flee the country (labour is immobile). Domestic capital outflows increase, and foreign capital inflows decrease if elasticities of substitution between labour and capital are sufficiently high in both countries. This is due to the fact that for high elasticities of substitution between labour and capital, country A will adopt a more labour-intensive input combination, while country B will adopt a more capital-intensive input combination in production. An additional result of the model is that negative transboundary externalities will affect the tax impact on production. An increase in the domestic pollution tax reduces domestic production and increases foreign production because capital has moved to the foreign country. Negative transboundary externalities affect domestic productivity negatively and domestic production decreases. Hence negative transboundary externalities exacerbate the decrease of the domestic product. This escalates environmental capital flight and thus enhances the increase in foreign production.

4.   EMPIRICAL STUDIES

The conclusion reached above from the theoretical discussion was rather blurred. Under some parameter constellations strict environmental policy may lead to environmental capital flight; under other parameter constellations this may not be the case. We now turn to empirical studies. This section consists of two parts. The first deals with the effects of environmental regulation on trade. In the second we discuss studies of international capital movement and changes in foreign direct investment as a response to environmental policy.

4.1.   Trade

There are two approaches by which to analyse empirically the relationship between environmental regulation and trade: the Leontief approach and the HO approach. Leontief (1954) measured whether American exports were labour or capital intensive relative to imports. Contrary to what was expected, Leontief found that the US exports were less capital intensive than its imports. If environmental policy is introduced into Leontief's model, one measures whether the export of a country is more or less pollution intensive than its import.

Walter (1973) uses the Leontief approach to measure whether US environmental policy is 'trade neutral' or export or import biased. He estimates the 'overall environmental control loadings' (OECL), which measure the proportion of the product's final value attributable to environmental regulation. This measure is then multiplied by the value of the US imports and exports to obtain the environmental cost component of US trade. The result is that the average annual OECL of US exports during 1968–70 was about 1.75 per cent of total exports. The US average annual OECL of imports is estimated to be 1.52 per cent of total imports, or 13 per cent lower than the exports. Walter concludes that this difference does not appear to be very significant and the result suggests that environmental control measures bearing on the respective suppliers of US exports and imports will be trade neutral, or at worst only marginally biased against the US trading partners. However, at the level of individual industries there may be a basis for a loss in competitiveness as a consequence of a more strict US environmental policy. The most sensitive industries turned out to be ordnance and accessories, construction and mining equipment, and plastics. It is difficult to say something about differences in environmental policy between the USA and its trading partners. An indicator could be the difference in OECL. In 1968–70, US exports to Japan had an OECL value of 1.70, whereas imports had a value of 1.50. The corresponding values for Canada were 1.75 and 1.70, respectively. Thus, relative to imports from Japan, US exports to Japan appear to be relatively pollution intensive, which is much less the case for US–Canadian trade.

More recent data for several years were analysed by Robison (1988). By means of a partial equilibrium model similar to that of Walter (1973), Robison measured the impact of marginal changes in industrial pollution-abatement cost on the US balance of trade in general and the balance of trade with Canada in particular. Walter (1973) measured price changes caused by environmental regulation by multiplying the abatement-cost vector by the total requirements matrix. Robison (1988) notes that this approach misses the abatement costs implicit in capital goods used in the production process. Robison takes this into account by adding a capital flow coefficient to the total requirements matrix. By means of this model, the average abatement content of US trade is estimated for the years 1973, 1977 and 1982. The ratio of abatement content of imports to abatement content of exports rose from 1.151 in 1973 to 1.389 in 1982. From this it is concluded that a more stringent environmental policy in the USA has changed the comparative advantage in such a way that more high-abatement-cost commodities have been imported and more low-abatement-cost commodities exported. There is no significant change in the abatement content ratio for US–Canadian trade, implying no major shift in trading patterns between these two countries.

Sorsa (1994) analysed the links between environmental expenditures and trade in environmentally sensitive commodities in seven countries that have high environmental standards – Austria, Finland, Germany, Japan, Norway, Sweden and the USA. Two approaches were used. First, she compared world trade shares in environmentally sensitive commodities in the period 1970–90. Second, revealed comparative advantage (RCA) indices were calculated for the seven countries within the sensitive industries. The RCA measures changes in the share of a country's exports of a product in world exports of the product, compared to changes in the country's total share in world exports, that is, relative to the size of the country. If this ratio is more (less) than unity it means that the country is at a comparative (dis)advantage in the trade of the product.

With respect to the first, the analysis shows that world market shares in environmentally sensitive commodities have not changed much over the last two decades. The industrialized countries' share in the world trade of environmentally sensitive commodities was 81.3 per cent in 1970 and 81.1

per cent in 1990. However, at country level there have been some changes. Austria, Finland and Germany have increased their share, while Japan, Norway, Sweden and the USA have reduced their shares. Correlation coefficients based on time series for Austria, Germany, Japan and the USA, between changes in world trade shares of the sensitive commodities and changes in environmental expenditures, confirm that there is no significant impact of higher environmental expenditures on trade performance in environmentally sensitive commodities. For Germany, Japan and the USA the correlation coefficient was statistically insignificant. Austria was the only country for which the correlation coefficient was significant. However, it was found to be positive.

With respect to the second approach, a comparison of RCA indices also showed that stricter environmental policy in the countries has not reduced their comparative advantage in pollution-intensive commodities. The RCA for the industrialized countries was 1.1 in 1970 and 1.0 in 1990. Thus, they have roughly maintained their comparative advantage in environmentally sensitive commodities. The same is true for the developing countries. Their RCA in 1970 was 0.8 and 0.9 in 1990. Again there is more divergence at the country level. Austria and Finland have a comparative advantage in environmentally sensitive commodities and have actually increased their competitiveness from 1970 to 1990. Norway has a comparative advantage, but the RCA has dropped from 2.3 in 1970 to 1.5 in 1990. Japan has lost its comparative advantage in the period. Sweden has a comparative advantage that has not changed over the period. The German and US RCAs are 1.0 and 0.8, respectively, and have not changed from 1970 to 1990. The decrease in Japanese and Norwegian RCAs may be due to other factors than stricter environmental policy. In the case of Japan, the decline in RCA might be caused by the increase of other exports. The reason for the decline in Norwegian RCA may reflect the increase in oil revenues in total exports.

Low and Yeats (1992) focused on secular changes that occurred in developed and developing countries' actual trade, and on RCA in heavily polluting industries. This approach is quite similar to that of Sorsa (1994). Low and Yeats (1992) computed RCA indices for some 109 countries and provided an almost complete profile of changing national comparative advantages within polluting industries. The results suggest that 'dirty' industries account for a growing share of exports of some developing countries. This has occurred against the background of a reduction of such exports in world trade. However, the study does not identify the different factors underlying this development. Differences in environmental policy could be just one out of a large array of other significant factors. For instance, for metal manufactures the relative labour intensity could explain 'dirty' industry location. Natural resource endowments turned out to be an important factor for industries such as pulp and waste paper, petroleum refining, cement and non-ferrous metals.

There are some drawbacks to the Leontief approach. First, the three studies mentioned do not take into account differences in strictness of environmental policies between countries, and, second, it is a bivariate analysis. We now turn to the HO approach, which may overcome the problems inherent in the Leontief approach. In the HO model it is possible to include several factors which might influence trade patterns. Further, if it is possible to construct a measure indicating the stringency of environmental policy applicable in all countries, cross-country comparisons can be made.

Murrell and Ryterman (1991) developed a procedure that can be used when some variables of interest are difficult to measure or unavailable, which frequently occurs in the case of measuring effects of environmental policy. The approach is an omitted variable procedure based on Ryterman (1988). The procedure is applied to test whether high environmental damages in Eastern Europe can be explained by a tendency to export pollution-intensive commodities. The basic assumption is that Eastern Europe has a more lax environmental policy than its trading partners, and should therefore have a comparative advantage in pollution-intensive products. The authors use 1975 statistics on imports and exports of pollution-intensive commodities, defined as commodities the production of which produces more than average levels of pollution or requires more than average amounts of pollution-abatement cost. The trade statistics relate to nine East European countries, seven low-income Organization for Economic Cooperation and Development (OECD) countries and ten Latin American countries. The null hypothesis is that differences in environmental policy do not affect the structures of trade. The test comes down to a comparison of each group with the seven OECD countries. The null hypothesis was accepted for all nine East European countries. Thus the relatively lax environmental policy in Eastern Europe does not show up in a tendency to export commodities intensive in pollution.

Kalt (1988) examines the power of domestic regulatory costs in explaining aggregate trade performance. He focuses on the environmental control costs because these form the bulk of the regulatory costs. His point of departure is that the imposition of stringent environmental regulations in the USA can be viewed as a decline in the relative abundance of environmental resources. According to the HO model, the US exports of environment-intensive products would decline. In the regression analysis the dependent variable is the net exports from a specific industry and among the five independent variables are expenditures on pollution services by each industry. These expenditures are defined as the annualized capital, operating and administrative costs of pollution abatement in 1977, representing the direct impact of environmental regulation. Kalt notes that an indirect impact of environmental regulation arises when direct pollution-control costs are not entirely absorbed by the directly spending industry and become embodied in the output of industries that purchase the output of the directly spending industries. A cross-section analysis for all 78 industries shows that pollution-abatement regulations have an insignificant influence on net exports in 1977. However, for the 52 manufacturing industries the influence is negative and significant. This result is also obtained if the dependent variable is specified alternatively as the change in net exports over the period 1967–77 and the independent variable is specified as the change in expenditures on pollution services over the same period. In order to obtain an estimate of the total pollution-abatement costs, that is, both the direct and the indirect, Kalt multiplies the direct abatement costs by the total requirements 1977 input–output matrix. The analysis shows that including the indirect costs as well does not change the conclusion. Pollution-abatement regulations have an insignificant influence on net exports in 1977 when all industries are included but a negative and significant influence when the analysis is narrowed by including only manufacturing industries.

Tobey (1990) tests whether trade patterns for pollution-intensive commodities, which are produced by the world's 'dirtiest' industries, are affected by environmental policy. The test is conducted by using a cross-section Heckscher–Ohlin–Vanek (HOV) model, which is a multi-factor, multi-commodity extension of the classic HO model. Pollution-intensive products are defined as the products of industries in the USA where the pollution-abatement costs are greater than or equal to 1.85 per cent of total costs. In 1977 there were 34 such industries, which Tobey divides into five commodity groups. Net export in a specific commodity is regressed on country characteristics. Data are from 1975 and are obtained from a mix of 13 OECD countries and ten developing countries. The test is applied in two ways. First, trade is regressed on country characteristics, including an index measuring the stringency of pollution-control measures. This measure is based on a 1976 United Nations Conference on Trade and Development (UNCTAD) survey, ranking the countries in seven categories, from 'strict' (7) to 'tolerant' (1). The measure of environmental policy stringency is not found to be statistically significant in the regressions of polluting industries' exports. The second approach is the omitted variable test based on Ryterman (1988) and is quite similar to that in Murrell and Ryterman (1991). The idea is that if the stringency of environmental policy affects exports, it will affect the constant and disturbance term if it is omitted. The result is similar to the first approach: the stringency of environmental policy does not affect HOV trade patterns. Tobey (1990) also relaxes two of the HOV assumptions. First, non-homothetic preferences are allowed.

Then consumption is a function of population and income. Second, scale economies are allowed. None of these extensions makes the stringency of environmental policy significant. Hence Tobey does not find any support at all for the hypothesis that environmental policy affects trade. The negative results may be due to a time lag between the introduction of environmental policy and the subsequent effect on trade. Therefore he conducts a 'fixed effects' test where he examines the change in trade patterns before and after the introduction of environmental measures. In this test, Tobey finds a significant effect in only one of the five commodity groups. However, the sign is positive.

At first glance Kalt (1988) and Tobey (1990) obviously derive contrasting conclusions. However, the conclusions from the two approaches are not directly comparable because the dependent and the independent variables are not defined in the same way. Kalt defines his dependent variable as net exports of all industries, or alternatively net exports of the manufacturing industries. The dependent variable in Tobey is a subset of Kalt's because he concentrates on the net exports from the 24 most pollution-intensive industries. Also the environmental policy variable differs between the two studies. Kalt uses expenditures on pollution-abatement services as a proxy for environmental policy. Tobey uses a qualitative variable measured on a scale from one to seven. The purpose of Kalt's study was to examine the power of domestic regulatory costs in explaining aggregate trade performance. Hence the perspective is much broader than the one in Tobey which is more focused on environmental policy.

Van Beers and Van den Bergh (1997) is in several respects an extension of Tobey (1990). First, a disadvantage of the multilateral approach in Tobey is that effects of differences in environmental policy on trade flows may cancel out because multilateral trade is an aggregate of bilateral trade flows. Therefore Van Beers and Van den Bergh analyse bilateral trade flows made up of imports and exports from one country to another measured in thousands of US dollars. Second, the results may be strongly dependent upon the choice of the indicator measuring strictness of environmental policy. Van Beers and Van den Bergh use two such measures. The first measure reflects a large array of environmental indicators, including ones that do not directly reflect private environmental costs. The second is a narrow measure that more adequately reflects private environmental costs. In terms of both measures, countries are ranked between 0 (weak environmental policy) and 1 (strict environmental policy). Moreover, the UNCTAD environmental policy measure used in Tobey is an input-oriented indicator, whereas Van Beers and Van den Bergh use an output-oriented environmental policy measure. The former is an *ex-ante* measure that does not take into account counterbalancing financial assistance, such as export rebates and import surcharges, and therefore may exaggerate the costs of environmental regulations. The output-oriented policy measure takes these counterbalancing financial compensations into account. The third difference compared to Tobey is that three types of dependent variables (bilateral trade flows) are used. The first is an aggregate bilateral trade flow including all industries. The second is bilateral trade flow in highly pollution-intensive sectors. The third is bilateral trade flow in highly pollution-intensive sectors that are not resource based. The non-resource-based industries (the 'footloose' industries) are highly mobile industries that are very sensitive to inter-country differences in environmental policy. Naturally, these industries are of great interest here.

The first group of regression analyses which Van Beers and Van den Bergh (1997) perform is quite similar to the Tobey regression, but now the three bilateral trade flows are used as the dependent variable. As in Tobey, data are from 1975 and include 14 OECD countries and nine developing countries. The result is that the environmental policy indicator is significant for the exports, but has a positive sign. Hence more strict environmental regulation increases the export of the country. A possible explanation is that in this regression the environmental policy indicator is input oriented because Van Beers and Van den Bergh wanted to approximate the Tobey regression as closely as possible (except from the bilateral trade flows as the dependent variables). By using the input-oriented environmental policy indicator, possible effects from subsidies are not captured. The environmental policy indicator is insignificant for the imports.[7]

If a distinction is made between industries according to their capability to relocate, the analysis shows that the environmental policy indicator is significant and positive for exports, but only for the footloose industries. The environmental policy indicator is insignificant for imports.

The second group of regression analyses is related to 1992. Data are obtained from 21 OECD countries. Both the broad and the narrow environmental policy measure are used. The former has an insignificant effect on exports as well as imports, irrespective of which trade flow is used. The narrow measure is significant and negative for exports if aggregate trade flows and trade flows from the footloose sectors are used. It is insignificant if trade flows from the highly pollution-intensive sectors, including both footloose and non-footloose industries, are used. The impact on imports is significant and negative for all types of sectors. This is in contrast to what trade theory would predict and may indicate the presence of import barriers.

There are, however, some problems with the operationalization of strict environmental policy. The most important problem is that the main indicator used is energy use, while others relating to, for example, waste, are ignored. According to the energy use indicator, countries like Norway and

Sweden are found to have lax environmental policies. This can be explained in terms of the availability of hydropower in these countries. As is well known, the environmental impacts of hydropower are quite different from the impacts of coal. Hence it is doubtful if energy use is a correct indicator. Moreover, the negative impact on exports from the footloose sectors raises some questions. Because of its very nature, for the long run one would expect this sector to locate in regions with lax environmental policies. Hence if there were to be a significant policy effect one would expect it for the resource-based rather than the footloose sectors.

4.2. International Capital Movements

In this section, capital migration in the form of foreign direct investment is analysed. This form of investment is characterized by a relatively strong commitment and a relatively long time-horizon and, hence, is expected to be sensitive to environmental policy.

Walter (1982) examines whether differences in environmental policy between countries will favour incremental industrial restructuring. Three types of data are used. First, data about plant closures, based on a US Department of Commerce sample survey, are examined. In the period 1974–76, 130 plants were closed in the USA. In 87 cases the entire establishments closed down permanently. In 80 per cent of the cases air pollution requirements were given as the main pollution-related reason for the plant closure. Naturally, other factors, such as age or obsolescence, also contributed to the plant closures, but unfortunately it is not possible to determine the relative weight of the environmental considerations. However, plant closings for environmental reasons seem to differ widely for US industries. In the mining industry the shutdown rate was 8.72 per cent and in the chemical industry it was 0.79 per cent. Walter concludes that the results suggest that no significant migration of productive capital may be expected to result from closures. This conclusion, however, seems to rest on a slender foundation. Data for more than three years are needed and more precise evidence for the importance of environmental regulations relative to other factors is necessary. The second type of statistics examines whether environmental control costs give a relocation 'push'. An indicator of the 'push' is a comparison between domestic and overseas investments in pollution control. For seven major pollution-intensive industries in 1974–75, the percentage capital investment required for pollution control abroad is significantly lower than in the USA. Thus in the USA there is a strong 'push' for the polluting industries to relocate. However, it does not say whether they actually relocate. An indicator of this could be the flows of foreign direct investment. Walter examines the regional differences of the capital expenditures of US companies. Data on domestic and overseas capital expenditures of US companies are examined for the period 1970–77. Overseas investments are also differentiated by regions. The data show that the industries vary greatly in the direction of their foreign direct investment. However, there is no significant increase in foreign direct investment by pollution-intensive industries in developing countries. In summary, Walter's analysis does not find support for the hypothesis that pollution-intensive industries have moved towards less-regulated countries.

Leonard (1988) seeks to establish some recent trends in foreign investment by US industries that might ascertain whether industries with high pollution-control costs have recently increased investments in countries with low environmental standards. Based on pollution-abatement expenditures and the extent of the ease with which industries can relocate, he selects the chemical and the mineral processing industries for further analysis. The aggregate investment and trade figures indicate that the years immediately following emergence of stringent environmental regulations in the USA did not witness widespread relocation of industries to countries with drastically lower environmental regulations. Nor in the long run could Leonard find any significant effects, and not even when countries have tried to attract 'dirty' industries. The few industries that moved out of the USA had few incentives to improve production facilities because demand for their products was reduced as a result of product obsolescence or hazards. There are no examples of healthy and growing US industries that have been forced to move abroad because of environmental regulations. In recent years, however, among pollution-intensive industries, some trends, which could be related to increased environmental regulations, seem to occur. Of greatest potential significance, Leonard remarks, are the large increases in recent years in overseas investment and refined imports by US mineral processors.

Rowland and Feiock (1991) do not consider international migration, but migration across states in the USA. The purpose is to investigate to what extent the interstate allocation of new chemical and allied producers' (CAP) capital can be accounted for by interstate variance in CAP pollution-abatement costs. The federal states in the USA differ greatly from each other in terms of environmental regulation of the CAP as well as share of new CAP capital. Rowland and Feiock come to the opposite conclusion of Walter (1982) and Leonard (1988): pollution-abatement costs have a significant negative influence on the states' ability to attract new CAP capital in the period 1977–81. However, this relationship is non-linear. There appears to be a threshold. Capital relocates if a state exceeds the threshold, but below it there is no relocation. This means that while states that impose high pollution-abatement costs tend to compete unsuccessfully for new capital, those states with the lowest marginal pollution-abatement costs are not necessarily the most successful in attracting new CAP capital. Rather, there seems to be a pollution-abatement expense threshold. When a state exceeds it, the state loses capital to states that remain below it. Rowland and Feiock do not discuss whether or not their result can be generalized to an international setting.

Hettige et al. (1992) and Lucas et al. (1992) examine whether environmental regulation in the OECD countries has displaced toxic industrial production towards less-regulated less developed countries (LDCs). They find support for the replacement hypothesis by studying measures of the toxic intensity of manufacturing in 80 countries from 1960 to 1988. The data are divided into subsets for each decade and show that, in the 1960s, toxic intensities grew most quickly in high-income countries. After the introduction of stricter environmental regulation in the OECD countries in the 1970s and 1980s, the pattern was sharply reversed: toxic intensity in the LDCs grew most quickly. Further, the authors conclude that pollution intensity has grown most rapidly in developing countries, which are relatively closed to world market forces. The same conclusion is reached in Birdsall and Wheeler (1992), who find that in Latin America, pollution havens are to be found in the most protectionist economies. Openness promotes cleaner industries. However, a major drawback of Hettige et al. (1992) and Lucas et al. (1992) is that the regressions do not include any environmental policy variables. Thus one cannot be certain of a causal connection between the decade patterns and the shifts in OECD environmental policies.

5. CONCLUSION

The purpose of this chapter was to review the literature on capital flight and trade impacts of environmental regulations. The theoretical analysis starts from the general HO model of international trade and from models of international capital movements. In the HO model, international trade is explained by differences in factor endowments. The model predicts that the relative prices of commodities converge, which leads to the convergence of relative factor prices. According to the theory of international capital movements, in the absence of trade, capital relocates internationally on the basis of marginal return. Consequently, factor prices converge. It follows that in these standard models with perfect competition and no scale economies, international trade and factor movements are substitutes.

The simplest possible model with environmental effects included assumes international capital movements and ignores consumption externalities and external effects on production. In this model, the result is obtained that a country repels mobile capital by imposing a restrictive environmental policy. However, in a more realistic model with consumption externalities and external effects on production, results become ambiguous. Then no clear-cut relation between the strictness of environmental policy and capital movement can be found. The same is true for trade models. The trade models are more complicated than the models with international capital movements because trade models include at least two commodities. If environmental policy is introduced in the simplest possible trade model, the standard HO result is obtained: the country well endowed with environmental resources exports the environmentally intensive produced commodity. However, in more realistic models with different technologies or external effects on production, the impact of stricter environmental policy on trade flows becomes ambiguous and dependent on specific parameter constellations.

The empirical studies also give mixed results. This applies to the Leontief approach, which focuses on the problem of whether or not strict environmental policy gives a comparative disadvantage in the production of pollution-intensive commodities. Robison (1988) finds that a comparative disadvantage will occur; Walter (1973) and Sorsa (1994) do not. On the contrary, Sorsa finds that in some instances, more strict environmental policy results in a comparative advantage.

There are some drawbacks to the Leontief approach. First, this type of study does not take into account differences in strictness of environmental policies between countries. The second major drawback is that it is bivariate. It is assumed that environmental costs are the only factor that explains the patterns of specialization.

The empirical studies using the HO model do not find much support for the claim that strict environmental policy in a country has a negative influence on the country's export of pollution-intensive commodities. Tobey (1990) finds an insignificant output-oriented environmental policy measure for 1975 data, using both the standard HO model and a modified model with scale economies and non-homothetic preference. For the same data, Van Beers and Van den Bergh (1997), who use bilateral trade flows and an input-oriented environmental policy measure, confirm these results. They even find a significant and positive relationship between strictness of environmental policy and exports. However, on the basis of 1992 data, and an environmental policy measure that better reflects the private environmental costs of production, they find a significant and negative relation between the stringency of environmental policy and trade. This applies in particular to industries that relocate relatively easily.

Empirical research with respect to international capital movement does not provide much evidence for the hypothesis that more strict environmental policy has affected international capital movements. Walter (1982) and

Leonard (1988) reject the hypothesis. Rowland and Feiock (1991) find support for the hypothesis, but only consider capital movements within the USA. There seems to be some evidence that LDCs have a growing share of toxic industrial production. It is, however, not clear whether changes in environmental policy have induced this change.

The general conclusion that emerges from the literature reviewed is that highly simplified theoretical models of international trade and capital movements support trade effects and large-scale capital flight. However, when these models are made more realistic, the clear-cut conclusions disappear. If, for instance, several different externalities are included, or differences between the countries other than environmental policy are considered, then stricter environmental policy does not necessarily lead to trade effects or capital flight. The empirical studies are also somewhat mixed in their conclusions. The majority of the studies find an insignificant relationship between environmental policy and environmental capital flight. Some studies even find a significant positive relationship. Other studies, however, do find a significant negative relationship.

The empirical studies show that there are many methodological problems. First of all, there is a scarcity of data. Second, some of the studies relate to years when environmental policy was in its infancy and costs of environmental regulation were relatively low. This leads to the more general hypothesis that the costs of environmental regulation need to exceed a certain threshold in order to have an impact on capital flight and trade. Although several of the empirical studies find that in general there is little support for trade effects or environmental capital flight, this does not hold for industries where the environmental cost component is much larger than average. This supports the hypothesis that with a continued increase in the strictness of environmental policy in the future, trade effects and environmental capital flight may occur.

Jeppesen et al. (2001) shed some light on how methodological problems affect empirical results. They use a meta-analysis to examine the methodological impacts on the results obtained in empirical studies. Using results from 11 studies that examine the effect of environmental regulations on new plant location decisions, the authors examine how different methodological aspects (such as regression method, aggregation, time period covered, and definition of environmental stringency) affect empirical results. They show that methodological differences are important in explaining the different results obtained in the literature. For example, cross-sectional regression models produce less evidence of a pollution haven effect than panel data models. Moreover, studies using data from the late 1980s and 1990s tend to find more significant negative results than studies using earlier data. Finally, studies pooling pollution-intensive and non-pollution-intensive industries find less evidence for the pollution haven hypothesis than studies that examine purely 'dirty' industries. Hence Jeppesen et al. (2001) show that mixed results from the empirical studies can to a large extent be explained by methodological differences.

NOTES

1. Markusen (1983), Ruffin (1984) and Wong (1986) consider situations where they are complements.
2. Foreign emissions might be variable because the country has implemented emission taxes.
3. Alternatively, it can be assumed that the agency maximizes a social welfare function with the three arguments: the output from the two countries and environmental quality.
4. Pollution-impact parameters reflect the capability of the country's natural resources to assimilate or withstand environmental disruption.
5. Non-homothetic preferences reverse this effect.
6. In the large-country case, tighter environmental policy in the export industry improves the terms of trade and tighter environmental policy in the import industry worsens them (Rauscher, 1997).
7. One might expect that domestic consumers would substitute domestic products for foreign ones because a strict environmental policy is expected to raise domestic production costs and hence prices. The result indicates that this substitution effect does not take place.

7. Strategic environmental policy

1. INTRODUCTION

It is often believed that a government can influence the competitiveness of an economy through its environmental policy. A strict environmental policy will distract internationally mobile factors and cause a relocation of mobile factors. Conversely, a lax environmental policy may attract internationally mobile factors. As a consequence it is believed rational for a government to engage in a 'race to the bottom' and implement lax environmental regulations in pursuit of industry and jobs.

This belief is supported by two groups often considered as being opposed. The first group, environmentalists, have used it as an argument against free-trade agreements. In the USA, for instance, environmentalists have claimed that NAFTA would result in industrial relocation from the USA to Mexico because of more lax environmental protection regulations there. The environmentalists have feared that the threat of industrial exoduses would motivate governments not to push their environmental regulations too far. The second group, industrialists, have also supported the belief. Industries have threatened governments that they would move abroad if environmental regulations were strengthened.

This chapter examines whether governments have incentives to implement a lax environmental policy in order to either attract new firms or reduce production costs for domestic firms so that they can then dump their products on international markets. This phenomenon is often referred to as the 'ecological dumping hypothesis'. In presenting an overview of the literature dealing with ecological dumping and firm relocation, this chapter argues that even though fear of ecological dumping and firm relocation has a high position on the political agenda, the scientific evidence is weak.

If Governments have the competences to set and enforce environmental regulations they may engage in a 'race to the bottom' implementing environmental regulations that could critically undermine efficient pollution control standards. Thus, it may be optimal to place these competences centrally, creating a 'level playing-field'.

Throughout the chapter, imperfect competition prevails. Ulph (1997) and Rauscher (1994, 1997) argue that under perfect competition there is little evidence for the ecological dumping hypothesis. A small country has no incentive to use environmental policy strategically, essentially because the country cannot influence its terms of trade. A large country which has some market influence may have incentives to use its environmental policy strategically. However, this does not necessarily mean that it will relax its environmental policy. If the country is a net exporter of a product which causes pollution in production, it will desire to set too strict environmental policies as a proxy for the optimal export taxes.

With imperfect competition this outcome may change because imperfect competition creates rents, motivating governments to capture these rents for their domestic producers. Wilson (1996), Ulph (1997), and Rauscher (1994, 1997), among others, present a number of scenarios under which governments may race to the bottom. This chapter, therefore, gives a concise review of the literature on imperfect competition and ecological dumping to examine under which circumstances ecological dumping may occur.

The chapter is organized as follows. Section 2 examines the question of environmental capital flight from a theoretical perspective. If industry location is affected by differences in environmental policy, there is good reason for governments to use environmental policy strategically. This does not mean, however, that if industry location is unaffected there is no basis for ecological dumping. As Cropper and Oates (1992) note, governments may engage in ecological dumping because they fear that firms will relocate. Section 3 examines whether ecological dumping is a rational response for a government that wants to attract new business investment or avoid environmental capital flight. Section 4 discusses whether ecological dumping is a rational choice for a government wanting to help domestic firms expand market shares in international markets. The conclusions are presented in section 5.

2.   ENVIRONMENTAL CAPITAL FLIGHT

This section focuses on whether or not differences in environmental policy induce firms to relocate. It does not discuss the incentives for governments to implement a lax environmental policy. Instead it deals with the environmental policy effects on plant location, taking the environmental policy as given. Hence this section discusses the effect of environmental policy on plant location in conditions where environmental policies or environmental targets are exogenous, that is, where only the producers engage in strategic behaviour.

Markusen et al. (1993) carried out the first study of environmental policy effects on plant location in a model with imperfect competition. The point of departure is that the Pigouvian tradition is inappropriate when it comes to analysing environmental policy effects on plant location. The Pigouvian tradition assumes constant returns to scale and perfect competition, and it applies marginal analysis. However, in a world of increasing returns to scale and imperfect competition, firms face the discrete choice of whether to serve another country by exports or by building a plant in that country. When deciding plant configuration, the producers compare the total profit arising from the different configurations. This means that at some point a small change in an environmental tax may be so critical as to cause the plant to relocate, which changes the welfare in the countries.

Markusen et al. construct a model with two countries and two firms that produce three goods. Each firm produces a good (X and Y) which generates purely local pollution, and both firms produce the same homogeneous good which does not generate any pollution. The cost functions for the firms are identical. The firms face firm-specific fixed costs as well as plant-specific fixed costs. There are constant marginal costs and there are transportation costs of shipping output between regions. Multi-plant economies of scale occur because the fixed costs of a two-plant firm are less than the combined fixed cost of two one-plant firms. The producer must therefore trade off the high fixed-cost option and production in both regions with the high variable-cost option and a plant in one country exporting to the other. The firms face a pollution tax in one of the countries, which can be interpreted as an added marginal cost of production in that country. The firms play a two-stage game. In Stage One, the two firms decide between three plant configurations: one plant, two plants (one in each country), or no entry (zero plants). In Stage Two, the firms play a one-shot Cournot output game. Solving this game shows how environmental policy affects the equilibrium market structure.

In the numerical analysis, Markusen et al. begin with the market structure (2,2) which means two plants in two countries. This configuration has low plant-specific costs, high firm-specific costs and high transport costs. By increasing the tax, critical tax levels are reached where the plant structure is changed. The first critical value for the tax is reached where it is unprofitable for one of the two firms to produce. This gives the market structure (2,0) or (0,2). If we assume that the market structure is (2,0), further increases in the tax may make it profitable for the Y producer to re-enter the market and serve the two markets from one plant. This yields the market structure (2,1), which emerges because an increased tax reduces the output of X and increases demand for Y. A continued increase in the tax rate reduces the profits of the X producer and increases the profits of the Y producer. Eventually, the profits of the X producer will become negative, and we will reach the final market structure (0,1), where all production takes place in the country without the tax. A sufficiently high tax may thus drive domestic producers out of the country.

The welfare effects are more complex because they depend on a number of factors, such as level of pollution, disutility of pollution, consumers' surplus, tax revenues and profits of the local firm. These factors may change in opposite directions. By using specific parameters, however, it is possible to calculate the optimal tax. The optimal tax may result in market structure (0,1) or (2,1), depending on the initial market structures and the specific parameters, such as the disutility of pollution. The most important findings in Markusen et al. are that plant location is a function of environmental policy, and the costs of overlooking this fact may be quite high.

Markusen et al. (1993) assume that the firms are not established when the game begins. Naturally, relocation is much more likely to occur in this situation than under the alternative assumption that the firms are already established from the beginning. This is the point of departure for Motta and Thisse (1994), who believe that firms are linked to their mother country for historical, cultural and economic reasons. This means a firm which sets up a plant abroad to supply the home market must deal with fixed set-up costs already sunk in the domestic plant.

Motta and Thisse consider a model with two countries and two firms, producing a homogeneous good. Firm 1 is located in Country A and Firm 2 in Country B. The fixed costs are sunk when the game begins, which means that Firm 1 does not have to incur any fixed costs when it operates its domestic plant. Motta and Thisse examine the relative impact of Country A's environmental policy on Firm 1's choice comparing three plant configurations: (1) supply of both markets from Country A (1,0); (2) establishment of a subsidiary in Country B (1,1); and (3) closing of plant in A and setting up a new plant in B (0,1). The market size (S) is variable, marginal costs of production in country A (c_A) are affected by the country's environmental policy, and trading costs per unit of output (t) are included. In their model, Motta and Thisse analyse how combinations of the market size in B (S_B) and c_A influence the plant configuration.

The results are as follows. First, when the two markets are equally small, Firm 1 never invests abroad. If the environmental policy becomes sufficiently strict, Firm 1 closes. Second, when the equally small markets become larger, equilibrium solutions appear in which Firm 1 invests abroad. For sufficiently large markets and strict environmental policy, Firm 1 closes its operations in A, moves to B and exports the goods back to A. Third, if the market in A is larger than the market in B, the critical value of S_B, at which Firm 1 invests abroad, decreases. This is because the larger the market in A, the more competitive it is and the more sensitive the firms are to changes in c_A. Fourth, as one might expect, an increase in the trading costs protects the domestic markets from foreign competition. This means that when the trading costs increase, the critical value of c_A at which Firm 1 invests abroad increases. This has the very relevant implication that the creation of a common market favours the relocation of production when one country imposes a stricter environmental policy.

However, Motta and Thisse also show that for certain values of c_A, a rise in the trading costs will cause Firm 1 to close, and the high t value will prevent the firm from relocating. In this situation, a protectionist trade policy does not necessarily allow A's government to implement a more strict environmental policy. Fifth, if we assume that the fixed costs are endogenous to the market structure, and we assume stronger scale economies, the possibility that the firm will operate two plants becomes much higher. This is because the joint savings in fixed costs and transportation costs exceed the increased marginal costs in country A. In fact, for sufficiently high values of c_A, the situation where the firm would concentrate all its activity abroad (configuration $(0,1)$ or $(1,0)$) may no longer exist. Finally, the welfare effects are considered. Although highly dependent on the definition of the welfare function and the specific parameter values, it is possible that a stricter environmental policy is welfare-improving. Even if there is complete relocation, the welfare level in the country which the firm has left is higher than the welfare if the firm does not relocate. In short, it may be welfare-improving if the firm in a country is 'footloose', that is, if it is relatively easy for it to relocate.

Ulph (1994), like Markusen et al. (1993), seeks to analyse the relationship between environmental policy and firm location. Ulph generalizes Markusen et al. by introducing a larger number of countries and firms. He uses a model with M countries and a fixed number of firms (F). The firms have fixed costs in setting up a plant, and variable costs, which exhibit constant returns to scale. It is assumed (1) that the firms have organized their domestic production to exploit economies of scale, and (2) that it is more expensive to set up a plant in foreign markets than in domestic markets. The firms face a unit cost of transport which is identical for all firms. Hence, as in Markusen et al. (1993), the firms are trading off economies of scale and transport costs.

This model specification is quite similar to that of Markusen et al. (1993). What differs is the governments' behaviour. Ulph assumes that some governments have joined an international agreement and thereby committed themselves to a specific target for reductions in CO_2. All governments in the agreement will use a carbon tax to achieve the target. In this way the target is determined exogenously, while the tax is determined endogenously. As in Markusen et al. (1993), the tax affects the firms' profits and hence their location choice. The governments recognize that they can influence this choice, and their strategic weapon is the extent to which carbon tax revenues are rebated back to the producers.The focus in Ulph (1994) is how the strategic choice of rebating tax revenues affects firm location. The model defines a four-stage game: in Stage 1 the governments announce their targets and choose their rebates; in Stage 2 the firms choose their locations; in Stage 3 the government chooses a tax rate; and in stage 4 the firms decide how much to sell and from where it shall be supplied.

There are many similarities between Markusen et al. (1993) and Ulph. Both have the same objective, their models have many of the same characteristics, and Markusen et al. (1993) have exogenous environmental policy, whereas Ulph has an exogenous environmental target. However, disparities also exist. Ulph endogenizes the environmental tax and turns the focus to how the tax revenues are rebated. Further, he deals with transboundary pollution, which makes it relevant to divide the countries into two groups: a group of countries which have signed an international environmental agreement; and a group of countries which have chosen not to enter the agreement. Ulph does not directly discuss whether transboundary pollution increases or reduces the incentive to relocate compared to local pollution. Instead he discusses the effects of transboundary pollution on 'carbon leakage', that is, the proportion of reduced CO_2 emissions achieved by the group taking action which is offset by the expansion of the output and hence by CO_2 emissions in those countries which do not take action. Clearly, if imperfect competition increases the incentives for the industries to relocate, the extent of carbon leakage will increase.

Before turning to the results, Ulph emphasizes that relocation can affect the degree of competitiveness in different markets. The fact that a plant is moving out of a market will protect the remaining plants through transport costs. The market to which the plant is moving will become more competitive, and one can expect the prices in that market to fall. If a country imposes a tax, one normally expects the price to increase. However, the reverse may actually be the case if more plants enter the market in response to even higher taxes in other countries. This will make the market more competitive. In order to reach precise results, it is necessary to resort to numerical solutions with specific functional forms and specific values of various parameters. Ulph chooses two firms and three countries in which only two countries have signed an environmental agreement. Data from the fertilizer industry are used to calibrate the parameter values.

The analysis indicates that despite substantial taxes in some markets, prices in these markets actually fall because of increased competition (in response to higher rebate rates or higher taxes elsewhere). The greatest price increases occur in markets with the lowest environmental tax rates. There is no longer a simple relationship between costs and price. Strategic behaviour by producers (relocation) offsets the direct effects of pollution taxes. The strategic responses by producers affect their market shares quite substantially and thus affect welfare, too. Because of possible relocation effects, the model also generates much larger estimates of carbon leakage, which questions the appropriateness of unilateral action. Ulph reaches the same result as Motta and Thisse (1994): a country with producers who are relatively 'footloose', that is, producers who are very willing to relocate, does much better than countries whose industries are less footloose. One may conclude that countries should think twice before they implement rebate policies. Rebate policies give producers an incentive not to relocate, that is, they turn them into less footloose producers, which, as noted, is quite undesirable.

3. ECOLOGICAL DUMPING AS A RESPONSE TO ENVIRONMENTAL CAPITAL FLIGHT

In this section, the environmental policy is endogenized, which means that we allow for strategic actions by both producers and governments. The purpose of this section is to analyse whether or not governments have an incentive to engage in ecological dumping. The fear, of course, is that too lax environmental regulation results in low environmental quality. It is not clear, however, what is meant by too lax environmental regulation.

Rauscher (1994) provides an excellent discussion of three definitions of ecological dumping. First, ecological dumping could be characterized as a situation in which environmental standards are lower in one country than in any of the other countries. However, this definition ignores differences in environmental endowments and preferences, which should be reflected in differentiated environmental measures. Second, ecological dumping could also be defined as a situation where a government prices environmental harmful activities at less than the marginal cost of environmental degradation (or less than environmental damage). The major problem with this definition is that suboptimal internalization may be due to many other reasons than ecological dumping, for example influential lobby groups. The third definition takes a non-traded-goods sector as a point of departure and defines ecological dumping as a scenario in which environmental standards are tighter in the non-traded-goods sector than in the tradables sector. The problem with this definition is that different sectors might not be discharging the same pollutant and the pollutant may not cause the same environmental damage at the margin. It then becomes difficult to compare the tightness of environmental standards across sectors. The first definition of ecological dumping does not make much sense. The latter two definitions are more sensible, but there does not seem to be any reason, a priori, to choose one or the other. The second definition assumes full internalization of external costs, which is not necessarily the case in the third definition.

Hoel (1994b) sets up a quite simple model which makes it possible to derive some qualitative results. In the model there are two countries and a single firm producing a product which generates a purely local negative environmental externality. There are fixed costs of setting up a plant and constant unit operation costs. There are no transport costs, so the firm will serve either both markets from one country, or not produce at all. In a two-stage game, the governments of each country choose emission taxes (t), and the firm decides where to locate in the second stage. The share of the firm owned by the residents in each country is denoted by α. Initially it is assumed that the countries are identical in this respect ($\alpha = 0.5$). The welfare in the country without the firm ($W(t,0)$) is consumers' surplus plus the firm's profit: $W(t,0) = V(t) + \alpha\pi(t)$. In addition to the country without the firm, welfare in the country in which the firm is located ($W(t,1)$) is dependent on the tax revenue, $R(t)$, and the environmental costs, $E(t)$. If $R(t) - E(t) = Z(t)$, such that the welfare of the country with the firm is $W(t,1) = W(t,0) + Z(t)$. Depending on the environmental costs, three possible outcomes are generated: (1) low environmental costs; (2) intermediate environmental costs; and (3) high environmental costs.

3.1.   Low Environmental Costs

The socially optimal tax, t^0, maximizes $W(t,0) + W(t,1)$. If there is a positive surplus at the socially optimal tax level ($Z(t^0) > 0$), there is an incentive for the countries to compete to have the plant located in their country. This is done by cutting their emission taxes below the socially optimal level. As Figure 7.1 shows, the Nash equilibrium is where the two countries are setting the same tax $t^* < t^0$. This is the equilibrium tax level because as long as $W(t,1) > W(t,0)$, it will benefit the country without the plant to undercut the other country. On the other hand, if $W(t,1) < W(t,0)$, it would benefit the country with the plant to raise its tax level until the plant moves out of the country. Hoel does not say whether t^* is above or below MD; he examines only whether t^* is above or below t^0.

3.2.   Intermediate Environmental Costs

The situation where $W(t,1)$ reaches its maximum at t^* for which $Z(t^0) < 0$ and $W(t^*,1) < W(t^*,0)$ is shown in Figure 7.2. In this situation the country where the plant is located will set the tax t^*, and the country without the plant will choose any tax at least as great as t''. In the situation shown in

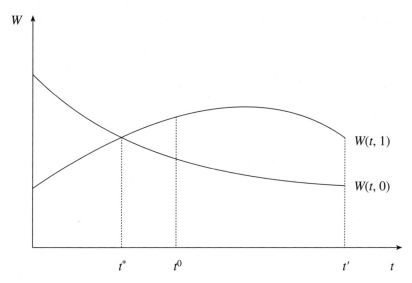

Source: Hoel (1994b).

Figure 7.1   Nash equilibrium (t^*) with low environmental costs

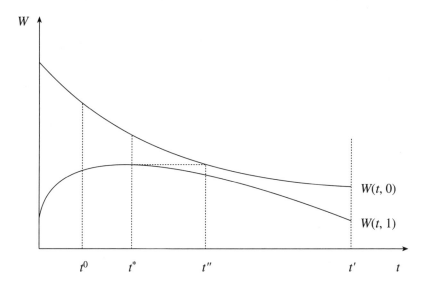

Source: Hoel (1994b).

Figure 7.2   Nash equilibrium (t^* and t'') with intermediate environmental costs

Figure 7.2 there will be no competition to attract the plant because the country with the plant is worse off than the country without the plant. To ensure the Nash equilibrium, the country without the plant sets $t \geq t''$, where $W(t^*,1) = W(t'',0)$. Given that the country without the plant has chosen t'', the country with the plant cannot do better than choose t^*.

3.3.   High Environmental Costs

The environmental costs may be so large that $W(t,1) < 0$ for all $t < t'$, as shown in Figure 7.3. In this situation, no country wants the plant, and the Nash equilibrium is where both countries choose prohibitively high taxes ($t > t'$). This is the NIMBY (Not In My Back Yard) case. As shown in Figure 7.3, the two countries would be better off if they behaved cooperatively. With appropriate transfers, the socially optimal solution is the situation in which the plant is located in one of the countries.

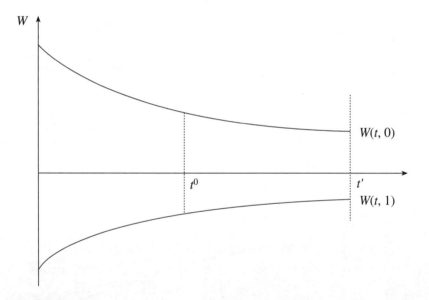

Source: Hoel (1994b).

Figure 7.3   Nash equilibrium (t') with high environmental costs

Rauscher (1995b) generalizes Hoel (1994b) by considering a large number of countries, and in Rauscher (1997) a two-country version is developed. Both of Rauscher's models obtain the same results as Hoel's model.

The model in Markusen et al. (1995), though quite similar to that of

Hoel (1994b), extends the model by introducing transport costs. The consequence is that it may be optimal for a firm to locate in both countries in spite of its fixed production costs. Markusen et al. build upon their previous model (Markusen et al., 1993), but turn their attention to the governments themselves, by considering the fact that the governments can compete in terms of their environmental policies. As noted above, in Markusen et al. (1993) the environmental tax introduced in one of the two countries is exogenous, and the two-stage game is played only by the firms.

In Markusen et al. (1995) there are two identical countries, a single imperfectly competitive firm producing a good with increasing returns to scale. The firm faces firm-specific fixed costs as well as plant-specific fixed costs. There is also a non-polluting industry in each country. The object of each government is to maximize its welfare, which is the consumers' surplus, plus the tax revenue, minus the disutility from pollution. In contrast to Hoel (1994b), it is assumed that all the profits go to owners outside the two countries. Hoel (1994b) assumes that $\alpha = 0.5$, but Markusen et al. assume that $\alpha = 0$. This assumption is also made in Rauscher (1995b). The competition between the governments is a two-stage game. In the first stage, the two countries simultaneously determine the values of their pollution taxes. In the second stage the firms choose one of four plant configurations: a plant in both countries (1,1); a single plant in one of the two countries (1,0) or (0,1), respectively, or zero plants (0,0). The model by Markusen et al. (1995) is a slightly more complex model than Hoel's (1994b), which has the consequence that large discontinuities arise. Consequently, Markusen et al. have to use fully specified functional forms and derive the equilibria numerically.

Pollution taxes affect the firm's location in two ways. First, high taxes in both countries may cause the firm to shift from the high fixed-cost option of two plants to the high variable-cost option of a single plant. Second, low taxes in one country may induce the firm to locate in that country. These two effects are discussed by constructing three cases. In the first case the disutility from pollution is moderate, and the plant-specific fixed costs are large relative to the transportation costs. The plant then chooses a single plant. Markusen et al. show that in this situation the country without the plant has an incentive to cut taxes, and tax competition occurs.

The Nash equilibrium occurs with taxes lower than the non-strategic taxes and a plant in one, or both, of the countries. Thus the tax competition may result in more plants and more pollution. This result focuses on the first effect mentioned above, where the firm shifts from the high fixed-cost option of two plants to the high variable-cost option of a single plant. In case two, the disutility from pollution is still moderate, but the fixed costs are now low relative to the transportation costs (that is, making two plants more attractive). In this case, the firm continues to have plants in both countries; however, if the added tax revenue from export sales exceeds the disutility of added pollution, then both countries have an incentive to undercut in order to make the firm close its foreign plant.

The Nash equilibrium is reached with plants in both countries, but at tax levels below the non-strategic taxes. Thus the tax competition may result in the right number of firms, but too much pollution. This result focuses more on the second effect mentioned above, where low taxes in one country may induce the firm to locate in that country. In the third case, the disutility of pollution is high (but not so high as to prevent the good from being produced) and the fixed costs are also high relative to the transportation costs. In this situation, neither country wants the plant in their country (a NIMBY situation). Hence the third case has the opposite Nash equilibrium to the first one, an equilibrium with too few plants and too little pollution.

As mentioned in the introduction (section 1), environmentalists in the USA feared that free-trade agreements would cause the multinationals to move to those countries having less strict environmental regulation. This fear seems to be based on two concerns. The first is that trade barriers insulate domestic production and welfare from costly environmental regulation. The second is that it is easier for multinationals to move production abroad, thereby intensifying the effects of strict environmental regulation. In order to analyse these two concerns, Markusen (1995) develops a standard oligopoly model with two symmetric countries producing two goods. Multinationals can arise endogenously. One of the goods is produced in the imperfectly competitive sector with increasing returns to scale, and the other good is produced in the competitive sector with constant returns to scale. There are constant marginal production costs and transport costs. There are firm-specific fixed costs, and plant-specific costs in the imperfectly competitive sector, creating economies of scale and a basis for multinational production.

Markusen shows that trade barriers do in fact insulate production from the cost increase but do not insulate welfare. In other words, the favourable production effects are offset by unfavourable effects on consumers through higher prices. Markusen's study shows no support for the second concern. It is no easier for multinationals to move production abroad. Hence the presence of multinationals does not intensify the effects of strict environmental regulation. Finally, the way in which environmental regulation is implemented is very important. Regulations which impact on plant fixed costs are more easily absorbed by the exit of firms and by higher outputs by the remaining firms. Regulations which impact on marginal costs cannot easily be absorbed by production decreases, which result in larger production and welfare effects. In summary, trade liberalization increases the degree to which production is internationally relocated in response to environmental regulation. However, investment liberalization, leading to multinational firms, does not necessarily increase the production and welfare responses to costly environmental regulation.

But what if we have more than one sector? The previous literature deals only with a single sector. By introducing different industries and sectors we allow for linkages between the industries which more accurately reflect the input–output structure of the economy. This makes it possible to analyse the agglomeration of industry. Ulph and Valentini (1996) construct a model with two countries, two industries, an upstream and a downstream sector, and two firms in each industry. The upstream industry produces an intermediate input to the production of the downstream industry. Firms face constant unit costs of production and a fixed cost of locating a plant in a particular country. For the upstream sector there are constant transport costs, while transport costs for the downstream sector depend on the volume shipped. Pollution is purely domestic. To control pollution the countries use a pollution tax. Furthermore it is assumed that the countries have introduced a profit tax. Each firm is wholly owned by the shareholders located in the country in question (that is, $\alpha = 1$, where $\alpha = 0.5$ in Hoel (1994b), and $\alpha = 0$ in Rauscher (1995b) and Markusen et al. (1995)). Welfare is consumer surplus (from consumption of the downstream good), plus net-of-tax profits of the firms owned by shareholders in that country plus emission tax revenues and profit tax revenues minus pollution damage costs. In Stage 1, governments set their emission taxes and profit taxes (profit taxes are set exogenously). In Stage 2 producers choose their locations, and in Stage 3 they choose output.

In this type of model, it is possible to analyse the incentives for agglomeration. Firms in different sectors are connected to each other through the input–output relationship in the economy. This makes the demand for intermediate goods endogenous because demand depends on the location of firms. As a consequence, environmental taxes in one industry can affect other industries. If, for instance, emission taxes cause firms in one industry to relocate, they may take with them firms in other closely related industries.

Ulph and Valentini include these intersectoral linkages and show that the imposition of environmental regulation in one sector may spill over into other sectors. A negative spillover effect occurs when an emission tax causes a firm to relocate, and this may cause other firms in related sectors to move as well. However, a positive spillover effect may also occur. If a country imposes a small environmental tax, the affected firms do not necessarily relocate, and the emission tax may then attract firms in related sectors in the foreign country. This result arises because the environmental tax raises the price that downstream firms must pay for the intermediate good in both markets, and reduces the importance of transport costs of downstream goods relative to the cost of production. This causes a firm in another sector to be more concerned about proximity to sources of supply than to final customers. Moreover, such a model may also generate hysteresis effects. Hysteresis occurs when there is a threshold by which a large tax differential causes relocation which is not reversed by a small move back below that threshold. Because the equilibrium choice of plant location in Ulph and Valentini's model involves agglomeration of all firms in the same country, the strategic incentives for governments are rather similar to Hoel's (1994b) model, which uses a single industry with a single firm. Hence Ulph and Valentini derive the same three types of equilibria: (1) a tax-cutting equilibrium; (2) an asymmetric equilibrium; and (3) a NIMBY equilibrium.

4.   ECOLOGICAL DUMPING AND INTERNATIONAL TRADE

The fear of environmental capital flight or the desire to attract new business investment is not the only rationale for ecological dumping. If domestic industries are operating in international markets, it may be rational for governments to design their environmental policies so as to confer competitive advantage upon the domestic industry at the expense of competitive disadvantage abroad.

The point of departure for Conrad (1993) is that subsidies introduced to improve environmental quality may be an indirect export subsidy for the final product. Conrad shows that governments have incentives to introduce subsidies into abatement efforts, or to a heavily taxed polluting input, because this enables the domestic firm to capture a larger share of the world market.

The model consists of two countries and two competing firms located in different countries. The two countries are competitors in third-country markets. A two-stage game is played whereby the governments in Stage 1 choose emission tax rates to regulate the environmental quality. In Stage 2, firms determine the degree of abatement of their abatement technology and then choose output levels. Pollution is transboundary. The government maximizes profit of the domestic firm, minus the damage from global emissions plus or minus revenues or costs of the environmental policy. In this model Conrad first finds that the optimal non-cooperative tax rate is set below marginal damage in order to keep a greater share of the output of domestic industries. A high tax depresses domestic output and increases the revenue of the competing country.

Next, Conrad considers two kinds of subsidies: (1) a subsidy to abated emissions; and (2) a subsidy to a pollution-intensive input which is taxed by an emission tax. If the subsidy in (1) is introduced, the optimal non-cooperative tax rate is higher than the tax rate without the subsidy. The subsidy depends only on the impact of foreign gain in market share and the corresponding change in environmental damage. The firm pays a high tax (but not equal to marginal damage) and receives a subsidy as a refund for losing profit from lower market shares. Thus, for a single government, a tax-subsidy scheme increases domestic welfare and improves the global environment compared to the situation with the emission tax alone. If the subsidy in (2) is introduced, the emission tax rate need not be adjusted downward to correct two kinds of market failures. In this case, the input subsidy increases domestic exports while the emission tax restores cost efficiency in environmental policy. The conclusion is that irrespective of the type of subsidy, there are national incentives to introduce them in order to capture a larger share of the world market.

Barrett (1994b) also examines the proposition that environmental policy may be used strategically by a government to confer competitive advantage on the home-country industry at the expense of competitive advantage abroad. Barrett's model is similar to that of Conrad (1993) except that it considers standards and purely local pollution, whereas Conrad's model considers taxes and international pollution. Barrett's model involves two governments and their respective industries, which sell all their output in a third market. In a two-stage game governments move first by choosing their standards, and in the second stage firms choose their output or price.

Barrett defines the environmentally optimal standard (EOS) as one at which $MD = MC$. However, the government can depart from the EOS and set a new strategical optimal standard (SOS). At this standard, the firm can make higher profits than at the EOS standard. This set-up makes it possible to compare the EOS and the SOS. Ecological dumping exists (does not exist) if the SOS is weaker (stronger) than the EOS. Hence, in this model ecological dumping refers to a situation where $MD > MC$. Barrett shows that if the domestic industry consists of one firm, the foreign industry is imperfectly competitive, and competition in an international market is Cournot, then ecological dumping exists. However, this conclusion is not robust. If more domestic producers are introduced, the incentives to implement a lax environmental policy are reduced or reversed. If firms compete on prices and not quantities, governments have an incentive to implement a stringent environmental policy. Hence, in contrast to Conrad, Barrett's study provides little support for ecological dumping. Rather, ecological dumping increases.

Kennedy (1994) deals with the same question as Conrad and Barrett.

Kennedy's model has two countries with a symmetric oligopolistic industry with n firms. The governments choose their tax rate, and, using these tax rates, the industry equilibrium is then calculated. Unlike the models in Conrad and Barrett, the firms are selling their output in the two countries. Pollution may be local or transboundary, depending on the parameter $\alpha \in [0,1]$. If $\alpha = 1$, then pollution is transboundary, as in Conrad's model. If $\alpha = 0$, then pollution is strictly local, as in Barrett's model.

Kennedy compares the strategic pollution taxes with the efficient pollution taxes. If the strategic pollution taxes are lower than the efficient taxes, ecological dumping exists. It should be noted, however, that the efficient taxes in Kennedy's model are not first best. With two market failures (pollution and market failures) and only one instrument (pollution tax), the pollution tax is second best but is none the less efficient given the limited availability of instruments. Hence Kennedy's benchmark is not, as it is in Barrett's model, a first-best pollution tax if $MD = MC$. Kennedy's analysis shows that each country has an incentive to set its pollution taxes below the efficient tax rate. This incentive can be decomposed into a rent capture effect and a pollution shifting effect. The rent capture effect arises because each country attempts to gain a competitive advantage by undercutting the other country's tax rate in order to boost exports.

The pollution shifting effect works in the opposite direction to the rent capture effect. Here the countries raise the pollution taxes in order to transfer production and pollution to the other country. This effect vanishes if $\alpha = 1$ and pollution is transboundary, because exported pollution causes as much damage to the domestic environment as does domestic pollution. A precondition for the existence of ecological dumping is that the net effect is negative, that is, the rent capture effect exceeds the pollution shifting effect. Kennedy shows that this is in fact the case. Transboundary pollution increases the incentive for ecological dumping because a switch in production from foreign to domestic firms reduces foreign production and thereby pollution.

In Kennedy's model, incentives for ecological dumping decrease when α decreases, but they do not vanish. Even when $\alpha = 0$, where pollution is strictly local, there is an incentive for the country to implement pollution taxes below the efficient level. Kennedy's model, however, does not give a broader scope for ecological dumping than Barrett's model. On the one hand, Barrett notes that when there are oligopolies in both countries, as in Kennedy, the incentives to weaken standards are reduced and may even be reversed. On the other hand, Kennedy includes domestic consumers, which means that the government must realize that raising prices and restricting output are not only beneficial to producers, but also damaging to consumers. Thus, introducing consumers into the models reinforces the incentive for lowering pollution taxes. A comparison of Barrett's and Kennedy's models indicates that increasing the number of firms reduces the scope for ecological dumping, but if domestic consumers are introduced at the same time, it more than offsets this effect, and ecological dumping may thus well be the outcome. It should be noted that if Bertrand competition is used, more domestic consumers mitigate the case for ecological dumping.

Ulph (1997) develops a model with two identical firms each located in a separate country. There are no domestic consumers. The market structure is Cournot competition and pollution damage is entirely domestic. Hence the model differs from Kennedy's model in its absence of domestic consumers and from Barrett's model because the instrument choice is endogenized. Ulph uses a three-stage game whereby the governments in Stage 1 choose the policy instruments (taxes or standards). In Stage 2 the governments choose the level of taxes (or standards), and in Stage 3 the firm chooses output.

Ecological dumping is a possible outcome in this model. Governments in countries which export pollution-intensive goods have incentives for relaxing environmental policy. However, Ulph notes (as does Barrett) that the result is by no means robust. Allowing for a larger number of domestic producers or for Bertrand competition could reverse the conclusion and even provide incentives for governments to set too tough environmental policy. However, if domestic consumers are introduced (as in Kennedy), or if pollution damage is transboundary, incentives for ecological dumping are reinforced. Ulph also shows that the choice of policy instrument has a strategic dimension. This effect, however, is not clear. Depending on the marginal cost, the result is derived that in some cases taxes dominate standards while in other cases the reverse holds true.

5. CONCLUSION

This chapter has examined a number of recent studies dealing with environmental capital flight and ecological dumping. The analysis concentrates on literature based on imperfect competition. Perfect competition provides little support for the ecological dumping hypothesis. While it might be expected that imperfect competition would increase the scope of ecological dumping, this hypothesis is not fully confirmed in this chapter.

In duopoly models like those of Markusen et al. (1993) and Motta and Thisse (1994), firms' choice of location is in fact a function of national environmental policy. Hence the necessary condition for ecological dumping is fulfilled. High environmental taxes may actually induce the plants to (re)locate in countries with lower taxes. In some specific range, even small tax increases may have dramatic consequences for the plant configuration. The structure of fixed costs turns out to have strong implications for relocation. Welfare effects, however, are even more complex because they depend on a large number of factors which may change in opposite directions.

The presence of sunk costs means that it may not be possible for a firm to set up a new plant abroad since a part of the foreign incumbent's fixed costs are already sunk. The result is that the welfare loss is greater when the sunk costs are included. If the firm is moving, the firm in the home country becomes a monopolist. Consequently, the home country then loses the domestic firm's profit *and* a part of its consumers' surplus. Finally, it is shown that the result may not be completely negative if the producers in a country are very sensitive to environmental regulation. Countries with relatively footloose producers may do much better than countries with less footloose producers. These results are quite different from the results obtained in models with perfect competition, due to the presence of fixed costs in the models with imperfect competition. In this case, the traditional marginal analysis derived from perfect competition models is inappropriate. Marginal changes in environmental policy will lead to non-marginal changes in the allocation of capital.

The fact that environmental policy affects industry location could provide sufficient motivation for governments to lower their emission taxes in order to attract plants. The literature reviewed here shows that this may actually be the result when governments act strategically, but not the only result. In monopoly models such as those of Rauscher (1997), Markusen et al. (1995) and Hoel (1994b), strategic actions by governments may lead to emission taxes below or above the socially optimal tax. This conclusion also appears if transport costs (Markusen et al., 1995), asymmetries (Hoel, 1994b), or intersectoral linkages (Ulph and Valentini, 1996) are added. Hence the literature reviewed here indicates some support for the ecological dumping hypothesis, but it is highly dependent on specific parameter constellations. Allowing for a larger number of domestic producers or for Bertrand competition gives incentives for governments to set too tough environmental policy. But if domestic consumers are introduced, or if pollution damage is transboundary, incentives for ecological dumping are reinforced.

The general conclusion that emerges is that the literature on imperfect competition provides predictions about ecological dumping that differ from those in the literature on perfect competition. In the case of imperfect competition there may be incentives for governments to lower their environmental policy in order either to attract firms to their country or to capture market shares in international markets. This result, however, is not robust. It may also be rational for a government to implement an environmental policy which is too strict. Policy conclusions are therefore difficult to draw, but it is evident that the fear of environmental capital flight and ecological dumping is based more on conventional wisdom than on scientific evidence.

8. Commitment and fairness in environmental games

1. INTRODUCTION

It is generally believed that the presence of transboundary externalities makes a strong case for centralized decision-making and paves the way for International Environmental Agreements (IEAs). Many economic models predict, however, that IEAs will be threatened by free-riding, perhaps thereby undermining the arguments for centralized decision-making. This chapter examines free-riding behaviour in IEAs and presents two reasons why these agreements may be less vulnerable to free-riding behaviour.

In 1990, one could read that the topics of environmental and resource economics were now very cold as topics for analytical investigation, and dead as research problems (Dasgupta, 1990). Dasgupta's somewhat provocative statement implies that not much new could be developed as regards the analytical foundation of, for instance, environmental taxes. Embedded in Dasgupta's article, however, is also the view that the neoclassical approach to environmental economics has in many ways failed to explain even the basic problems. Dasgupta's statement was mainly directed to the partial analysis of economic instruments in environmental policy, and the statement does not include a distinction between *local* and *international* environmental problems. If this distinction is made, it may be that Dasgupta's statement is a bit harsh. The statement may be valid for local environmental problems, but international environmental problems are surely not 'dead' as research problems. This is evident if one makes even a brief review of the research topics in environmental economics in the first half of the 1990s.

There are two properties that distinguish international environmental problems from local environmental problems:

- *Global aggregate emissions.* In the case of international environmental problems, global aggregate emissions are at the heart of the matter. This generates a kind of contradiction: what one country emits is diminishing compared to the total emissions, but at the same time the emissions from one country affect all other countries.

Countries are thus highly interdependent, which is not the case with local environmental problems. For example, two obvious cases with a high degree of interdependence are global warming due to emissions of CO_2 and the rarefaction of the ozone layer due to emission of chlorofluorocarbons (CFCs).

- *Absence of a supranational institution.* Environmental taxes or pollution permits must be set by some kind of institution, for instance a government. In the case of international environmental problems, such an institution does not exist.[1] Environmental problems are instead managed by voluntary agreements among a group of countries. Thus environmental economics must deal with such important questions as: under what conditions are these agreements signed? How can agreements be induced? How can they be made stable?

These two circumstances have shifted the focus in environmental economics from government interventions to negotiations and coordination. These issues and problems are neither 'cold' nor 'dead', as Dasgupta stated; they are 'hot' and 'alive and kicking'.

International environmental problems have the same properties as a communally owned good. In the absence of specified property rights, there is an incentive for each individual to over-use the good in order to maximize individual welfare. This is the well-known 'tragedy of the commons' and contains one of the core issues in this chapter: it is in the common interest to agree to cooperate and reduce the consumption of common resources. Cooperative agreements are not stable, however, because every country will profit even more by free-riding. For instance, it will be in Denmark's interest to have an international agreement on reducing the world's emissions of CO_2 by introducing a tax on those emissions. But it will be even better for Denmark to withdraw from the agreement and not to introduce an emissions tax. In this way, Denmark will still benefit from improved environmental quality due to the actions taken by the other countries, but it will obtain these benefits at a lower cost than the cooperating countries. In the parlance of game theory, this can be described as the classic prisoner's dilemma, where we, for simplicity, illustrate the problem in a two-country context.

Figure 8.1 illustrates the incentives in the prisoner's dilemma in a global CO_2 agreement: if both A and B initially cooperate in a CO_2 agreement, country A will prefer to drop out, earning profits of 5 instead of 4. However, country B decides that if country A defects, B will not cooperate either, earning 1 instead of 0. This is the key point in the prisoner's dilemma: each country will prefer to defect, whatever the other country does. Thus the solution (1,1) is an equilibrium strategy for both countries.

Country B

	Cooperates in a CO_2 agreement	Defects from the CO_2 agreement
Country A Cooperates in a CO_2 agreement	4,4	0,5
Defects from the CO_2 agreement	5,0	1,1

Figure 8.1　The prisoner's dilemma in a global CO_2 agreement

The paradox is that both countries would be better off if both chose to cooperate. Put simply: the prisoner's dilemma shows that an international CO_2 agreement will either not be reached in the first place, or, if it is reached, it will inevitably be undermined by free-riding behaviour. This behaviour is the origin of the instability of the IEAs.

The solutions to this rather unfortunate conclusion are few and not easy to implement in practice. Despite this, however, more than 140 IEAs exist today (Barrett, 1991), with the Montreal Protocol for phasing out ozone-depleting substances as one of the most prominent. The Montreal Protocol was first signed in 1987 by 24 countries, but by 1995, about 140 countries had ratified the protocol. Thus, even though the prisoner's dilemma leads to non-cooperation, countries do cooperate in reality. In order to induce cooperative behaviour, the key issue is to build incentives into voluntary environmental agreements. These incentives should induce cooperative behaviour and make the coalition stable. In order to identify the incentives, it is first of all helpful to distinguish the static one-shot game from dynamic games where negotiation takes place continuously. The incentives in these two groups may be different depending upon the type of game. Second, it is important which type of regulation the game is about, for example eco-taxes, standards, emission targets and so on (Barrett, 1992a; Hoel, 1991a). Third, it can be shown that it is of major importance for international agreements whether or not the environmental issue is linked to some other policy issues (see for example, Kroeze-Gil and Folmer, 1998; Carraro and Siniscalco, 1993; Cesar and De Zeeuw, 1994). This third issue is, however, not dealt with in this chapter. Neither do we deal with dynamic games, and we do not discuss issues concerning different economic instruments.

Instead we concentrate on static games. Our point of departure is the work done by Scott Barrett (Barrett, 1990, 1992a, 1992b, 1993, 1994a). A somewhat rigid conclusion from this work is that IEAs are unavoidably undermined by free-riding and thus become very insignificant. However, IEAs do exist, and the purpose of this chapter is to elaborate on why reality contradicts (economic) theory. We do this by introducing two factors into Barrett's model which enhance the possibilities of reaching and maintaining an IEA. These two factors are commitment and fairness.

The chapter is structured as follows: in section 2, we present Barrett's (1994a) model on which we base our work. In section 3, we introduce one kind of commitment and illustrate how it affects the size of an IEA. In section 4, we present the concept of fairness in environmental policy, inspired by Rabin (1993). In section 5, we incorporate fairness into the model and again illustrate how this may actually enlarge the IEA. The concluding remarks are presented in section 6.

We should initially emphasize that our work so far is only indicative. We work with a simple version of commitment, and we have specified a very simple form of fairness. Our purpose in this chapter is to focus on the policy issues rather than the technicalities. The aim is to identify some preliminary suggestions as to how game theory can be improved and become more applicable as a policy-oriented tool.

2. BARRETT'S MODEL

The tradition of looking at IEAs from a prisoner's dilemma point of view gives a rather pessimistic outlook on the possibility of creating and maintaining IEAs.

The purpose of this section is to review briefly the conclusions from the literature on static environmental games. The model we present here is from Barrett (1994a), but work by Mäler (1989) and Hoel (1993a, 1993b, 1993c, 1994a, 1994b, 1994c) also provides some valuable insights into static environmental games. In the remaining part of this chapter, we use the Barrett (1994a) model as a point of departure for discussing the importance of commitment and fairness in IEAs.

First, it is assumed that there are N identical countries (that is, identical size and identical benefit and cost functions connected to the emission reduction). Further, assume that the benefit function can be specified as

$$B_i(Q) = b\left(aQ - \frac{Q^2}{2}\right)/N, \qquad (8.1)$$

where i is the $1 \ldots N$ countries, Q is the global emission abatement ($Q = \Sigma q_i$), and a and b are parameters, where b is the slope of the global marginal benefit function.

Country i's abatement cost function can be specified as

$$C_i(q_i) = cq_i^2/2, \qquad (8.2)$$

where c is the slope of each country's marginal abatement cost curve.

The choice of the functional forms makes it possible[2] to identify global emission abatement in the cooperative solution

$$Q_c = \frac{a \cdot N}{N + \gamma}, \qquad (8.3)$$

where $\gamma = c/b$. If the countries maximize their own net benefits, the global emission reduction in the non-cooperative Nash solution[3] will be obtained, where

$$Q_o = \frac{a}{N(1 + \gamma)}. \qquad (8.4)$$

Further, the global net benefit under full cooperation and non-cooperation is denoted Π_c and Π_o, respectively.

With this starting-point, the question arises whether or not it is possible to obtain some degree of cooperation between many countries. To answer this question, it is necessary to specify how the agreement is entered. It is assumed that the countries which do so maximize their combined net benefits under the assumption that the other countries adapt their emission abatement. It is necessary to require that the gains of being a member of an IEA are larger than those of being outside. When this is the case, the IEA is said to be stable and self-enforcing. The equilibrium fraction of signatories is denoted α^*, where $0 \le \alpha^* \le 1$ (where $\alpha = 0$ is the non-cooperative solution, and $\alpha = 1$ is the full-cooperative solution). In this framework, Barrett (1994a) analyses the possibilities for signing an IEA and the gains from cooperation. Figure 8.2 shows the size of the stable IEA for various values of c and b. It is clear that the result can be categorized as:

- $\gamma \ge 1$: the IEA consists of no more than three countries
- $\gamma < 1$: the IEA consists of more than three countries.

The intuitive explanation for the results in the first category is that if one has an environmental problem where one additional unit of abatement is very expensive and the benefits are low, the countries will be unwilling to form an IEA. This is caused by a strong incentive to free-ride due to the relatively high abatement costs. In the second category, with very high benefits accruing from one additional unit of abatement and very small costs,

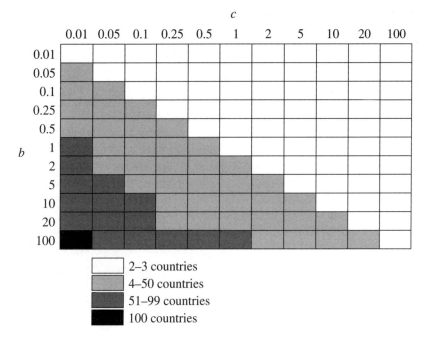

Figure 8.2   Number of signatories for various values of c *and* b, *homogeneous countries*

the countries will be very willing to form an IEA because there is a weak incentive to free-ride.

The next step is to show what happens with the global effects when the relative size of b and c is changed. Table 8.1 shows the outcomes under full cooperation (Π_c), non-cooperation (Π_o), and the outcome when an equilibrium number of countries has signed (Π_{α^*}). As in Figure 8.2, Table 8.1 illustrates that an IEA cannot consist of more than three countries when γ is large, and notice that when γ is large the difference between the full-cooperative and the non-cooperative outcome is quite significant. On the other hand, when a large IEA is possible, the IEA does not contribute to the global net benefits. The paradox here is obvious: when cooperation is possible, it does not matter; and when it does matter, cooperation is not possible.

The most interesting case is when both c and b are large. In this case, the difference between the cooperative and the non-cooperative outcome is actually quite significant, but, as noted before, when $\gamma \approx 1$ the IEA comprises no more than three countries. However, here we are on a border-line, and with a declining c, the size of the IEA will rise, and the global benefits

Table 8.1   The size of an IEA, global abatement and global net benefits with homogeneous countries

	Number of signatories out of 100 countries	Global abatement	Global net benefits
$\gamma = c/b = 100/0.01 = 10\,000$	2	$Q_o = 0.1$ $Q_* = 0.1$ $Q_c = 9.9$	$\Pi_o = 1$ $\Pi_* = 1$ $\Pi_c = 50$
$\gamma = c/b = 1/1 = 1$	2	$Q_o = 500.0$ $Q_* = 503.9$ $Q_c = 990.1$	$\Pi_o = 373\,750$ $\Pi_* = 375\,659$ $\Pi_c = 495\,050$
$\gamma = c/b = 0.01/1 = 0.01$	51	$Q_o = 990.1$ $Q_* = 990.2$ $Q_c = 999.9$	$\Pi_o = 499\,902$ $\Pi_* = 499\,903$ $\Pi_c = 499\,950$
$\gamma = c/b = 0.01/100 = 0.0001$	100	$Q_o = 999.9$ $Q_* = 1000.0$ $Q_c = 1000.0$	$\Pi_o = 49\,999\,949$ $\Pi_* = 49\,999\,950$ $\Pi_c = 49\,999\,950$

Source: Barrett (1994a), pp.885–6.

will fall. Nevertheless, it is in this case that the most promising possibilities exist for a relatively large IEA, and relatively large global net benefits.

Barrett (1993) extends his analysis to the more realistic case where the countries differ with respect to the cost and benefit parameters. However, the conclusions remain the same: it is the exception rather than the rule that the IEA consists of more than three countries. Thus the conclusion for the case with heterogeneous countries is identical to the case with homogeneous countries: *where the relative gains from cooperation are largest, cooperation is absent, and where cooperation takes place, the absolute gain to cooperation is negligible.*

As noted earlier, more than 140 IEAs exist, which at first glance seems to contradict (economic) theory. It should be noted, however, that many of the IEAs are ineffective, because it is the non-affected parties which have joined the agreement, or because the agreement is not effectively enforced. What remains is, however, that the agreements are signed and established. It would therefore be of great interest to see why the theoretical conclusions above are not the whole truth. Something is missing.

In the remaining part of this chapter we include two aspects which both increase the probabilities of signing IEAs. As noted earlier, there are a number of other aspects which also point in the same direction, where the most promising aspect is to link environmental policy to other policy areas. Here we only deal with commitment and fairness, which are taken from a large array of relevant aspects.

3. COMMITMENT

The preceding results were based on the idea that IEA must be self-enforcing, and clearly, the first results are discouraging, independent of whether the countries are homogeneous or heterogeneous. Stable coalitions consist of a small number of signatories compared to the number of potential signatories. An instrument for obtaining larger IEAs is if some countries are committed to environmental politics. It can then be shown that the committed countries can give additional countries an incentive to sign the agreement.

It is an empirical fact that some countries are focusing more on environmental issues than other countries (see for instance Andersen, 1994 for a discussion about the differences in the EU), and it is well known that some countries have taken unilateral actions to reduce emissions. This could be modelled by assuming that some countries are committed to environmental cooperation. In other words: if ten countries agree to cooperate to reduce their emissions, regardless of what other countries do, these ten countries are said to be committed. This definition of commitment is equivalent to the definition in Hoel (1991b), where he discusses the consequences of a country's 'setting a good example'. In the case of global warming, the EU countries seem to be committed to some extent, but the USA doesn't appear to be, and certainly not China, India, and so on. Of course, this commitment can take several forms. Carraro and Siniscalco (1991) use the Nash-bargaining solution for emission setting among the cooperating countries, whereas Barrett (1994a) uses maximization of net abatement benefit among cooperators. He does not consider the possibility of commitment and is in fact critical about it:

> The snag in this proposal [about the existence of a number of committed countries] . . . is that the commitment is not credible; the expanded agreement is not self-enforcing. If commitment could be made credible, then the full cooperative outcome would be easy to sustain: every country would simply commit to choose the full cooperative abatement level (q_c). (Barrett 1994a, p. 883)

We do not agree with Barrett's statement that commitment is not credible. In fact, it is our suggestion that one of the explanations of why more than 140 IEAs exist today is that commitment exists and certainly is credible. It would be nice to have a theory about conditions for commitment.

However, we do not try to provide such a theory, we simply take commitment for granted.

In order to illustrate the consequences of credible commitments, we continue with Barrett's (1994a) model. Table 8.2 illustrates the stability of a coalition consisting of four signatories. In the table α is the fraction of signatories, q_s is the abatement level of any individual signatory, q_n is the abatement level of any individual non-signatory, π_s is the net benefit of any individual signatory, and π_n is the net benefit of any individual non-signatory. Q and Π denote, as mentioned above, global abatement and global net benefits. The signatories are assumed to choose q_s in order to maximize their collective net benefits, whereas non-signatories maximize their individual net benefits. The signatories are assumed to have a Stackelberg-leader role, and the other countries are followers.

Table 8.2   Stability analysis, hypothetical example, homogeneous countries

α	q_s	q_n	π_s	π_n	Q	Π
0.0	–	8.0	–	472.0	80.0	4720.0
0.1	1.9	8.5	476.8	468.1	78.7	4690.0
0.2	4.2	8.7	474.0	466.6	78.2	4681.2
0.3	6.7	8.4	472.3	468.9	78.9	4699.4
0.4*	8.9*	7.6*	472.2*	474.9*	81.1*	4738.1*
0.5	10.5	6.3	473.7	482.5	84.2	4781.2
0.6	11.3	4.9	476.4	489.4	87.7	4816.0
0.7	11.5	3.6	479.5	494.3	91.0	4839.8
0.8	11.1	2.5	482.7	497.3	93.8	4855.9
0.9	10.5	1.6	485.4	498.8	95.9	4867.8
1.0	9.8	–	487.8	–	97.6	4878.0

Note: $N=10$, $a=100$, $b=1$, $c=0.25$.

Source: Barrett (1994a), table 1.

The equilibrium fraction of signatories ($\alpha^*=0.4$) can be found by starting at $\alpha=1.0$. Here $\Pi_s(\alpha=1.0)=487.8$, but any country could do better by withdrawing from the agreement. According to the stability definition above, a country compares the profit from taking part in the agreement with the profit from withdrawing from the agreement. Starting from a point where all countries are signatories, they obtain a profit of $\Pi_s(\alpha=1.0)=487.8$. However, if any single country leaves the agreement, it obtains a profit of $\Pi_n(\alpha=0.9)=498.8$. Clearly there is an incentive to leave the agreement. This means that an agreement consisting of ten countries is unstable. Next, by comparing the profit of $\Pi_s(\alpha=0.9)=485.4$ with $\Pi_n(\alpha=0.8)$

$= 497.3$, we see again that the agreement is unstable. Following this line of argument we end up with a stable agreement consisting of four countries. Note that none of these four countries has an incentive to leave the agreement since $\Pi_s(\alpha = 0.4) = 472.2$ is greater than $\Pi_n(\alpha = 0.3) = 468.9$.

Suppose now that only one country is committed in the sense that it would choose the value of q_s corresponding to the number of signatories, and that the country would willingly use the increase in net gain to 'bribe' the non-cooperating countries to participate.[4] At first sight, Table 8.2 seems to indicate that it is unnatural to have an agreement with one member. The reason is that the member is assumed to have the leader role in a Stackelberg game, whereas the other countries are followers. Note that the committed country would lose by trying to expand the coalition to fewer than seven members, because $\Pi_s(\alpha = 0.1) = 476.8$ is greater than $\Pi_s(\alpha = 0.6) = 476.4$. Thus the committed country would not earn a net profit if the agreement were expanded up to six countries. Further, the committed country would be unable to finance larger coalitions. If it tried to use its net gain to maintain a coalition of, say, nine members, its own net gain from the expansion ($\Pi_s(\alpha = 0.9) = 485.4 - \Pi_s(\alpha = 0.1) = 476.8$) should be distributed so that each of the other eight countries prefers to stay in the coalition rather than dropping out. However, if we have a coalition of nine members, each country could earn a profit of $\Pi_s(\alpha = 0.9) = 485.4 - \Pi_s(\alpha = 0.8) = 497.3$. The net gain from the enlarged coalition is obviously too small to bribe the uncommitted countries. In this sense, unilateral actions are not necessarily welfare increasing.

Next, consider a stable coalition (that is, with four members) where all members are committed. They would gain in total from full cooperation $4(\Pi_s(\alpha = 1.0) = 487.8 - \Pi_s(\alpha^* = 0.4) = 472.2) = 62.4$, but to compensate each new member for not leaving the agreement, it must pay the new member ($\Pi_n(\alpha = 0.9) = 498.8 - \Pi_s(\alpha = 0.9) = 487.8) = 11$, that is, in total $6*11 = 66$, which is greater than 62.4. Hence it is not possible to establish full cooperation but, using the same argument, it is possible to establish a coalition of six members, since $4(\Pi_s(\alpha = 0.6) = 476.4 - \Pi_s(\alpha^* = 0.4) = 472.2) = 16.8 > 2(\Pi_n(\alpha = 0.5) = 482.5 - \Pi_s(\alpha = 0.6) = 476.4) = 12.2$.

Using the same technique, we have calculated the maximum probable size of a coalition as a function of the number of committed countries in Table 8.3. We see that five committed countries are necessary for full cooperation, but we also see that with less than four committed countries, it is impossible to expand the coalition.

Table 8.3 illustrates the possibilities for obtaining full cooperation in the specific case of Barrett's (1994a) model. Carraro and Siniscalco (1991) use slightly different specifications of the cost and benefit functions, and they conclude that the slope of the reaction functions is of critical importance. If the reaction functions are orthogonal, or near-orthogonal, a fraction of

Table 8.3   Committed countries and the expanded coalitions

Committed countries	1	2	3	4	5	6	7	8	9	10
Size of expanded coalition	1	2	3	6	10	10	10	10	10	10

Note: The table draws on the specific example in Table 8.2.

committed countries is sufficient for expanding the coalition to full cooperation, but if the reaction functions are sufficiently sloped, then attempts
to cooperate are undermined by incentives to free-ride.

4.   FAIRNESS IN ENVIRONMENTAL POLITICS

The partial success of commitment has its limitations as in itself it does not
explain where commitment comes from. It is obvious that the committed
countries can leave the agreement with advantage. This leads to a possible
criticism of models based on countries which solely take care of their own
interests. Empirical results from negotiation games indicate that agents
even in static games make choices which contradict self-interest alone. This
is documented in the extensive literature on public-good provision (see for
example, Marwell and Ames, 1981), and in the literature on ultimatum
games (see for example, Thaler, 1988).

   One possible specification could be that one or more countries has global
gains as an argument in its welfare function. Another insight is achieved by
introducing the concept of 'fairness equilibria', where the individual countries in their investments want to sacrifice their own profit in order to
benefit others or to sacrifice their own profit to hurt others. In relation to
environmental agreements, the emission abatement in country i depends
positively on the emission abatement in country j. Countries will hereafter
do their part of the job, if enough of the others do theirs as well. In such a
game, various Nash equilibria may occur. In a cooperative equilibrium,
countries may forego profit-increasing moves if that would hurt others who
'behave well'.

   In Rabin (1993), a model is set up where the individual agents take care
of things other than their own material interests. A simple version is a
model where the agents have altruistic preferences, that is, they are worried
about payoffs to others. The problem is that individual agents are typically
not altruists in general. Altruism is more complex; many agents want to be
altruistic towards others who treat them well, but will be motivated to hurt
those who try to hurt them.

Rabin constructs a game in which two players, beyond the material payoffs, worry about how the other player acts depending on that other player's motives. In the following, the model will be used in an economy where there are two agents who can enter into an environmental agreement (and observe it), or not. As the profits of an environmental agreement are collective and the costs individual, conventional game theory suggests that this will end up in a prisoner's dilemma situation (unless the collective profits are very large in relation to the individual costs), that is, a payoff matrix with the structure as shown in Figure 8.3. In the figure, x represents a scale variable for material payoff. A change in x changes the scale of payoffs without changing the structure of the game.

Player 2

		Cooperation in an agreement	No agreement
Player 1	Cooperation in an agreement	$4x,4x$	$0,5x$
	No agreement	$5x,0$	x,x

Figure 8.3   Environmental game for two agents

Following Rabin, two expectations are crucial here:

- what player 1 expects player 2 to choose;
- what player 1 expects player 2 expects player 1 to choose.

If we assume that player 1 expects that player 2 chooses 'no agreement', and that player 1 thinks that player 2 thinks that 1 plays 'no agreement', then player 2, by having chosen agreement, could have benefited player 1 considerably. As player 2 is not expected to do that, player 1 has no particular reason to be nice to player 2, that is, there is every reason to believe that the result will be the usual prisoner's dilemma solution ('no agreement', 'no agreement').

If, alternatively, we assume that player 1 expects that player 2 chooses agreement, and that player 1 thinks that player 2 thinks that player 1 chooses agreement, then player 2 is nice to player 1, as player 2 relinquishes $1x$ so that player 1 can win $4x$.

It is natural to believe that player 1 would consider rewarding player 2's kindness by giving up the materially dominating strategy and instead use the materially dominated strategy. Rabin gives a specific definition of the concept of kindness and uses this as an argument in the utility function of the individuals. In Rabin's specification, the immaterial aspects will dominate by small material payoffs (small values of x in Figure 8.3), while the immaterial aspects are dominated if the material payoffs are sufficiently large (large values of x in Figure 8.3).

Notice the central role of expectations: player 1's payoffs do not depend simply on the actions taken, but also on player 1's beliefs about player 2's motives. Rabin shows that it is impossible to model these emotions (immaterial payoffs) by transforming immaterial payoffs into material payoffs.

The force of Rabin's model is that it makes several equilibria possible, which appears to be a good description of reality.[5] Sometimes the game ends up in a negative equilibrium, where the material payoff is low, and where the agents get their negative expectations to the counterpart confirmed. Other times the game ends more satisfactorily, that is, the players realize a high material payoff and enjoy the reciprocity of kindness.

In most IEAs there are many participants and, due to the public-good character of environmental externalities, it is not possible to be nice to someone and less nice to others, so that countries are either nice to everybody, or to nobody (unless environmental political instruments are supplemented with other instruments). It is natural to assume that a country will join an agreement if it expects that sufficient other countries are joining the agreement.

We assume that a country expects $\tilde{n}$ countries to enter into and observe the agreement, and where $B(\tilde{n})$ is the material profit without participation and $B(\tilde{n}) - A$ is the material profit with participation, where A is the loss in net benefits by entering the agreement.

Assume now that there is a loss f by not signing, when $\tilde{n}$ is large (and a profit, when $\tilde{n}$ is small), that is:

$$f(0)>0\,,f(n)<0\,,f^{i}(\tilde{n})<0$$

This means that a country experiences a loss by staying inside the agreement if it expects many other countries to participate. This loss presents the stigma of not being a part of a generally accepted agreement. In the same way, the country experiences a profit if it stays out of an agreement which very few countries sign. If $|f(\tilde{n})|>A$, the country will sign the agreement, if it expects that $\tilde{n}$ countries will do so. If it is assumed that all countries are identical, they will all sign.

In more realistic conditions, the countries are different in several respects. It cannot therefore be expected that all countries will necessarily sign. This has the derivative effect that one might fear that some of the countries which would have signed, if other countries had signed, now withdraw, which further undermines the accession to the agreement (for example, nuclear testing). In such situations, a diversified treatment of diversified countries will not only impel the individual countries to sign, but will also prevent derivative effects from the fact that some withdraw.

Above it is assumed that the possibilities of action are two-sided. It is more realistic to look at the possibilities as continuous (degrees of an environmental improvement). In future work, it will undoubtedly be fruitful to combine Rabin's approach (adequately modified) with Barrett's excellent analyses of IEAs. In section 5 below, we have made a small beginning in order to illustrate some initial results.

5.   INCORPORATING FAIRNESS INTO BARRETT'S MODEL

How would Barrett's rather pessimistic results be affected if we incorporated fairness into the model?

When analysing this, we use Table 8.2 above, where a coalition consisting of four countries is self-enforcing. In addition to the material payoffs, countries are concerned about their behaviour relative to others.

Barrett (1990) touches on this issue in his discussion about morality in non-cooperative environmental games. As an illustration, he refers to the deliberations of the House of Commons Environment Committee (1984), recommending that the UK join the Thirty Per Cent Club:

> As our inquiry has progressed, the stance of the United Kingdom has become increasingly isolated by its refusal to legislate to reduce SO_2 and NO_x emissions. . . . The other European nations are reducing their emissions, so we should, too. (Barrett, 1990, pp. 73–4)

The argument seems to be a moral one, unrelated to material payoffs. It is the committee's opinion that the UK ought to reduce its emissions. This argument captures exactly Rabin's idea of fairness.

In order to incorporate this into Barrett's model, we assume that this concern about other countries' behaviour is captured in the f function, where two alternative specifications are used:

$$f_1(n) = 10 - 2n, f_2(n) = 20 - 4n$$

The f function is the loss from not joining an agreement and should be added to the Π_s column in Table 8.2. This gives Table 8.4. Hence Π_n^1 now denotes the non-cooperative global net benefit when fairness is incorporated ($\Pi_n^1 = \Pi_n + f_1(n)$, and $\Pi_n^2 = \Pi_n + f_2(n)$). $F(n)$ is increasing in n, that is, the more countries that sign the agreement, the larger the loss from not joining the agreement.

Table 8.4　Global net benefits with fairness incorporated

α	Π_s	Π_n^1	Π_n^2
0.0	–	482.0	492.0
0.1	476.8	486.1	474.1
0.2	474.0	472.6	478.6
0.3	472.3	472.9	476.9
0.4	472.2	476.9	478.9
0.5	473.7	482.5	482.5
0.6	476.4	487.4	485.4
0.7	479.5	490.3	486.3
0.8	482.7	491.3	485.3
0.9	485.4	490.8	482.8
1.0	487.8	–	–

Note:　The table is based on the specific example in Table 8.3.

Consider the case with $f_1(n)$ and consider the coalition with four countries. Since $\Pi_n^1 > \Pi_s$ (472.9 > 472.2), it is no longer stable. In fact, it is seen that no coalition is stable with the new payoff structure. For example, a full coalition is not stable, since $\Pi_n(\alpha = 0.9) = 490.8 > \Pi_s(\alpha = 1.0) = 487.8$.

On the other hand, if the non-material part has a higher weight, as in $f_2(n)$, it is seen that full cooperation is a stable coalition, since $\Pi_s(\alpha = 1.0) = 487.8 > \Pi_n(\alpha = 0.9) = 482.8$; that is, if a country expects all others to be signatories, it will join the agreement.

If a country expects all others not to sign an agreement, it will choose to act non-cooperatively. In that sense, it is possible to have two equilibria and, as Rabin notes, sometimes cooperation is obtained, and sometimes it fails. This seems to describe IEAs very well. In some cases IEAs are seen as codifications of what the countries would have done anyway, but the agreements may also be seen as an attempt to end up in the cooperative equilibrium by ensuring support from all important countries. In fact, many treaties are contingent on a certain number of countries signing the treaty.

The model including fairness allows for multiple equilibria without any explanation of which equilibrium is realized. This can be considered a weakness, but also a challenge, since it would be nice to identify factors increasing the probability of successful cooperation. Happily, recent research addresses these questions in relation to common-pool resources (Ostrom et al., 1994). They study how individuals have been able to overcome the 'tragedy of the commons'. They conclude that players both in experimental designs and field studies are able to develop stocks of social capital, such as trust and norms of reciprocity, that tend to be self-reinforcing and cumulative, especially when the players are able to communicate, and when they have relatively symmetric interests. On the other hand, absence of these trusts is also self-reinforcing. In Sethi and Somanathan (1996) it is shown that cooperation can be stable against invasion by narrowly self-interested behaviour. With respect to IEAs there are no serious problems with communication, but different countries have very different interests, due to differences in income levels, location and availability of natural resources. These differences lead to different criteria for reductions in CO_2 emissions, which could serve as focal points for negotiations, ranging from emissions allocated according to the population size or according to GNP. This complicates the use of the fairness concept, since signing one type of agreement might be considered more or less fair than signing another agreement. A rich country could sign an agreement with associated net costs relative to staying outside the agreement without being considered fair, if the agreement is based on emission entitlements related to GNP.

In many models, as for instance Carraro and Siniscalco's (1991) and Barrett's (1994a), a self-reinforcing coalition consists of two or three countries. Do these results have a counterpart in real-life IEAs? Probably not. An explanation could be that two or three countries do not like to help other countries even though it is in their own (self-)interest. As an old proverb reads:

Next to own fortune, the misfortune of others is not to be despised.

6. CONCLUSION

This chapter has introduced to a subset of the literature on international environmental policy. Common to the literature used here is the extensive use of game theory. Game theory is strong as an analytical and theoretical tool when it comes to analysing the dynamic in strategic interactions when countries are forming IEAs. However, we think that when it comes to real negotiations and cooperation, there are so many factors that influence the games that it seems evident that game theory is unable to describe more than small parts of the process. Additionally, game theory still suffers from the paradigm that it uses archetypical games such as the prisoner's dilemma, the battle of the sexes, or the chicken game. Like game theory in general, these games serve very well as analytical and theoretical instruments, but are very distant from reality. Much work still has to be done in applying the game structure in a more realistic way.

It is well known from the literature that commitment enhances the success of IEAs. This we have illustrated here by introducing a very simple form of commitment into one of Barrett's models. This shows how an increasing number of committed countries increases the size of the IEA and finally is able to establish full cooperation. However, commitment does not just come out of thin air, and future research will have to examine how different forms of commitment affect the IEAs.

Further, we have tried to apply Rabin's (1993) ideas of fairness to environmental games. This application turns the focus away from the rather simple Nash equilibria to the more realistic fairness equilibria where countries are rewarding the 'good ones' and punishing the 'bad ones'. The work so far is, however, very preliminary, but it seems promising to combine Barrett's and Hoel's work with Rabin's ideas. We have introduced a very simple form of fairness into Barrett's model and show that if the countries are highly concerned about the welfare of other countries, full cooperation may be established.

In short, we argue here that fairness is a new aspect which has to be added to the list of different aspects, such as commitment and issue-linkage, which all increase the size and stability of IEAs.

NOTES

1. The United Nations does not have a mandate to introduce environmental taxes, and the European Union is limited to only 15 countries.
2. The derivations of (8.3) and (8.4) are given in the Appendix.
3. Barrett (1994a) denotes this 'thew open access solution'; this is the reason for the 'o' subscript.
4. This is equivalent to the idea of side payments.
5. Depending on viewpoint, this lack of predictability could be seen as a weakness.

APPENDIX

Derivation of global emission abatement in the cooperative solution (8.3).

Since the N countries are assumed to be identical, we can write the global optimization problem as:

$$\text{Max}_{qi} \quad b\left(aQ - \frac{Q^2}{2}\right) - Nc\frac{q_i^2}{2}. \tag{A.1}$$

The first-order conditions are:

$$ba - bQ - Ncq_i = 0. \qquad i = 1, \ldots, N \tag{A.2}$$

Solving these equations, we obtain:

$$Q = \frac{QN}{N + \gamma}, \tag{A.3}$$

where $\gamma = c/b$.

Derivation of global emission abatement in the non-cooperative solution (8.4).

The non-cooperative solution can be computed by assuming that each country chooses its abatement level given the abatement levels of all other countries; that is, each country solves the following problem:

$$\text{Max}_{qi} \quad \frac{b\left(aQ - \frac{Q^2}{2}\right)}{N} - C\frac{q_i^2}{2} \qquad i = 1, \ldots, N \tag{A.4}$$

The first-order conditions are:

$$\frac{b(a - Q)}{N} - C_{q_i} = 0. \qquad i = 1, \ldots, N \tag{A.5}$$

Solving the equations, we obtain:

$$Q_0 = \frac{a}{N(1 + \gamma)}. \tag{A.6}$$

9. Conclusion

How can environmental regulatory authority be allocated most efficiently among federal and state governments? There are no easy answers to this question, even though it has been a central issue in environmental federalism research for 25 years (see, for example, Revesz, 1992, 1997; Oates, 1994, 1998, 1999; Oates and Schwab, 1988, 1989; List and Gerking, 2000). The driving force behind this book has been to find the answers. It is, however, hard to reach a general conclusion because the answer depends on so many things.

The public finance literature provides a standard answer: if the economy is perfectly competitive and distortion free and if available tax instruments are unconstrained, then both regional and national governments have incentives to implement efficient environmental policies. But in a second-best world with initial distortions locally determined, environmental regulations may be suboptimal when jurisdictions compete to attract capital (List and Gerking, 2000).

For several reasons this standard answer is much too simple. First, the advantages of competition in the private sector are well understood. In the public sector, however, the implications of competition are less clear. Two divergent strands in the public finance literature point in opposite directions. The first strand argues that competition among governments leads to distorted outcomes (see, for example, Cumberland, 1979, 1981), while the other strand argues that such competition is efficiency-enhancing (see, for example, Tiebout, 1956). When competition promotes efficiency and when it is detrimental to social welfare is still an unresolved question. Second, when political institutions are included in the analysis, things become murkier. The normative analysis in the public finance literature asks questions such as: what is the potential for interjurisdictional competition? Does the potential for interjurisdictional competition justify central governments in implementing and enforcing environmental regulations? Does interjurisdictional competition enhance social welfare? Answers to these questions are based on economic efficiency and thus may help to identify the optimal level of authority. They tell us little, however, about the actual patterns of regulation that are likely to develop in federal systems, because these are determined by politics, not efficiency.[1] Moreover, if we accept that agents (that is, governments) in a federal system have other factors than self-interest in their utility function, things may change. Third, the relations and interactions between central and local governments are complex and contingent upon each other. This makes the question not so much about either/or, but more about sharing competence at both governmental levels.

This book examined how these three modifications affect the optimal institutional arrangements for pollution control in federal systems. The first part of the book focused on aspects of the second point above. These chapters examined how a political system, such as the EU, has shaped the concept of environmental federalism. The second part challenged the standard answers from public finance in different ways, and analysed the first point above. Chapters 6 and 7 examined whether capital does relocate in response to changes in environmental regulations, and under what circumstances governments may engage in interjurisdictional competition. Chapter 5 examined the third point above by examining cooperation between central and local governments in controlling local pollutants in a federal system. Despite the presence of local pollutants, central government nevertheless plays a central role, because it provides needed information to local government. Finally, the last chapter examined how international environmental cooperation is affected if we allow governments to maximize aspects other than self-interest. Below, the results will be briefly summarized, structured around the two parts.

Chapter 2 examined how the Treaty of the European Union limits Member States' possibilities to enact environmental regulations that are more stringent than Community measures. Environmental policy in the Community can be based on two different articles in the Treaty. An environmental measure affecting both the internal market and the environment should be based on Article 95 EC if the main aim of the measure is to improve the internal market and reduce distortions of competition. 'Genuine' environmental measures should be based on Article 175 EC. It makes a difference which legal basis an environmental measure has. Article 175 EC aims at minimum harmonization, allowing Member States to maintain or introduce more stringent protective measures. These measures must, however, be compatible with the Treaty, and must constitute neither a means of arbitrary discrimination nor a disguised restriction on trade between Member States. The purpose of minimum harmonization is to ensure a certain minimum level of environmental quality and to avoid a situation whereby Member States introduce less stringent protective measures in order to gain a comparative advantage. Article 95 EC aims at complete harmonization, and, in principle, does not allow Member States to maintain more stringent protective measures unless they can be justified on grounds mentioned in the environmental guarantee.[2]

The Danish Bottles Case is a good example of how more stringent protective national measures may affect the internal market. The case showed that there must be a balance between the internal market and environmental protection, even if, in achieving this balance, a high level of environmental protection is reduced. In other words, environmental protection is a legitimate objective which can justify certain obstacles to the internal market, but Member States are not necessarily allowed to achieve the highest level of environmental protection.

The Danish Bottles Case is an example of an area without common rules in the Community. If these are harmonized, a Member State has some possibility of maintaining or introducing more stringent protective measures than a harmonized measure adopted under Article 95 EC. This possibility is defined by the environmental guarantee, which was introduced to ensure that Member States did not lose sovereignty over their respective environmental policies; that is, a Member State voted down in the Council would not be forced to lower its environmental standards. The environmental guarantee was introduced in the SEA in 1987, but clarified and enlarged by the Amsterdam Treaty in 1997. First, in the SEA it was possible only to maintain national measures. With the Amsterdam Treaty it also became possible for Member States to introduce new measures. Second, in the SEA the environmental guarantee applied only to Council directives. The Amsterdam Treaty has determined that it also applies to Commission directives. Third, in the SEA, a Member State intending to apply the environmental guarantee was required to have voted against the harmonized measure. This is no longer required in the Amsterdam Treaty. In addition, the Amsterdam Treaty expands the Parliament's veto-power to cover measures adopted on the basis of Article 175, and it has become easier for the Parliament to use this power. In other words, the Amsterdam Treaty has expanded the framework for environmental policy in the Community. The amendments to the environmental guarantee have increased Member States' possibilities to apply protective measures more stringent than the harmonized measures.

Chapter 3 examined how subsidiarity has affected the division of environmental powers between different governmental layers in the EU. Subsidiarity was introduced in 1992 by the Maastricht Treaty and is defined by Article 5 EC. It determines an ambiguous balance between proximity of government and efficiency of Community action. A literal reading of Article 5 EC results in Community action being abandoned even where the envisaged Community action would produce clear benefits compared to action by the Member States. This may explain why Community institutions have interpreted subsidiarity as a test of comparative efficiency. Would the Community or the Member States achieve the goal most efficiently? This interpretation reduces the ambiguities but may be criticized as sacrificing proximity of government to the altar of efficiency. The Community institutions' interpretation contains a very low threshold with regard to justifying the need for Community action. It is difficult to find any examples of environmental policy measures where there are no interstate spillovers involved or risks of distortion of competition.

The development of Community legislation in the 1990s has been in accordance with the Commission's intentions to 'do less but do it better'. Subsidiarity has had the effect that the number of Commission proposals, particularly proposals for new legislation, has decreased quite rapidly. Following this drop in proposals, the number of adopted instruments should be expected to drop after 1994. This has also occurred, but the number of adopted instruments has started to increase again, especially in the internal market and the environment. This increase in the last couple of years may indicate that after a 'subsidiarity shock' in 1992–94, the Community is on its way back to 'business as usual'.

Subsidiarity means that the directive should be preferred to the regulation. It was demonstrated in Chapter 3 that the Commission has not been successful in achieving this. On the contrary, the number of adopted directives has actually decreased after 1993. Moreover, compared to regulations and decisions, the relative importance of directives has also decreased. Hence the proportion of the most binding instruments (regulations and decisions) has increased.

Chapter 4 examined the relationship between the public finance literature and subsidiarity. In the public finance literature it is argued that a decentralized authority may have an advantage over a centralized authority in that it can better tailor environmental policies to the particular circumstances of individual regions. Therefore varying endowments, preferences and cultural traditions call for a considerable degree of decentralization of environmental policy in the Community. However, a decentralized approach may be inappropriate in the presence of transboundary externalities, scale economies or relatively homogeneous endowments and preferences. In these cases centralized government should be preferred.

Subsidiarity does not, however, determine such a clear rule for how powers should be exercised in the Community. Rather, subsidiarity requires that the Commission examine the efficiency of Community action compared to action by the Member States. In this examination, arguments in favour of Community action and action by the Member States are identified. From the way in which subsidiarity has been applied, and from the recitals of the directives, it is possible to identify four groups of arguments for Community action: (1) transboundary externalities; (2) prevention of unequal competition; (3) free movement of goods; and (4) general concern about the environment and human health. Economic theory and subsidiarity have a lot in common in their arguments for Community action. However, there are also major differences. The economic approach examines whether the powers should be placed at a Community level or the level of the Member States. Subsidiarity, on the other hand, involves a mixture of powers at different levels. A regulatory system with harmonized target standards and differentiated emission standards may combine the advantages of central rules with the advantages of decision-making by Member States. In such a system, the Community can set the necessary rules in order to guarantee the citizens of Europe a minimum level of environmental and health protection, and the differentiated emission standards may guarantee optimal specificity and at the same time avoid, for instance, incomplete internalization of externalities.

The revision of Community water policy legislation in light of subsidiarity has been carried out in a way which corresponds quite closely to this system. This is most clearly expressed in the proposed drinking water directive and bathing water directive, which state that the Community should only set objectives that are of universal relevance, that is, objectives for which the preferences do not vary between different areas, since they are essential to human health and based on scientific knowledge. This means that the Community should set minimum standards for water quality and leave it to the Member States to choose the means to reach those objectives. The Commission has developed a list of seven questions which must be answered to justify a proposal. The Commission's responses to the Community water policy show that they contain a low threshold with regard to the assessment of the need for Community action. It has been quite easy to justify that the action involves a transboundary element, but the documentation proving that the transboundary elements are significant has been weak. Moreover, many benefits of Community action have been difficult to quantify, and the costs of inaction have proven to be equally difficult to estimate. Thus the degree to which a proposal is seen to comply with subsidiarity seems to depend to a larger extent on the degree to which Member States are allowed to choose the means, and to a lesser extent on the seven subsidiarity questions.

The chapters in the second half of this book scrutinize the standard result from public finance in different ways. Chapter 5 challenges the result that central governments should let local governments control local externalities. This result is based on the assumption that information is perfect and symmetrical. But what if the central authority possesses private information which ideally should be used by the local authority to design environmental policies? This situation occurs in many cases in both the USA and in the EU. Environmental competences have been delegated to the local authorities, but the central authority still plays a part because it possesses relevant information. The central authority may be better informed about, say, scientific aspects related to changes in environmental quality and human health. If this is the case, the local authorities should be induced to make use of central information. A simple transmission of information from the central to the local level may not always be possible.

Chapter 5 shows that in order to overcome these problems, the central authority can introduce a grant-in-aid system that induces the local author-ity to take central authority information into account and combine it with local information. This system should be flexible so that the local author-ity is induced to use a weighted combination of local and central informa-tion. At one extreme, the central authority is highly uncertain of the environmental and health effects of a specific pollutant. In this case, the tax subsidy scheme may be designed to allow local information to play an essential role in the environmental policy. At the other extreme, the central authority is quite certain that a specific pollutant must not exceed a certain limit. In this case, the tax subsidy scheme is designed to allow local infor-mation little influence on environmental policy. Thus the central authority could, in principle, use a 'forcing contract', but since it recognizes that its information is imperfect, it will use a flexible grant-in-aid system involving a weighted combination of local and central estimates. The weight should reflect the relative quality of the two estimates. If the central authority is weighting its estimate higher (lower) than its quality indicates, we could call the system relatively over-centralized (under-centralized), even though the competence is delegated to the local level.

Chapters 6 and 7 examine interjurisdictional competition. This is done first by analysing whether environmental regulations affect economic activ-ity, and second, by analysing under which circumstances interjurisdictional competition may occur.

Chapter 6 presents an overview of theoretical and empirical work exam-ining whether environmental regulations affect international trade and capital movements. The literature on the theory of environmental capital flight departs from the general Heckscher–Ohlin (HO) model of interna-tional trade and from models of international capital movements. In the HO model, international trade is explained by differences in factor endow-ments. The model predicts that the relative prices of goods converge, which leads to the convergence of relative factor prices. According to the theory of international capital movements, in the absence of trade, capital relo-cates internationally on the basis of marginal return. Consequently, factor prices converge. The simplest possible model of international capital move-ments with environmental effects included ignores consumption external-ities and external effects on production. In this model, the result is that a country repels mobile capital by imposing a restrictive environmental policy. In a more realistic model, however, with consumption externalities and external effects on production, results become ambiguous. No clear-cut relation between the strictness of environmental policy and capital movement is found here. The same is true for the HO model of international trade. Trade models are more complicated than models with international capital movements because the former include at least two commodities. If environmental policy is introduced in the simplest possible trade model, the standard HO result is obtained: the country well endowed with environmental resources exports the environmentally intensive produced good. In more realistic models with different technologies or external effects on production, the impact of stricter environmental policy on trade flows becomes ambiguous and dependent on specific parameter constellations.

Empirical studies also gave mixed results. Leontief-based approaches conclude that more strict environmental policy has not generated a comparative disadvantage. On the contrary, some studies found that more strict environmental policy may result in a comparative advantage. Nor did the empirical studies using the HO model find much support for the claim that strict environmental policy in a country has a negative influence on the country's exports. By using regression analysis, where the dependent variable is trade flows and the stringency of environmental policy is one of the explanatory variables, the studies showed that the environmental policy coefficient is in most cases insignificant. Empirical research with respect to international capital movement did not provide much evidence for the hypothesis that a more strict environmental policy has affected international capital movements. However, there is some evidence that less developed countries (LDCs) have a growing share of toxic industrial production. Unfortunately, it is not clear whether changes in environmental policy have induced this change. Hence the general conclusion that emerges from the literature on international trade and capital movements is that neither the theoretical nor the empirical analysis supports trade effects and large-scale capital flight as a response to more strict environmental policies.

Conclusions in Chapter 6 were based on studies assuming perfect competition. It might be expected that imperfect competition could increase the scope for environmental capital flight, and thereby also for ecological dumping. This was examined in Chapter 7. Contrary to the situation with perfect competition, the conclusion from the duopoly models reviewed was that firms' choice of location is a function of the state's environmental policy. High environmental taxes in a country may actually induce firms to locate plants in countries with lower taxes. In some specific range, even small tax increases may have dramatic consequences for the plant configuration.

However, the welfare effects are ambiguous. They are much more complex because they depend on a large number of factors which may change in opposite directions. The structure of fixed costs turns out to have strong implications for relocation. The presence of sunk costs makes it impossible for a firm to set up a new plant abroad since a part of the foreign incumbent's fixed costs is already sunk. As a consequence, the welfare loss is greater when the sunk costs are included. In addition to the loss of the domestic firm's profit, the home country also loses a part of its consumers' surplus because the foreign firm is now a monopolist. Moreover, it may not be so bad if the producers in a country are very sensitive to environmental regulation ('footloose' producers). Countries with relatively 'footloose' producers may do much better than countries with less 'footloose' producers. These results are quite different from the results obtained in models with perfect competition. The reason is the presence of fixed costs in models with imperfect competition. In this case, the traditional marginal analyses from the perfect competition models are inappropriate. Marginal changes in environmental policy will lead to non-marginal changes in the allocation of capital.

The fact that differences in environmental policies affect firms' choice of location provides a good reason for governments to lower their emission taxes in order to attract plants. The literature reviewed here showed that this may actually be the result when governments act strategically, but it is not the only result. The monopoly models reviewed show that strategic actions by governments may lead to emission taxes below or above the socially optimal tax. Thus it may be rational for a country to lower its environmental standards in order to attract business investment. It may also, however, be rational for a country to increase its environmental standards in order to drive the polluting firm out of the country. This conclusion also appears if transport costs are added, if countries differ, for example in their valuation of the environment, or if there are intersectoral linkages. Hence the literature reveals some support for the ecological dumping hypothesis, but it is highly dependent on specific parameter constellations. Allowing for a larger number of domestic producers or for Bertrand competition gives incentives for governments to set too tough environmental policy. If domestic consumers are introduced, however, or if pollution damage is transboundary, incentives for ecological dumping are reinforced.

The general conclusion is that the literature on imperfect competition provides a range of predictions about ecological dumping from the literature on perfect competition. There may be incentives for governments to lower their environmental policy in order to either attract firms to their country or to capture market shares in international markets. This result, however, is not robust. It may also be rational for a government to implement an environmental policy which is too strict.

Basic economic reasoning argues that IEAs are undermined by free-riding. This is challenged in Chapter 8, where commitment and fairness are introduced as two concepts that reduce free-riding behaviour. An international environmental problem has the same properties as a communally owned good and is therefore subject to 'the tragedy of the commons': it is in the common interest to agree to cooperate and reduce consumption of common resources. Cooperative agreements are not stable, however, because every country will profit even more by free-riding. For instance, it will be in a country's interest to have an international agreement on reducing the world's emission of CO_2, perhaps by introducing a CO_2 tax. But it would be even better for the country to withdraw from the agreement and not introduce the tax. In this way, the country would still benefit from improved environmental quality due to the actions taken by the other countries, but it would obtain these benefits at a lower cost than the cooperating countries. Despite this, there exist more than 140 IEAs. Thus the reality seems to contradict the basic view. One explanation could be that the basic view generally assumes that governments behave like rational individuals who maximize their own welfare. By introducing commitment and fairness in the analysis a more sophisticated description of governments' behaviour is obtained. Moreover, commitment and fairness may be some of the explanation for the fact that countries seems to participate in voluntary IEAs.

A group of countries is said to be committed if they agree to reduce emissions regardless of what other countries do. This is equivalent to the situation where a country is a 'forerunner' or is 'setting a good example'. If this group were expanded, a net gain would be generated because a larger group of countries can abate more pollution. This net gain could be used to expand the coalition even more by making side payments, inducing non-cooperative countries to cooperate. The more committed countries, the more net gains and the larger the coalition. At some point, where a sufficiently large number of countries are committed, full cooperation can be obtained.

Fairness was defined as a situation where a country's behaviour is partly determined by how 'fair' the country believes other countries are. The country may be willing to sacrifice its own profit in order to reward another country that 'behaves well', or it would be willing to forego its own profit in order to hurt countries that do not 'behave well'. In other words, if a country believes that other countries will enter an IEA, it may refrain from free-riding and choose to enter the IEA. However, if the country believes that other countries will not cooperate in an IEA, it will choose not to cooperate in order to 'punish' the non-cooperating countries. Hence, if fairness is introduced, it imposes a loss on a country which is not part of an IEA in which many countries are expected to cooperate. It also imposes a loss on a country which is part of an IEA in which few countries are expected to cooperate. This mechanism leads either to the formation of large IEAs or to the situation where no IEA is signed. In this way, fairness allows for multiple equilibria without accounting for which equilibrium is realized. This can be considered as either a weakness or a challenge, since it would be nice to identify those factors which increase the probability of successful cooperation. None the less, fairness may be one of the reasons that large IEAs can become stable and successful.

In conclusion, the question of how to allocate environmental regulatory authority efficiently among federal and state governments is still unresolved after this book was written – perhaps even more so. The main conclusion from the book is that answers from public finance are not as clear and straightforward as they appear. Federal systems are political systems and these affect the allocation of environmental regulatory authority in a way that cannot be understood in merely economic efficiency terms. The most fruitful way to go in the search for better answers is probably a way that combines law, economics and political science.

NOTES

1. Elliot et al. (1985) and Rose-Ackerman (1981) provide some good insights into the positive theory of environmental federalism.
2. Article 95, paras 4–10.

References

Andersen, Mikael Skou (1994), 'From Narvik to Naples: Environmental Policy in an Enlarged European Union', paper presented at the conference 'Governing Our Environment', Copenhagen, 17–18 November 1994.

Asako, K. (1979), 'Environmental Pollution in an Open Economy', *Economic Record*, **55**: 359–67.

Bär, S. and R.A. Krämer (1998), 'European Environmental Policy after Amsterdam', *Journal of Environmental Law*, **10**: 315–30.

Barrett, Scott (1990), 'The Problem of Global Environmental Protection', *Oxford Review of Economic Policy*, **6**: 68–79.

Barrett, Scott (1991), 'Economic Analysis of International Environmental Agreements: Lessons for a Global Warming Treaty', in OECD, *Climate Change: Selected Economic Topics*, Paris: OECD.

Barrett, Scott (1992a), 'Free-rider Deterrence in a Global Warming Convention', in OECD, *Convention on Climate Change. Economic Aspects of Negotiations*, Paris: OECD.

Barrett, Scott (1992b), 'International Environmental Agreements as Games', in Rüdiger Pethig, *Conflicts and Cooperation in Managing Environmental Resources*, Berlin: Springer-Verlag.

Barrett, Scott (1993), 'Heterogeneous International Environmental Agreements', CSERGE Working Paper, University of East Anglia and University College London.

Barrett, Scott (1994a), 'Self-Enforcing International Environmental Agreements', *Oxford Economic Papers*, **46**: 878–94.

Barrett, S. (1994b), 'Strategic Environmental Policy and International Trade', *Journal of Public Economics*, **54**: 325–38.

Baumol, W.J. (1971), *Environmental Protection, International Spillovers, and Trade*, Stockholm: Almkvist & Wicksell.

Baumol, W.J. and W.E. Oates (1988), *The Theory of Environmental Policy*, 2nd edn, Cambridge: Cambridge University Press.

Becker, Randy and Vernon Henderson (2000), 'Effects of Air Quality Regulation on Polluting Industries', *Journal of Political Economy*, **108**: 379–421.

Beghin, J. and M. Potier (1997), 'Effects of Trade Liberalization on the Environment in the Manufacturing Sector', *The World Economy*, **20**(4): 435–56.

Bermann, G.A. (1994), 'Taking subsidiarity seriously: Federalism in the European Union and the United States', *Columbia Law Review*, **94**: 331–456.

Birdsall, N. and D. Wheeler (1992), 'Trade Policy and Industrial Pollution in Latin America: Where are the Pollution Havens?', in P. Low (ed.), *International Trade and the Environment*, World Bank Discussion Papers 159, Washington: World Bank.

Braden, J.B. and S. Proost (1997), *The Economic Theory of Environmental Policy in a Federal System*, Cheltenham, UK and Lyme, USA: Edward Elgar.

Braden, J.B., H. Folmer and T.S. Ulen (1996), *Environmental Policy with Political and Economic Integration*, Cheltenham, UK and Brookfield, USA: Edward Elgar.

Brinkhorst, L.J. (1993), 'Subsidiarity and European Community Environment Policy: A Panacea or a Pandora's Box?', *European Environmental Law Review*, **2**: 16–22.

Cameron, J., P. Demaret and D. Geradin (1994), *Trade and the Environment: The Search for Balance*, London: Cameron May.

Carraro, Carlo and Domenico Siniscalco (1991), 'Strategies for the International Protection of the Environment', CEPR Working Paper No. 568.

Carraro, Carlo and Domenico Siniscalco (1993), 'Policy Coordination for Sustainability: Commitments, Transfers, and Linked Negotiations', FEEM *Nota di Lavoro 63.93*.

Cass, D.Z. (1992), 'The Word that Saves Maastricht? The Principle of Subsidiarity and the Division of Powers Within the European Community', *Common Market Law Review*, **29**: 1107–36.

Cesar, Herman and Art de Zeeuw (1994), 'Issue Linkage in Global Environmental Problems', FEEM *Nota di Lavoro 56.94*.

Chichilnisky, G. (1994), 'North–South Trade and the Global Environment', *American Economic Review*, **84**(4): 851–74.

Commission of the European Communities (CEC) (1993), *European Economy*, No. 5.

Commission of the European Communities (CEC) (1995), *Europeans and the Environment*, survey conducted in the context of the Eurobarometer 43.1 bis.

Conrad, K. (1993), 'Taxes and Subsidies for Pollution-Intensive Industries as Trade Policy', *Journal of Environmental Economics and Management*, **25**: 121–35.

Copeland, B.R. (1994), 'International Trade and the Environment: Policy Reform in a Polluted Small Open Economy', *Journal of Environmental Economics and Management*, **26**: 44–65.

Copeland, B.R. and M.S. Taylor (1994), 'North–South Trade and the Environment', *Quarterly Journal of Economics*, **109**: 755–87.

Copeland, B.R. and M.S. Taylor (1995), 'Trade and Transboundary Pollution', *American Economic Review*, **85**(4): 716–37.

Craig, P. and G. de Búrca (1995), *EC Law. Text, Cases, and Materials*, Oxford: Clarendon Press.

Cropper, M.L. and W.E. Oates (1992), 'Environmental Economics: A Survey', *Journal of Economic Literature*, **30**: 675–740.

Cumberland J.H. (1979), 'Interregional Pollution Spillovers and Consistency of Environmental Policy', in H. Siebert et al. (eds), *Regional Environmental Policy: The Economic Issues*, NY: NYU Press, pp. 255–81.

Cumberland J.H. (1981), 'Efficiency and Equity in Interregional Environmental Management', *Review of Regional Studies*, **2**: 244–57.

D'Arge, R.C. and A.V. Kneese (1972), 'Environmental Quality and International Trade', *International Organization*, **26**: 419–65.

Dasgupta, Partha (1990), 'The Environment as a Commodity', *Oxford Review of Economic Policy*, **6**: 51–67.

Dean, J.M. (1992), 'Trade and the Environment: A Survey of the Literature', in P. Low (ed.), *International Trade and the Environment*, World Bank Discussion Papers 159, Washington: World Bank.

Dehousse, R. (1993), 'Does Subsidiarity Really Matter?', EUI Working Paper Law No. 92/32.

Dinan, T.M., M.L. Croppe and P.R. Portney (1999), 'Environmental Federalism: Welfare Losses from Uniform National Drinking Water Standards', in A. Panagariya and P. Portney (eds), *Environmental and Public Economics. Essays in Honor of Wallace E. Oates*, Cheltenham, UK and Northampton, USA: Edward Elgar, pp. 13–31.

Dockner, E. and N. van Long (1993), 'International Pollution Control: Cooperative versus Noncooperative Strategies', *Journal of Environmental Economics and Management*, **24**: 13–29.

Duffy-Deno, Kevin (1992), 'Pollution Abatement Expenditures and Regional Manufacturing Activity', *Journal of Regional Science*, **32**: 419–36.

Earnshaw, D. and D. Judge (1996), 'From Co-operation to Co-decision: The Parliament's Path to Legislative Power', in J.J. Richardson (ed.), *European Union: Power and Policy-making*, London: Routledge, pp. 96–126.

Elliot, Donald E., Bruce A. Ackerman and John C. Milian (1985), 'Toward a Theory of Statutory Evolution: The Federalization of Environmental Law', *Journal of Law, Economics and Organization*, **1**: 313–40.

Farrell, J. (1987), 'Information and the Coase Theorem', *Journal of Economic Perspectives*, **1**: 113–29.

Faure, M. and J. Lefevere (1999), 'Integrated Pollution Prevention and Control: An Economic Appraisal', in C. Backes and G. Betlem (eds), *Integrated Pollution Prevention and Control*, The Hague: Kluwer Law International, pp. 93–120.

Flynn, J. (1987), 'How Will Article 100A(4) Work? A Comparison With Article 93', *Common Market Law Review*, **24**: 689–707.

Folmer, H. and C.W. Howe (1991), 'Environmental Problems and Policy in the Single European Market', *Environmental and Resource Economics*, **1**: 17–42.

Freeman III, A.M. (1990), 'Water Pollution Policy', in P.R. Portney (ed.), *Public Policies for Environmental Protection*, Washington: Resources for the Future.

Friedman, Joseph, Daniel A. Gerlowski and Jonathan Silberman (1992), 'What Attracts Foreign Multinational Cooperations? Evidence From Branch Plant Location in the United States', *Journal of Regional Science*, **32**: 403–18.

Gandolfo, G. (1987), *International Economics I. The Pure Theory of International Trade*, Berlin: Springer-Verlag.

Golub, J. (1996), 'Sovereignty and Subsidiarity in EU Environmental Policy', *Political Studies*, **XLIV**: 686–703.

Gray, Wayne B. (1997), 'Manufacturing Plant Location: Does State Pollution Regulation Matter?', Clark University.

Green, P. (1994), 'Subsidiarity and European Union: Beyond the Ideological Impasse? An Analysis of the Origins and Impact of the Principle of Subsidiarity Within the Politics of the European Community', *Policy and Politics*, **44**: 287–300.

Gulmann, C. (1987), 'The Single European Act – Some Remarks from a Danish Perspective', *Common Market Law Review*, **24**: 31–40.

Haigh, N. (1994), 'The Environment as a Test Case for Subsidiarity', in M. Dubrulle (ed.), *Future European Environmental Policy and Subsidiarity*, ESED & European University Press.

Heckscher, E.F. (1919), 'Utrikeshandelens Verkan på Inkomstfördelningen: Några Teoretiska Grundlinjer', *Ekonomisk Tidskrift*, **21**: 497–512.

Hettige, H., R.E.B. Lucas and D. Wheeler (1992), 'The Toxic Intensity of Industrial Production: Global Patterns, Trends, and Trade Policy', *American Economic Review* (Papers and Proceedings), **82**: 478–81.

Hildebrand, P.M. (1992), 'The European Community's Environmental Policy, 1957 to "1992": From Incidental Measures to an International Regime?', *Environmental Politics*, **1**: 13–44.

Hoel, Michael (1991a), 'Efficient International Agreements for Reducing Emissions of CO_2', *The Energy Journal*, **12**: 93–107.

Hoel, Michael (1991b), 'Global Environmental Problems: The Effects of Unilateral Actions Taken by One Country', *Journal of Environmental Economics and Management*, **20**: 55–70.

Hoel, Michael (1993a), 'Harmonization of Carbon Taxes in International Climate Agreements', *Environmental and Resource Economics*, **3**: 221–31.

Hoel, Michael (1993b), 'Cost-effective and Efficient International Environmental Agreements', Reprint Series No. 441, University of Oslo.

Hoel, Michael (1993c), 'Stabilizing CO_2-Emissions in Europe: Individual Stabilization versus Harmonization of Carbon Taxes', in Carlo Carraro and Domenico Siniscalco (eds), *The European Carbon Tax: An Economic Assessment*, Amsterdam: Kluwer.

Hoel, Michael (1994a), 'Efficient Climate Policy in the Presence of Free Riders', *Journal of Environmental Economics and Management*, **27**: 259–74.

Hoel, M. (1994b), 'Environmental Policy as a Game Between Governments When Plant Locations are Endogenous', paper presented at the 21st Annual AERIE Conference, Crete.

Hoel, Michael (1994c), 'International Coordination of Environmental Taxes', unpublished paper, University of Oslo.

Holzinger, K. (1994), *Politik des Kleinsten Gemeinsamen Nenners? Umweltpolitische Entsheidungsprozesse in der EG am Beispiel der Einführung des Katalysatorautos*, Berlin: Sigma.

Howe, C.W. (1993), 'The US Environmental Policy Experience: A Critique with Suggestions for the European Community', *Environmental and Resource Economics*, **3**: 1–21.

Jaffe, A.B., S.R. Peterson and P.R. Portney (1995), 'Environmental Regulation and the Competitiveness of U.S. Manufacturing: What Does the Evidence Tell Us?', *Journal of Economic Literature*, **33**: 132–63.

Jasay, A.E. (1960), 'The Social Choice Between Home and Overseas Investment', *Economic Journal*, **70**: 105–13.

Jeppesen, Tim and Henk Folmer (2001), 'The Confusing Relationship Between Environmental Policy and Location Behaviour of Firms: A Methodological Review of Selected Case Studies', *Annals of Regional Science*, forthcoming.

Jeppesen, Tim, John A. List and Henk Folmer (2001), 'Environmental Regulations and New Plant Location Decisions: Evidence from a Meta-Analysis', *Journal of Regional Science*, forthcoming.

Johnson, S. and G. Corcelle (1989), *The Environmental Policy of the European Communities*, London: Graham & Trotman.

Jordan, A. and T. Jeppesen (2000), 'EU Environmental Policy: Adapting to the Principle of Subsidiarity?', *European Environment*, **10**: 64–74.

Jordan, A., R. Brouwer and E. Noble (1999), 'Innovative or Responsive? A

Longitudinal Analysis of the Speed of the EU Environmental Policy Process', *Journal of European Public Policy*, **6**: 376–98.

Judge, D. (1992), 'Predestined to Save the Earth: The Environment Committee in the European Parliament', *Environmental Politics*, **1**: 186–212.

Kaitala, V., M. Pohjola and O. Tahvonen (1991), 'Transboundary Air Pollution Between Finland and the USSR – A Dynamic Acid Rain Game', in R.P. Hämäläinen and H. Ehtamo (eds), *Dynamic Games in Economic Analysis. Lecture Notes in Control and Information Sciences*, Berlin: Springer-Verlag, 157, pp. 183–92.

Kalt, J.P. (1988), 'The Impact of Domestic Environmental Regulatory Policies on U.S. International Competitiveness', in A.M. Spence and H.A. Hazard (eds), *International Competitiveness*, Cambridge, MA: Ballinger Publishing.

Keller, Wolfgang and Arik Levinson (1999), 'Environmental Regulations and FDI Inflows to U.S. States: The Potential for a "Race to the Bottom" of Environmental Stringency', paper prepared for the ISIT99 conference, 4–5 June.

Kemp, M.C. (1964), *The Pure Theory of International Trade*, Englewood Cliffs, NJ: Prentice-Hall.

Kennedy, P.W. (1994), 'Equilibrium Taxes in Open Economies with Imperfect Competition', *Journal of Environmental Economics and Management*, **27**: 49–63.

Kent, P. (1996), *Law of the European Union*, London: M&E Pitman Publishing.

Klibanoff, P. and J. Morduch (1995), 'Decentralization, Externalities, and Efficiency', *Review of Economic Studies*, **62**: 223–47.

Klibanoff, P. and M. Poitevin (1996), 'A Theory of (De)Centralization', unpublished working paper, Northwestern University.

Kolstad, C.D. (1987), 'Uniformity versus Differentiation in Regulating Externalities', *Journal of Environmental Economics and Management*, **14**: 386–99.

Komen, M.H.C. and J.H.M. Peerlings (1999), 'Energy Taxes in The Netherlands: What are the Dividends?', *Environmental and Resource Economics*, **14**: 243–68.

Koppen, I. J. (1993), 'The Role of the European Court of Justice', in J.D. Liefferink, P.D. Lowe and A.P.J. Mol, *European Integration and Environmental Policy*, London: Belhaven Press, pp. 126–49.

Krämer, L. (1987), 'The Single European Act and Environmental Protection: Reflections on Several New Provisions in Community Law', *Common Market Law Review*, **24**: 659–88.

Krämer, L. (1992), *Focus on European Environmental Law*, 1st edn, London: Sweet and Maxwell.

Krämer, L. (1993), 'Environmental Protection and Article 30 EEC Treaty', *Common Market Law Review*, **30**: 111–43.

Kroeze-Gil, Jardena and Henk Folmer (1998), 'Linking Environmental and Non-environmental Problems in an International Setting: The Interconnected Games Approach', in Nick Hanley and Henk Folmer (eds), *Game Theory and the Environment*, Cheltenham, UK and Northampton, USA: Edward Elgar, pp. 165–80.

Krugman, P.R. and M. Obstfeld (1997), *International Economics. Theory and Policy*, 4th edn, Reading, MA: Addison-Wesley.

Krutilla, K. (1991), 'Environmental Regulation in an Open Economy', *Journal of Environmental Economics and Management*, **10**: 127–42.

Lefevere, J. (1999), 'Integrating Groundwater Quantity Control into European Community Water Policy', *Reciel*, **8**: 291–300.

Lenaerts, K. (1994), 'The Principle of Subsidiarity and the Environment in the European Union: Keeping the Balance of Federalism', *Fordham International Law Journal*, **17**: 846–95.

Leonard, H.J. (1988), *Pollution and the Struggle for the World Product*, Cambridge: Cambridge University Press.

Leontief, W. (1954), 'Domestic Production and Foreign Trade: The American Capital Position Re-examined', *Economia Internazionale*, **7**: 9–45.

Levinson, Arik (1996), 'Environmental Regulations and Manufacturers' Location Choices: Evidence from the Census of Manufactures', *Journal of Public Economics*, **62**: 5–29.

Liefferink, D. (1996), *Environment and the Nation State. The Netherlands, the European Union and Acid Rain*, Manchester: Manchester University Press.

Liefferink, D. and M.S. Andersen (1997), 'Greening the EU: National Positions in the Run-up to the Amsterdam Treaty', *Environmental Politics*, **7**: 66–93.

List, J.A. (1997), 'Optimal Institutional Arrangements for Pollution Control: Evidence from a Differential Game with Asymmetric Players', unpublished working paper, University of Central Florida.

List, John A. and Catherine Co (2000), 'The Effects of Environmental Regulations on Foreign Direct Investment', *Journal of Environmental Economics and Management*, **40**: 1–20.

List, J. and S.D. Gerking (1996), 'Optimal Institutional Arrangements for Pollution Control', *Journal of Regional Analysis & Policy*, **26**: 113–33.

List, John A. and Shelby Gerking (2000), 'Regulatory Federalism and U.S. Environmental Policies', *Journal of Regional Science*, **40**: 453–71.

List, John A. and Mitch Kunce (2000), 'Environmental Protection and Economic Growth: What do the Residuals tell us?', *Land Economics*, **76**: 267–82.

Low, P. and A. Yeats (1992), 'Do "Dirty" Industries Migrate?', in P. Low (ed.), *International Trade and the Environment*, World Bank Discussion Papers 159, Washington: World Bank.

Lucas, R., D. Wheeler and H. Hettige (1992), 'Economic Development, Environmental Regulation and the International Migration of Toxic Industrial Pollution: 1960–1988', in P. Low (ed.), *International Trade and the Environment*, World Bank Discussion Papers 159, Washington: World Bank.

MacDougall, G.D.A. (1960), 'The Benefits and Costs of Private Investment from Abroad', *Economic Record*, **36**: 13–35.

Mäler, Karl-Göran (1989), 'The Acid Rain Game', in H. Folmer and E. van Ierland (eds), *Valuation Methods and Policy Making in Environmental Economics*, Amsterdam: Elsevier.

Mansoorian, A. and G.M. Myers (1993), 'Attachment to Home and Efficient Purchases of Population in a Fiscal Externality Economy', *Journal of Public Economics*, **52**: 117–32.

Markusen, J.R. (1975), 'International Externalities and Optimal Tax Structures', *Journal of International Economics*, **5**: 15–29.

Markusen, J.R. (1983), 'Factor Movements and Commodity Trade as Complements', *Journal of International Economics*, **14**: 341–56.

Markusen, J.R. (1995), 'Costly Pollution Abatement, Competitiveness, and Plant Location Decisions', paper presented at the workshop 'Environmental Capital Flight', Wageningen Agricultural University.

Markusen, J.R., E.R. Morey and N. Olewiler (1993), 'Environmental Policy When Market Structure and Plant Locations Are Endogenous', *Journal of Environmental Policy and Management*, **24**: 68–86.

Markusen, J.R., E.R. Morey and N. Olewiler (1995), 'Competition in Regional Environmental Policies When Plant Locations are Endogenous', *Journal of Public Economics*, **56**: 55–77.

Marwell, Gerald and Ruth Ames (1981), 'Economists Free Ride, Does Anyone Else?: Experiments on the Provision of Public Goods, IV', *Journal of Public Economics*, **15**: 295–310.

McGuire, M.C. (1982), 'Regulation, Factor Rewards, and International Trade', *Journal of Public Economics*, **17**: 335–54.

McLure, C.E. Jr (1970), 'Taxation, Substitution, and Industrial Location', *Journal of Political Economics*, **78**: 112–32.

Merrifield, J.D. (1988), 'The Impact of Selected Abatement Strategies on Transnational Pollution, the Terms of Trade, and Factor Rewards: A General Equilibrium Approach', *Journal of Environmental Economics and Management*, **15**: 259–84.

Mors, M. (1993), 'The Subsidiarity Principle and Environmental Policy in the Community', paper presented at the conference 'Environnement et

Economie: quelles perspectives pour la recherche dans les prochaines années?', Paris.

Motta, M. and J.-F. Thisse (1994), 'Does Environmental Dumping Lead to Relocation?', *European Economic Review*, **38**: 563–76.

Mundell, R.A. (1957), 'International Trade and Factor Mobility', *American Economic Review*, **47**: 321–35.

Murrell, P. and R. Ryterman (1991), 'A Methodology for Testing Comparative Economic Theories: Theory and Application to East–West Environmental Policies', *Journal of Comparative Economics*, **15**: 582–601.

Musgrave, R.A. (1959), *The Theory of Public Finance: A Study in Public Economy*, New York: McGraw-Hill.

Myers, G.M. (1990), 'Optimality, Free Mobility and the Regional Authority in a Federation', *Journal of Public Economics*, **43**: 107–21.

O'Keeffe, D. and P. M. Twomey (eds) (1994), *Legal Issues of the Maastricht Treaty*, London: Chancery Law Publishing.

Oates, W.E. (1972), *Fiscal Federalism*, New York: Harcourt Brace Jovanovich.

Oates, W.E. (1994), 'Federalism and Government Finance', in J.M. Quigley and E. Smolensky (eds), *Modern Public Finance*, Cambridge, MA: Harvard University Press.

Oates, W.E. (1998), 'Environmental Policy in the European Community: Harmonization or National Standards?', *Empirica*, **25**: 1–13.

Oates, W.E. (1999), 'An Essay on Fiscal Federalism', *Journal of Economic Literature*, **XXXVII**: 1120–49.

Oates, W.E. and R.M. Schwab (1988), 'Economic Competition Among Jurisdictions: Efficiency Enhancing or Distortion Inducing?', *Journal of Public Economics*, **35**: 333–54.

Oates, W.E. and R.M. Schwab (1989), 'The Theory of Regulatory Federalism: The Case of Environmental Management', unpublished paper, University of Maryland, Department of Economics.

Ohlin, B. (1933), *Interregional and International Trade*, Cambridge, MA: Harvard University Press.

Ostrom, Elinor, Roy Gardner and James Walker (1994), *Rules, Games and Common-Pool Resources*, Ann Arbor, MI: The University of Michigan Press.

Pagh, P. (1996), *EU-Miljøret*, Copenhagen: Christian Ejlers' Forlag.

Pethig, R. (1976), 'Pollution, Welfare and Environmental Policy in the Theory of Comparative Advantages', *Journal of Environmental Economics and Management*, **2**: 160–69.

Pfander, J.E. (1996), 'Environmental Federalism in Europe and the United States: A Comparative Assessment of Regulation through the Agency of Member States', in J. Braden, H. Folmer and T.S. Ulen (eds),

Environmental Policy with Political and Economic Integration, Cheltenham, UK and Brookfield, USA: Edward Elgar.

Porter, M.E. (1991), 'America's Green Strategy', *Scientific American*, April: 168.

Portney, P.R. (ed.) (1990), *Public Policies for Environmental Protection*, Washington, DC: Resources for the Future.

Rabin, Mathew (1993), 'Incorporating Fairness into Game Theory and Economics', *American Economic Review*, **83**: 1281–302.

Rauscher, M. (1991), 'Foreign Trade and the Environment', in H. Siebert (ed.), *Environmental Scarcity: The International Dimension*, Tübingen: Mohr.

Rauscher, M. (1992), 'Environmental Policy and International Capital Movements', paper prepared for the Task Force Meeting in Stockholm, 12–14 June 1992.

Rauscher, M. (1994), 'On Ecological Dumping', *Oxford Economic Papers*, **46**: 822–40.

Rauscher, M. (1995a), 'Environmental Regulation and the Location of Polluting Industries', *International Tax and Public Finance*, **2**: 229–44.

Rauscher, M. (1995b), 'Environmental Policy and International Capital Mobility – An Aggregate View', paper presented at the workshop 'Environmental Capital Flight', Wageningen Agricultural University.

Rauscher, M. (1995c), 'Environmental Regulation and the Location of Polluting Industries', *International Tax and Public Finance*, **2**: 229–44.

Rauscher, M. (1997), *International Trade, Factor Movements, and the Environment*, Oxford: Oxford University Press.

Rehbinder, E. (1996), 'Regulatory Federalism: Environmental Protection in the European Community', in I. Pernice (ed.), *Harmonization of Legislation in Federal Systems*, Baden-Baden: Nomos, pp. 61–80.

Revesz, Richard (1992), 'Rehabilitating Interstate Competition: Rethinking the "Race-to-the-Bottom" Rationale for Federal Environmental Regulation', *NYU Law Review*, **67**: 1210.

Revesz, Richard (1997), 'Federalism and Environmental Regulation: Lessons for the European Union and the International Community', *Virginia Law Review*, **83**: 1331.

Rob, R. (1989), 'Pollution Claim Settlements under Private Information', *Journal of Economic Theory*, **47**: 307–33.

Robison, H.D. (1988), 'Industrial Pollution Abatement: The Impact on Balance of Trade', *Canadian Journal of Economics*, **21**: 187–99.

Rose-Ackerman, Susan (1981), 'Does Federalism Matter? Political Choice in a Federal Republic', *Journal of Political Economy*, **89**: 152–65.

Rowland, C.K. and R. Feiock (1991), 'Environmental Regulation and Economic Development: The Movement of Chemical Production

Among States', in M.J. Dubnick and A.R. Gitelson (eds), *Public Policy and Economic Institutions*, Greenwich, CT: JAI Press, pp. 205–18.

Rubin, S.J. and T.R. Graham (eds) (1982), *Environment and Trade. The Relation of International Trade and Environmental Policy*, Allanheld & Osmun.

Ruffin, R.J. (1984), 'International Factor Movements', in R.W. Jones and P.B. Kenen (eds), *Handbook of International Economics*, Vol. I, Amsterdam: Elsevier.

Ryterman, R. (1988), 'Technological Flexibility and the Pattern of East–West Trade', Ph.D. Thesis, University of Maryland.

Samuelson, P.A. (1948),'International Trade and Equalisation of Factor Price', *Economic Journal*, **58**: 163–84.

Samuelson, P.A. (1949), 'International Factor Price Equalisation Once Again', *Economic Journal*, **59**: 181–97.

Scott, J. (1998), *EC Environmental Law*, London: Longman.

Segerson, K., T.J. Miceli and L.-C. Wen (1997), 'Intergovernmental Transfers in a Federal System: An Economic Analysis of Unfunded Mandates', in J.B. Braden and S. Proost (eds), *The Economic Theory of Environmental Policy in a Federal System*, Cheltenham, UK and Lyme, USA: Edward Elgar.

Sethi, Rajiv and E. Somanathan (1996), 'The Evolution of Social Norms in Common Property Resource Use', *American Economic Review*, **86**: 766–88.

Sevenster, H. (2000), 'The Environmental Guarantee After Amsterdam: Does the Emperor Have New Clothes?', in H. Somsen (ed.), *Yearbook of European Environmental Law*, Oxford: Oxford University Press, pp. 292–310.

Shapiro, P. and J. Petchey (1995), 'The Welfare Economics of Environmental Regulatory Authority: Two Parables on State vs. Federal Control', Working Paper in Economics #5–95, Department of Economics, University of California at Santa Barbara.

Siebert, H. (1974), 'Environmental Protection and International Specialization', *Weltwirtschaftliches Archiv*, **110**: 494–508.

Siebert, H. (1977), 'Environmental Quality and the Gains from Trade', *Kyklos*, **30**: 657–73.

Siebert, H. (1979), 'Environmental Policy in the Two-country Case', *Zeitschrift für Nationalökonomie*, **39**: 259–74.

Siebert, H. (1985), 'Spatial Aspects of Environmental Economics', in A.V. Kneese and J.L. Sweeney (eds), *Handbook of Natural Resource and Energy Economics*, Vol. 1, Amsterdam: North-Holland.

Siebert, H. (1991), 'Europe '92. Decentralizing Environmental Policy in the Single Market', *Environmental and Resource Economics*, **1**: 271–87.

Siebert, H., J. Eichberger, R. Gronych and R. Pethig (1980), *Trade and Environment: A Theoretical Inquiry*, Amsterdam: North-Holland.

Silva, E.C.D. (1997), 'Decentralized and Efficient Control of Transboundary Pollution in Federal Systems', *Journal of Environmental Economics and Management*, **32**: 95–108.

Silva, E.C.D. and A.J. Caplan (1997), 'Transboundary Pollution Control in Federal Systems', *Journal of Environmental Economics and Management*, **34**: 175–86.

Sloan, R.D. (1995), 'Exemptions From Harmonization Measures Under Article 100a(4): The Second Authorization of the German Ban on PCP', *European Environmental Law Review*, February: 45–50.

Somsen, H. (1994), 'Applying More Protective National Environmental Laws After Harmonization', *European Environmental Law Review*, August–September: 238–42.

Sorsa, P. (1994), *Competitiveness and Environmental Standards. Some Exploratory Results*, World Bank Policy Research Working Paper 1249, Washington: World Bank.

Steinberg, R. (1996), 'The Subsidiarity Principle in European Environmental Law', in I. Pernice (ed.), *Harmonization of Legislation in Federal Systems*, Baden-Baden: Nomos.

Steininger, K. (1994), 'Reconciling Trade and the Environment: Towards a Comparative Advantage for Long-Term Policy Goals', *Ecological Economics*, **9**: 23–42.

Stewart, R.B. (1992), 'Environmental Law in the United States and the European Community: Spillovers, Cooperation, Rivalry, Institutions', *University of Chicago Legal Forum*, **41**: 41–80.

Stolper, W.F. and P.A. Samuelson (1941), 'Protection and Real Wages', *Review of Economic Studies*, **9**: 58–73.

Tannenwald, Robert (1997), 'State Regulation Policy and Economic Development', *New England Economic Review*, Proceedings of a Symposium on the Effects of State and Local Public Policies on Economic Development, March–April, pp. 83–97.

Task Force (1990), '"1992" The Environmental Dimension', Task Force Environment and the Internal Market. Bonn: Economica Verlag.

Temmink, H. (2000), 'From Danish Bottles to Danish Bees: The Dynamics of Free Movement of Goods and Environmental Protection – A Case Law Analysis', in H. Somsen (ed.), *Yearbook of European Environmental Law*, Oxford: Oxford University Press, pp. 60–102.

Thaler, Richard H. (1988), 'Anomalies: The Ultimatum Game', *Journal of Economic Perspectives*, **2**: 195–207.

Tiebout, C.M. (1956), 'A Pure Theory of Local Expenditures', *Journal of Political Economy*, **74**: 416–24.

Tietenberg, T.H. (1978), 'Spatially Differentiated Air Pollutant Emission Charges. An Economic and Legal Analysis', *Land Economics*, **54**: 265–77.

Tietenberg, T.H. (1985), *Emissions Trading*, Washington, DC: Resources for the Future.

Tobey, J.A. (1990), 'The Effects of Domestic Environmental Policies on Patterns of World Trade: An Empirical Test', *Kyklos*, **43**(2): 191–209.

Ugelow, J.L. (1982), 'A Survey of Recent Studies on Cost of Pollution Control and the Effects on Trade', in S.J. Rubin and T.R. Graham (eds), *Environment and Trade. The Relation of International Trade and Environmental Policy*, Allanheld & Osmun.

Ulph, A. (1994), 'Environmental Policy, Plant Location and Government Protection', in C. Carraro (ed.), *Trade, Innovation, Environment*, Amsterdam: Kluwer.

Ulph, A. (1997), 'International Trade and the Environment: A Survey of Recent Economic Analysis', in H. Folmer and T. Tietenberg (eds), *The International Yearbook of Environmental and Resource Economics 1997/1998. A Survey of Current Issues*, Cheltenham, UK and Lyme, USA: Edward Elgar, pp. 205–42.

Ulph, A. and L. Valentini (1996), 'Plant Location and Strategic Environmental Policy With Inter-Sectorial Linkages', Discussion Paper No. 9623, University of Southampton.

Van den Bergh, R. (1994), 'The Subsidiarity Principle in European Community Law: Some Insights from Law and Economics', *Maastricht Journal of European and Comparative Law*.

Van den Bergh, R., M. Faure and J. Lefevere (1996), 'The Subsidiarity Principle in European Environmental Law: An Economic Analysis', in E. Eide and R.R. van den Bergh (eds), *Law and Economics of the Environment*, Oslo: Juridisk Forlag.

Van Beers, C. and J.C.J.M. Van den Bergh (1997), 'An Empirical Multi-country Analysis of the Impact of Environmental Regulations on Foreign Trade Flows', *Kyklos*, **50**: 29–46.

Vig, N.J. and M.E. Kraft (eds) (1990), *Environmental Policy in the 1990s. Toward a New Agenda*, Washington, DC: Congressional Quarterly.

Walsh, C. (1993), 'Fiscal Federalism: An Overview of Issues and a Discussion of Their Relevance to the European Community', *European Economy*, **5**.

Walter, I. (1973), 'The Pollution Content of American Trade', *Western Economic Journal*, **11**: 67–70.

Walter, I. (1974), 'International Trade and Resource Diversion: The Case of Environmental Management', *Weltwirtschaftliches Archiv*, **110**: 482–93.

Walter, I. (1982), 'Environmentally Induced Industrial Relocation to Developing Countries', in S.J. Rubin and T.R. Graham (eds), *Environment and Trade. The Relation of International Trade and Environmental Policy*, Allanheld & Osmun.

Wang, L.-J. (1995), 'Environmental Capital Flight and Pollution Tax', *Environmental and Resource Economics*, **4**: 273–86.

Weatherill, S. (1994), 'Beyond Preemption? Shared Competence and Constitutional Change in the European Community?', in D. O'Keefe and P.M. Twomey (eds), *Legal Issues of the Maastricht Treaty*, London: Chancery Law Publishing.

Wellisch, D. (1994), 'Interregional Spillovers in the Presence of Perfect and Imperfect Household Mobility', *Journal of Public Economics*, **55**: 167–84.

Wils, W.P.J. (1994), 'Subsidiarity and EC Environmental Policy: Taking People's Concerns Seriously', *Journal of Environmental Law*, **6**: 85–91.

Wilson, J.D. (1996), 'Capital Mobility and Environmental Standards: Is There a Theoretical Basis for a Race to the Bottom?', in J. Bhagwati and R. Hudec (eds), *Fair Trade and Harmonization: Prerequisites for Free Trade?* Vol. I, Cambridge, MA: MIT Press, pp. 393–427.

Wong, K.Y. (1986), 'Are International Trade and Factor Movements Substitutes?', *Journal of International Economics*, **21**: 25–43.

Zaelke, D., P. Orbuch and R.F. Housman (1993), *Trade and the Environment*, Washington, DC: Island Press.

Appendix

COMMUNITY LEGISLATION

Council Directive 70/220/EEC of 20 March 1970 on the approximation of the laws of the Member States relating to measures to be taken against air pollution by gases from positive-ignition engines of motor vehicles. *Official Journal* L 076, 06/04/1970, pp. 0001–0022.

Council Directive 73/404/EEC of 22 November 1973 on the approximation of the laws of the Member States relating to detergents. *Official Journal* L 347, 17/12/1973, pp. 0051–0052.

Council Directive 75/716/EEC of 24 November 1975 on the approximation of the laws of the Member States relating to the sulphur content of certain liquid fuels. *Official Journal* L 307, 27/11/1975, pp. 0022–0024.

Council Directive 75/442/EEC of 15 July 1975 on waste. *Official Journal* L 194, 25/07/1975, pp. 0039–0041.

Council Directive 76/464/EEC of 4 May 1976 on pollution caused by certain dangerous substances discharged into the aquatic environment of the Community. *Official Journal* L 129, 18/05/1976, pp. 0023–0029.

Council Directive 76/160/EEC of 8 December 1975 concerning the quality of bathing water. *Official Journal* L 031, 05/02/1976, pp. 0001–0007.

Council Directive 78/319/EEC of 20 March 1978 on toxic and dangerous waste. *Official Journal* L 084, 31/03/1978, pp. 0043–0048.

Council Directive 78/659/EEC of 18 July 1978 on the quality of fresh waters needing protection or improvement in order to support fish life. *Official Journal* L 222, 14/08/1978, pp. 0001–0078.

Council Directive 79/923/EEC of 30 October 1979 on the quality required of shellfish waters. *Official Journal* L 281, 10/11/1979, pp. 0047–0052.

Council Directive 80/779/EEC of 15 July 1980 on air quality limit values and guide values for sulphur dioxide and suspended particulates. *Official Journal* L 229, 30/08/1980, pp. 0030–0048.

Commission Decision 94/783/EC concerning the prohibition of PCP notified by the Federal Republic of Germany, *Official Journal* 1994 L 316, p. 43.

Commission Decision 96/211/EC concerning the prohibition of pentachlorophenol (PCP) notified by Denmark, *Official Journal* 1996 L 68, p. 32.

Council Decision 87/373/EEC laying down the procedures for the exercise of implementing powers conferred on the Commission. *Official Journal* 1987 L 197, p. 33.

Council Directive 70/157/EEC of 6 February 1970 on the approximation of the laws of the Member States relating to the permissible sound level and the exhaust system of motor vehicles. *Official Journal* L 042, p. 16.

Council Directive 84/360/EEC of 28 June 1984 on the combating of air pollution from industrial plants. *Official Journal* L 188, p. 20.

Council Directive 91/173/EEC, amending for the ninth time Directive 76/769/EEC on the approximation of the laws, regulations and administrative provisions of the Member States relating to restrictions on the marketing and use of certain dangerous substances and preparations. *Official Journal* 1991 L 085, p. 34.

Council Directive 91/173/EEC, amending for the ninth time Directive 76/769/EEC on the approximation of the laws, regulations and administrative provisions of the Member States relating to restrictions on the marketing and use of certain dangerous substances and preparations. *Official Journal* 1991 L 085, p. 34.

Council Directive 91/338/EEC amending for the tenth time Directive 76/769/EEC on approximation of the laws, regulations and administrative provisions of the Member States relating to restrictions on the marketing and use of certain dangerous substances and preparations. *Official Journal* 1991 L 186, p. 59.

Com/93/680 final. Proposal for a Council Directive on the ecological quality of water. *Official Journal* C 222, p. 6.

Council Directive 94/55/EC of 21 November 1994 on the approximation of the laws of the Member States with regard to the transport of dangerous goods by road. *Official Journal* L 319, pp. 0007–0013.

European Parliament and Council Directive 94/35/EC on sweeteners for use in foodstuffs. *Official Journal* 1994 L 237, p. 3.

European Parliament and Council Directive 94/36/EC of 30 June 1994 on colours for use in foodstuffs. *Official Journal* 1994 L 237, p. 13.

European Parliament and Council Directive 94/60/EC amending for the 14th time Directive 76/769/EEC on the approximation of the laws, regulations and administrative provisions of the Member States relating to restrictions on the marketing and use of certain dangerous substances and preparations. *Official Journal* 1994 L 365, p. 1.

European Parliament and Council Directive 94/62/EC of 20 December 1994 on packaging and packaging waste. *Official Journal* L 365, p. 10.

Com/94/612 final. Proposal for a Council Directive concerning the quality of water intended for human consumption. *Official Journal* C 131, p. 5.

European Parliament and Council Directive 95/2/EC on food additives other than colours and sweeteners. *Official Journal* 1995 L 061, p. 1.

Case 8/74 *Procureur du Roi* v. *Dassonville*, ECR 1974, 837.

Case 120/78 *Rewe* v. *Zentralverwaltung*, ECR 1979, 649.

Case 302/86 *Commission of the European Communities* v. *Kingdom of Denmark*, ECR 1988, 4607.

Case 319/97 *Criminal proceedings against Antoine Kortas*. ECR 1999, 3143.

Index